The ABCs of
Intranets

The ABCs of
Intranets

Peter Dyson
Pat Coleman
Len Gilbert

SYBEX®

San Francisco - Paris - Düsseldorf - Soest

Associate Publisher: Amy Romanoff
Acquisitions Manager: Kristine Plachy
Acquisitions & Developmental Editor: Dan Brodnitz
Editor: Lee Ann Pickrell
Technical Editor: Mark Butler
Book Designer: Catalin Dulfu
Graphic Illustrator: Inbar Berman
Electronic Publishing Specialist: Deborah A. Bevilacqua
Production Coordinator: Amy Eoff
Proofreaders: Jennifer Metzger, Theresa Gonzalez
Indexer: Lynnzee Elze Spence
Cover Designer: Design Site
Cover Illustration: Design Site

Screen reproductions produced with Collage Plus.

Collage Plus is a trademark of Inner Media Inc.

SYBEX is a registered trademark of SYBEX Inc.

TRADEMARKS: SYBEX has attempted throughout this book to distinguish proprietary trademarks from descriptive terms by following the capitalization style used by the manufacturer.

Netscape Communications, the Netscape Communications logo, Netscape, and Netscape Navigator are trademarks of Netscape Communications Corporation.

The author and publisher have made their best efforts to prepare this book, and the content is based upon final release software whenever possible. Portions of the manuscript may be based upon pre-release versions supplied by software manufacturer(s). The author and the publisher make no representation or warranties of any kind with regard to the completeness or accuracy of the contents herein and accept no liability of any kind including but not limited to performance, merchantability, fitness for any particular purpose, or any losses or damages of any kind caused or alleged to be caused directly or indirectly from this book.

Photographs and illustrations used in this book have been downloaded from publicly accessible file archives and are used in this book for news reportage purposes only to demonstrate the variety of graphics resources available via electronic access. Text and images available over the Internet may be subject to copyright and other rights owned by third parties. Online availability of text and images does not imply that they may be reused without the permission of rights holders, although the Copyright Act does permit certain unauthorized reuse as fair use under 17 U.S.C. Section 107.

Library of Congress Card Number: 97-65911
ISBN: 0-7821-2064-4

Manufactured in the United States of America

10 9 8 7 6 5 4 3 2 1

Acknowledgments

A modern book, especially a computer book, is never the work of one individual, and this book is a prime example. It took three writers and a talented team of editors, electronic publishing specialists, graphic designers, and production coordinators to get this book ready to go to press. We'd especially like to thank Dan Brodnitz, acquisitions editor, and Lee Ann Pickrell, editor, for their excellent work as editors, brainstormers, and guardians of quality. Their patience and diligence are an author's dream. Thanks for an excellent job also go to Debi Bevilacqua, electronic publishing specialist; Inbar Berman, graphic illustrator; Amy Eoff, production coordinator; Mark Butler, technical editor, Lynnzee Elze Spence, indexer; Kristine Plachy, acquisitions manager; Barbara Gordon, executive managing editor; and Amy Romanoff, associate publisher.

Finally a big thanks to our families, friends, and coworkers who put up with us and stood by us as we worked on this project.

Contents at a Glance

Table of Contents

PART 3: CONSTRUCTING YOUR INTRANET 159

Chapter 8: Installing Intranet Software 161

Chapter 9: Creating Intranet Pages with HTML 197

Introduction

You've heard about the Internet, the Web, intranets, and now extranets. You've heard the hype—you *need* an intranet for your business to succeed. You may not even know what an intranet is yet, but every magazine and newspaper with a technology column is turning up the heat on your intranet plans, making you feel that you're doomed without the latest technology.

Well, this book cuts through the intranet hype and helps you decide if an intranet is right for your business and if it is, what *kind* of intranet. We'll show you how you can set up different kinds of intranet sites, each meeting the specific needs of different types of businesses. How can we do that? By giving you the information you need in a concise, friendly little book.

NOTE   If you want even more information, *Mastering Intranets*, also from Sybex, covers more intranet territory.

What to Expect

This book isn't going to show you how to do everything required to set up an intranet; however, we'll give you all the basics you need to make decisions about your intranet from planning to implementation, and we'll point to other resources in print and on the Web that you can use to learn more about this expanding new technology. We're going to assume that you don't know much about intranets—maybe even not much about the related technologies of the Web and the Internet. But we also assume that you're smart, so we'll give you the explanations you need, plus clear, concise instructions beginning with using a browser, to creating an intranet business plan, to creating intranet pages, to setting up an intranet server, and more!

This book is ideal for a newly appointed Webmaster, the executive whose group is about to launch an intranet, or anyone else new to intranet technology and needing the essentials in a straightforward format.

We've divided the book into three parts: "Getting Started with Intranets," "Planning Your Intranet," and "Constructing Your Intranet." Each part builds on your knowledge of intranets, allowing you to make informed decisions about your company's intranet. Let's take a closer look.

Getting Started—What Is an Intranet?

An *intranet* is many things. It can be as simple as a Web server and some HTML pages your users access from their desktop or as complex as several specialized servers running multimedia applications, HR benefits enrollment, a technical support help desk, and collaborative meeting software connecting several remote locations over private networks. Part 1, "Getting Started with Intranets," will cover the basics, including a quick overview of the two most popular Web browsers used to access an intranet—Microsoft Internet Explorer and Netscape Navigator.

Planning to Plan

One area we'll spend some time on is planning. The stronger, more adaptive your intranet plan is, the better your intranet will meet its goals—even if those goals change, your plan will be flexible enough to make it work. Part 2, "Planning Your Intranet," shows you how to "plan to plan" as well as how to plan content, security, hardware, and software.

Building Things

Once you've become familiar with intranets and set out your intranet plan, you'll need to build your intranet's components. Those pieces of your intranet may be HTML pages, Acrobat files, multimedia, sound, or video. Part 3, "Constructing Your Intranet," explains just enough HTML to get you going and gives you tips on the tools you'll use to construct your intranet and on other types of content you can add. You'll also get a close look at some examples of different types of intranets.

Of course, the best intranet is only as useful as it is used, so we'll also explain how you can create a training plan to get your users started and establish connections within your company to keep your content current. Finally, we'll pass along some tips on where to look for the latest information for your intranet.

NOTE Just like the Web, intranet information changes rapidly. Much information about intranets is available on the Web and may have changed by the time this book is published. If you can't find the information you need, try using one of the Internet search engines mentioned throughout this book to find the latest info.

Understanding the Basics

We've also included two appendices to add to your intranet knowledge. Appendix A, "Intranet Glossary," helps you define all the terms and phrases you may come across as you implement your intranet. Appendix B, "Intranet Protocol—TCP/IP," gives you background information about the underlying "glue" that keeps the Internet and your intranet running seemlessly.

Conventions

Throughout this book, our goal is to give you the most information possible in the most useful format. We don't have a lot of space, so we won't waste any. When you need an Internet address, we'll put it in a special typeface, for example, `http://www.sybex.com`, so you can easily pick it out. New terms are italicized. We'll also pull important information from the text and put it into notes, tips, or warnings like this one.

TIP	Notes, Tips, and Warnings point you toward small bites of useful information. Pay special attention to Warnings, which help you sidestep potential problems.

Another way we've made information more useful is to include sidebars on mini-topics within a chapter. We've added them where they're useful, so some chapters won't have any while others have several. If you're in a hurry, you can skip the sidebars, but you'll want to come back to the information. You may also want to skim the book's sidebars for useful information.

We hope this book gives you all the essential information you need to plan, construct, and implement a successful intranet. If along the way you find new tips or suggestions, feel free to send them to us, so we can continue to improve this book in future editions.

Part 1

Getting Started
with Intranets

Chapter 1

WHAT IS AN INTRANET?

- **The difference between an intranet and the Internet**
- **Understanding intranets**
- **How intranets are being used**
- **What an intranet looks like**
- **Answers to frequently asked questions about intranets**

Intranet—it's the new trend in Internet-based technology. If you open any computer magazine or even the local Sunday paper, you'll read about intranets and intranet tools, trends, and possibilities. So what is this technological phenomenon, and why has it become part of America's business language at such a breakneck speed?

We'll start off by discussing how an intranet is the same as the Internet and how it differs. In the process, we'll cover some basic Internet and intranet terminology and concepts. As the discussion moves from the Internet to intranets, you'll see that much of the Internet's functionality is available for intranets, with the added benefits of a controlled, secure environment, a clearer target audience, and increased access speed. Because of these factors, intranets are much more productive business environments than the Internet.

Then we'll look at how some organizations are taking advantage of intranet technology and discuss the "look" of an intranet. The last part of this chapter answers some frequently asked intranet questions, including how you should determine if the Internet or an intranet is appropriate for your needs.

Depending on your background, some or most of this material may be familiar; however, you should still skim through this chapter to make sure you're clear on the fundamentals before proceeding on to Chapter 2, "Using a Web Browser to Access an Intranet."

Intranet or Internet: What's the Difference?

Any definition of an intranet starts, of necessity, with the Internet. The *Internet* is that network of networks that connects people and computers worldwide. Most users' contact points for the Internet are e-mail and the World Wide Web. However, Telnet and e-mail were available at my company long before Web access. Also users may have one kind of Internet access—e-mail—at work and another—the Web—at home. Some surveys estimate that there are more than 30 million Internet users today and that some 8 to 10 million of those users have access to the World Wide Web.

In addition to e-mail and the World Wide Web, many experienced Internet users communicate and share files over the Net using somewhat lesser-known approaches, such as Usenet and FTP. We'll discuss all four of these ways to access the Internet later in this section. But first you might be wondering what these pieces of the Net have to do with intranets.

NOTE You'll find an extensive glossary of Internet and intranet terms at the back of this book. When you encounter an unfamiliar word or phrase and you want more information than the text provides, check the glossary.

What's This Have to Do with Intranets?

You'll notice that much of what you learn about the Internet can also be accomplished using an intranet. Why set up an intranet if you already have an Internet presence? Or why not set up an intranet and make it available both inside and outside the company? We'll answer those questions later in this chapter and in Part II, as we cover planning for an intranet. First, let's define what an intranet is.

An *intranet* is an internal company network that uses the Internet standards of *HTML* (*HyperText Markup Language*) and *HTTP* (*HyperText Transfer Protocol*) and the *TCP/IP* (*Transmission Control Protocol/Internet Protocol*) communications protocol along with a graphical Web browser to support business applications and provide departmental, interdepartmental, and companywide communications solutions. That definition is only one of many intranet definitions. For example, an intranet can be as simple as an internal Web server that allows employees access to an employee handbook and a phone list. The intranet on the floor below could include sophisticated interactions with a database, video conferencing, private discussion groups, and multimedia. The exact definition of an intranet is impossible because you can set up so many kinds of intranets.

Here's how *PC Magazine* described an intranet:

> Building a private intranet accessed through a server you control is like living on an island that doesn't appear on any maps. The barbarians never see you.

An intranet uses a Web server, but unlike an Internet-based Web, an intranet Web server is only connected to a company's local area network. An intranet can also use news and mail servers to create private newsgroups for your intranet and to send and receive e-mail for your users. In other words, an intranet uses the tools and standards of the Internet to create an infrastructure that can be accessed only by those within a corporate enterprise. In many cases, those inside what's been called the "Web within" can venture out onto the Internet, but unauthorized users can't come in.

Some companies are creating private intranets that can be accessed by outside users on a selective basis. For example, if your company partners with a company whose intranet contains product information your company uses internally to place orders, your two companies may link intranets to save duplicating information.

NOTE There are several ways to selectively allow outside access to your intranet. We'll discuss those in Chapter 6, "Planning Your Intranet's Security."

Just like the Web, your intranet can use multimedia, sound, and fill-in forms to add functionality and interest. You can also incorporate private newsgroups and use FTP to extend your intranet's functionality. Unlike the Web, because your intranet is a closed environment, you control access and because your intranet is on a closed system, it usually runs significantly faster than an Internet Web site.

Now let's look more closely at the Internet technology you will use to build an intranet.

NOTE Although an intranet can use many aspects of Internet technology, you'll often hear an intranet referred to as simply *a Web*. Even though this book will focus on the Web aspect of intranets, we're going to use the term *intranet* instead of *Web* to avoid any possible confusion with the World Wide Web. While we're talking about names, we should mention that, although commonly used, the phrase *the intranet* is a bit of a misnomer. Unlike the Internet, in reality, there is no single intranet, but many, independent intranet implementations.

E-Mail

If the Web is the heart of the Internet, e-mail is its lifeblood. E-mail allows you to interact with the online world at your own pace. You can quickly dash off a note or take time to carefully craft and rework an idea before sending it. E-mail allows the spontaneity of the telephone with the luxury of time and thought that letter writing allows.

Most of you use e-mail daily; it's part of your routine. For those who've just connected, we'll quickly explain how e-mail works.

Let's start by clarifying the term *e-mail*. For the purposes of our discussion, we mean e-mail that is transported via the Internet or possibly your intranet. Your company or an online service may have a closed e-mail system that functions like regular e-mail and may even use the same e-mail program, but it limits you to users it knows about.

Now say you want to send e-mail to someone outside your company. To send and receive e-mail, you must have three things: an Internet connection, an Internet account, and an e-mail program. You may already have everything you need to send e-mail at your work or through school. Also, if you're connected to one of the major online services, such as CompuServe or America Online, you can send e-mail to the Internet just as you can send e-mail to other service users.

If you don't have everything you need, you must first establish an Internet account. A company called an *Internet service provider* (ISP) provides you with an Internet account and may also handle your e-mail connection. If not, your internal MIS department may manage your e-mail connection (the lines and mail server) that transports your e-mail from your desktop to the Internet.

Your e-mail program can be as sophisticated as your word processor, or it can be a simple command-line utility. You can even use a Web browser to send e-mail. Some e-mail systems allow you to create bulletin boards for group postings or public folders for shared information. If your company's e-mail system has those features, you already have a low-tech beginning for your intranet.

While using e-mail software is beyond the scope of this book, we will cover e-mail addressing conventions because those conventions are similar to Web addresses and Usenet newsgroups. We'll need to know how those addresses work as we discuss using the Internet and intranets.

E-mail uses a system that separately identifies the user from the place they are sending from or to and identifies the type of place that the message is coming from or to. For example, if you send e-mail to the address

`JDoe@MyCompany.com`

the structure tells you that mail should go to a user named `JDoe` at a company called `MyCompany`. The `.com` part tells you that the company is a commercial business. Other types of addresses, called *domains,* that you'll see are government (`.gov`), organizations (`.org`, usually nonprofit), and educational institutions (`.edu`). There are other domains and proposals to add even more, but these are the ones you'll come across most often as you send and receive e-mail using both the Internet and your intranet.

When you tell someone your e-mail address, you pronounce the period as *dot* and the ampersand as *at.* Most user names are made up of the first initial of the first name and then the last name. Normally you say the initial distinctly from the last name. Using the example address, you'd say "jay doe at my company dot com." Remember that most, but not all, addresses will work this way—some systems use numbers to identify users instead of real names.

The World Wide Web

Many people interchange the terms *Internet* and *World Wide Web*. These terms are different, though. You can think of the World Wide Web (also called *WWW* or just the *Web*) as a movie, and the Internet as both the hardware and the wires that get that movie into your home or office. In technical terms, the Web uses the HTTP protocol to deliver Web content, such as HTML pages, across the Internet. We'll discuss what this means in just a second.

You may already use the Web on a daily basis, but let's run through a few basic Web terms and concepts to make sure we're all speaking the same language. The Web is usually accessed via a *browser*, which is a program on your computer that knows how to read and display Web content. Netscape Navigator and Microsoft Internet Explorer are the two most popular browsers available today.

The Web was designed as a *client-server network.* In other words, Web content is distributed—or served—to the Internet from *Web servers*, computers that are connected to the Web and run Web server software, such as Netscape FastTrack Server or Microsoft Internet Information Server. This information is then received by *Web clients*. Even if you've never heard this term before, there's a good chance you've been operating one of these for some time. A Web client is just a computer that's connected to the Web and runs software (such as a browser) that can retrieve files from the Web.

NOTE
There are many other kinds of network servers besides Web servers. If you're connected to a corporate network, your company is probably using at least one server to help you access network resources, such as printers and shared hard drives, and another server to help you access your e-mail. Just as your computer can run more than one program at a time, a computer with enough power and memory, can run more than one server at the same time.

Web pages, e-mail, programs, pictures—all kinds of computer files—are sent over the Internet using *protocols*. These protocols are a set of common rules that allow computers running different operating systems to efficiently communicate with each other. These rules determine how information is sent from server to client and back again. Transmission Control Protocol/Internet Protocol, or TCP/IP, is the standard protocol for Internet communication. One of the other protocols you'll hear a lot about is HTTP or Hypertext Transfer Protocol. HTTP is the protocol used to distribute Web content on both the Internet and an intranet.

NOTE   When you see a Web or intranet address, also called a *URL* or *Uniform Resource Locator*, it usually begins with `http://` as a signal to your browser to use the HTTP protocol to transfer the file to your computer.

The word *Hypertext* in Hypertext Transfer Protocol refers to one aspect of the way information is organized on the Web. Although hypertext is a large part of what's made the Web and intranets so powerful and so popular, it isn't unique to them. If you have used a Windows Help file or a Macintosh hypercard stack, then you've already used a hypertext system. In its simplest terms, hypertext is just a way of presenting information in a nonlinear format. It lets you move through information based on context, rather than just following the kind of strict, predetermined sequence you'd find in a book. *Links* are special areas of text that you can click on to move through the document. A link is usually set off typographically so you know it's clickable. To design an effective intranet, you'll need to get a good feel for how to effectively organize hypertext content. We'll discuss hypertext in much more detail in Chapter 2.

The Web's hypertext is written in something called HTML. Although HTML stands for *Hypertext Markup Language*, it's really more of a set of text codes than it is a programming language. If you've used an older DOS-based word processor like WordPerfect 5.1 or WordStar, HTML will probably be a familiar concept. Early Web publishers had to create all their HTML code by hand, but today many authoring tools, like Microsoft FrontPage or Adobe PageMill, make creating HTML pages remarkably easy. We'll look at some of these authoring tools in Chapter 11, "Using Intranet Authoring and Management Tools."

Just as e-mail has an addressing scheme, the Web also has one. Web addresses or URLs are similar to the e-mail addresses we looked at earlier in this chapter. Let's take a typical URL, for example, the address of the Excite search engine:

```
http://www.excite.com/
```

The first section of the URL, the part up to the colon and double slashes, defines the protocol, in this case HTTP. Web browsers may support other protocols, including FTP, mail, or news.

After the double slashes, you'll find the the name of the server you'd like to connect to. In this example, we're connecting to a World Wide Web server at a company called Excite. The site is a commercial site. If we wanted to connect directly to a page, we'd add the page name after the single slash. Let's say you wanted to go to the advanced search page at the Yahoo Web site. You'd use the URL:

```
http://www.yahoo.com/search.html
```

Since most intranet access is via a Web browser, you'll need to use URLs to access the bulk of your intranet's information.

Usenet

Usenet is a network of computers that distribute Usenet newsgroups. *Newsgroups* are really discussion areas arranged hierarchically by subject. Newsgroup names follow standard patterns much like Internet mail addresses and Web addresses. There are eight primary categories:

`alt`—Alternative groups discussing some of the most interesting or bizarre things you've ever imagined.

`comp`—Computer-related topics including hardware, software, computer design, and so on.

`misc`—Miscellaneous topics not covered by other groups. This area may be duplicated by an `alt` newsgroup.

`rec`—Recreational interests, including the outdoors, hobbies, movies, television, and so on.

`sci`—Scientific topics from astronomy to zoology.

`soc`—Discussion of social topics, culture, and related issues.

`talk`—Conversational groups on a wide range of subjects.

Other categories exist; we've just listed the ones you're most likely to encounter. In each category, you'll find groups that aren't available on all networks, and groups sometimes quickly come and go, so don't be surprised if a newsgroup you hear about isn't available the next time you log on. Figure 1.1 shows you a sample of available Usenet newsgroups.

Like e-mail addresses and Web URLs, newsgroup addresses are divided into domains to identify where the information should be routed. Usenet newsgroups start at the highest level and work to more specific levels as you read from right to left.

The newsgroups shown in Figure 1.1 are in the comp category. Notice that we're using a browser, in this case Netscape Navigator, to access Usenet. You can also use a generic newsreader or special software that works only for your Internet provider.

If you decide to create a Usenet newsgroup that is only available via your intranet, you'll probably use a browser to read messages.

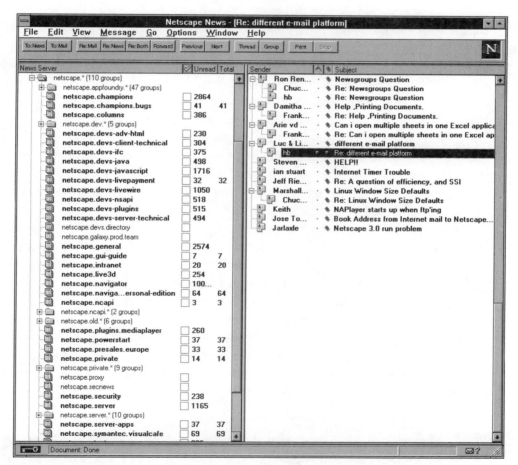

FIGURE 1.1: Sample Usenet newsgroups

FTP

The fourth Internet component that we'll discuss is *FTP*. FTP stands for *File Transfer Protocol.* This protocol was created to let different types of computers transfer files with each other in a standard way. Nowadays, many people send files via e-mail. Just a few years ago, the limitations of the technology made this a fairly painful and time-consuming process; FTP offered a much easier way to move files back and forth. FTP is still popular, particularly with companies, universities, and other organizations who want to make space on a hard drive accessible across the Internet.

Like Usenet, FTP can be accessed via a Web browser or by using a dedicated FTP utility, such as WS_FTP, an excellent shareware program.

When you use FTP through a browser or graphical FTP utility, you'll see a directory listing similar to the kind of listing you see when you open a folder on your Macintosh or use Explorer or File Manager on your Windows PC. Figure 1.2 shows a sample FTP listing. Command-line FTP utilities are also available for most platforms. On the Internet, you can access many machines as an *anonymous ftp* user.

When you use anonymous ftp, most sites track you in some way, but as a rule it's an unsecured world of unfiltered and uncensored information.

Now that you have a basic idea of the differences and similarities between the Internet and an intranet, we'll get a little more specific and give you some background on where this technology came from.

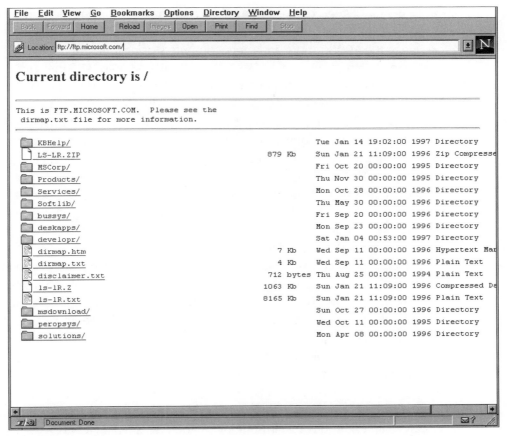

FIGURE 1.2: A sample FTP listing

A Brief History of Intranets and the Internet

Intranets are the big breakthrough in corporate communications that the Internet-based World Wide Web was hyped to provide. Internet Web technology took too long to create a stable, secure environment that businesses could rely on. If technology was not the primary driving force, it was, nevertheless, a vital component, and a little chronology can provide some perspective. Here are some Internet milestones that made intranets possible:

- In 1969, ARPAnet, an experimental four-computer network, was established by the Advanced Research Projects Agency (ARPA) of the U.S. Department of Defense so research scientists could communicate.

- By 1971, ARPAnet comprised almost two dozen sites, including MIT and Harvard. By 1974, ARPAnet comprised 62 sites and by 1981, more than 200 sites.
- During the 1980s, more and more computers using different operating systems were connected. In 1983, the military portion of ARPAnet was moved onto the MILnet, and ARPAnet was officially disbanded in 1990.
- In the late '80s, the National Science Foundation's NSFnet began its own network and allowed everyone to access it. It was, however, primarily the domain of techies, computer-science graduates, and university professors.
- In the late '80s and early '90s, Tim Berners-Lee and his coworkers at the European Particle Research Center (CERN) in Switzerland created what would become the World Wide Web. The goal was to improve the way people shared information and research by creating a system in which hypertext documents could be easily transmitted, displayed, and printed on almost any kind of computer hooked to the Internet.
- In 1992, the World Wide Web system and software were released, and in late 1993, NCSA (the National Center for Supercomputing Applications) released versions of Mosaic (the first graphical Web browser) for Microsoft Windows, for Unix systems running the X Window System, and for the Apple Macintosh.
- In February 1993, when President Bill Clinton visited Silicon Graphic's headquarters, employees around the world caught his address via an internal network based on Web technology—an early intranet.
- In 1994, Netscape Communications released the Netscape Navigator browser. Navigator was widely distributed across the globe via the Internet. It played an enormous role in spurring on the Web's rapid growth.
- In December 1994, Bill Gates ordered Microsoft to redirect its focus toward the Internet, and then in August 1995, the company introduced Internet Explorer, a browser that went into head-to-head competition with Netscape Navigator.
- By 1996, the hottest menu item in the cybercafe was Java, Sun's programming language for creating Internet and intranet applications. Meanwhile, Netscape, Microsoft, Apache, and others began to release inexpensive or free Web server software that made setting up feature-rich intranets much easier.

- And 1997 and beyond? Intranets are redefining the way the corporate world communicates. Walls between departments are being torn down, and companies are rethinking old ideas about how they work. Intranets are expanding into *extranets*, or internets that are blended with an Internet Web site to expand the type and range of information available.

How Intranets Are Being Used

The ways in which an intranet can be used by industries, corporations, or organizations are as numerous and as varied as the enterprises themselves. Figure 1.3 shows a recent estimate of how intranets are being deployed in corporate environments by percentage of use.

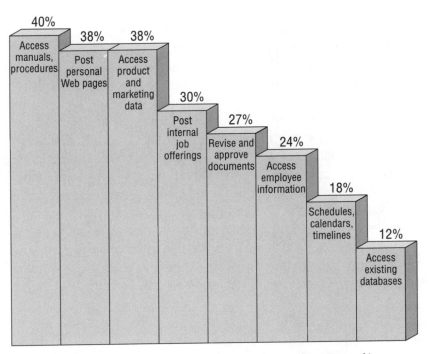

FIGURE 1.3: How corporations are using intranets (source: Zona Research)

> **TIP**
>
> For some interesting conversation with some people who are wild about intranets, go to http://www.intranut.com. You'll find a discussion group, case studies, and articles, including "A Practical Guide to Managing Intranet Projects" and "How Could the Intranet Redefine Corporate Life As We Know It?"

Here are some examples of how several companies use their intranet:

- At Genentech, the pharmaceutical company, employees can access the employee directory, find out how to get business cards, read company announcements, and get information on research seminars, building facilities, commuting options, benefits, and child care.
- At Compaq Computer, employees tap into an intranet to reallocate investments in their 401(k) plans.
- Silicon Graphics uses their intranet to connect several departmental intranets, allowing them to share data with other groups in the organization and to network with departments who may not have an on-site office but can dial in to the corporate intranet for sales and marketing information, online conferencing, or other tasks.
- At AT&T, employees stay in touch with one another via an intranet database that contains the phone numbers, addresses, titles, and organizational information for all 300,000 of them—an electronic phone book that contains data on more people than the directories for many medium-sized towns.
- At HBO, researchers, programmers, and high-level executives use an intranet to access a database that contains information on every movie ever made; it tracks a movie's cast, director, distributor, how much money it made, whether it's on videocassette, and when it's scheduled to air for the next two years.
- At Ford Motor Co., with the help of an intranet that linked design centers in Asia, Europe, and the United States, engineers created the 1996 Taurus.

Throughout this book, you will find many other examples of how companies are using intranets to increase productivity, improve employee morale, save money, save trees, and otherwise make better business decisions.

According to Zona Research, the market for Internet and intranet-related technologies and products topped $5.3 billion during 1995, exceeding industry projections.

Zona Research also predicts that intranet projects will outpace Internet spending by 4 to 1 and will reach up to $7.8 billion by 1998. The reason: faster-than-anticipated deployment of corporate intranets. Perhaps this helps explain a short statement by Sun CEO Scott G. McNealy: "Intranets are huge."

For example, Digital Equipment Corporation has more than 400 internal Web sites, Silicon Graphics has some 600 Web servers, and Sun Microsystems has more than 1,000. Frank Dietrich, former corporate Web systems manager at Silicon Graphics, said the intranet is "like a thousand flowers blooming." According to Dietrich, at Silicon Graphics there's "hardly a piece of information that's not online."

International Data Corporation reported that even in 1995 sales of Web servers for intranet use exceeded those for Internet use by 10 percent, and it forecasts that by the year 2000, server licenses for intranet usage will outdistance those for Internet usage by 10 to 1.

Netscape Communications Corporation says that about 80 percent of its revenue comes from companies that primarily use its technology to set up intranets. Microsoft, Netscape's arch rival in the browser war, reports that 80 percent of its Internet servers are used on intranets.

In 1995, the market for *Web authoring tools* (the software used to create Web pages) was $2 million; predictions are that it will hit $300 million by the close of the '90s, and Forester Research estimates that by 1999, the entire market for Internet software is expected to grow to $8.5 billion, with most of the growth coming from intranets.

That's quite a bit of hype about intranets. You can see that there is a lot of excitement gathering around intranets and that the potential for growth and productivity when using an intranet is much stronger than the business growth of Internet-based Web sites.

Now that we have explained how an intranet differs from the Web, given you some Web history, and shown you a glimpse of the future of intranets, we'll get hands-on and show you what an intranet might look like in your organization.

The Look of an Intranet

The two basic elements of an intranet are its *home page* and *links*. The home page is simply the first screen you see when you access a Web site. A link usually appears on the screen in some visually distinctive way, and a link can be text or a graphic. Text links are generally in a particular color (blue is the default for both Netscape's and Microsoft's Web browsers) and are underlined. When you place your mouse pointer over a graphical link, it often turns into a hand. When you click on a link, you go to the *page* (screen) that the link represents. And that's how you navigate an intranet. Figure 1.4 shows the home page of NatureLand's corporate intranet. Figure 1.5 shows the BusinessPlus home page. We'll use these two sample intranet sites to show how things work and how you can put some of the ideas we discuss into practice.

FIGURE 1.4: NatureLand's intranet home page

Some home pages are colorful and full of graphics; others are primarily text. (For step-by-step instructions on creating home pages and a thorough discussion of design

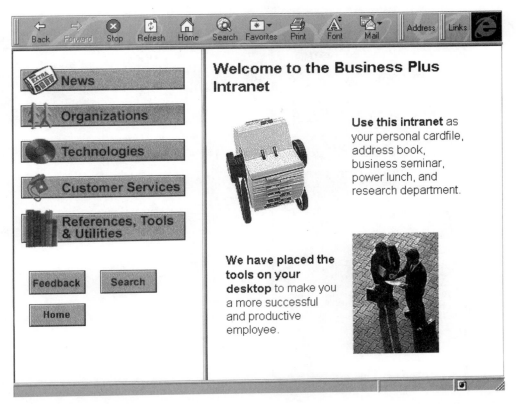

FIGURE 1.5: BusinessPlus's intranet home page

issues, see Part III, "Constructing Your Intranet." Throughout Part III, you'll find some ideas to get you started setting up your own intranet.) How a home page looks depends on its purpose, the corporate culture, and, of course, the talents of the designer. It can be as flashy or as staid as its developer wants. The only limits are good taste and the color and design of the corporate logo.

Earlier we mentioned that many of the things you can do on the Internet can be implemented in the more stable and secure environment of an intranet, including newsgroups, FTP, multimedia, sound, database access, and custom applications. Figure 1.6 shows you a sample *search page* that was added to the BusinessPlus intranet. The search page allows you to specify key words or concepts that you'd like to find.

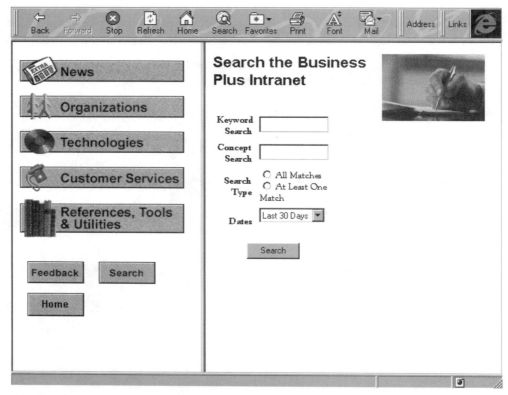

FIGURE 1.6: A sample search page

Figure 1.7 shows you a sample form that was added to the site to allow intranet users to send feedback. Users could just as easily send e-mail, but by using an HTML form, specific data can be captured using radio buttons, check boxes, and text boxes in a standard format.

Notice that the two intranets look very different and provide different functionality. NatureLand's intranet is primarily informational with little two-way interaction. BusinessWorld's intranet provides information but also gathers information from users—information that allows the site to grow and improve according to its plan. Each intranet has a plan that suits the style of the company and the users. Since these sites are fictional intranets, we've made some guesses on the companies' users and technical proficiency when planning the intranet sites. We'll go into further detail in the planning chapters in Part II.

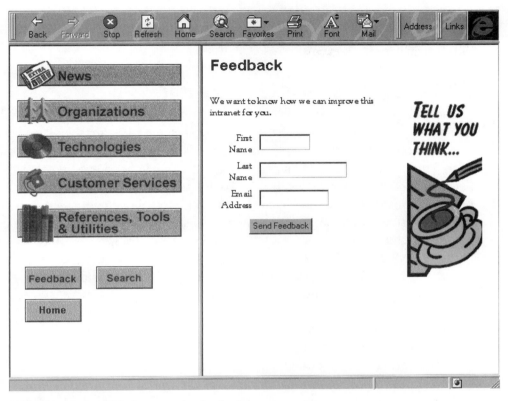

FIGURE 1.7: An HTML form to gather feedback

Some of the Most Frequently Asked Questions about Intranets

This section includes some of the questions we often encounter when intranets become the topic of conversation. Following each question is a brief answer and some ideas on how to deal with that intranet issue. All these questions, however, are multifaceted and lead to other questions and to answers that require much more detailed discussion, which is why we wrote this book. For in-depth information, see the cross-referenced sections of this book.

After you've read through these questions and answers, you'll have some of the high-level information you need to answer that last, big question, intranet or Internet: Which is right for my business?

What Hardware Do I Need to Get Started?

The hardware you need varies in direct relation to the number of users and the complexity of your intranet design. The more users, the more machines you'll need and the more sophisticated your hardware needs to be. If your intranet plans call for large, enterprise-wide use of intranet applications, you'll need even more high-end hardware. You also need to decide what platform will integrate best into your current network infrastructure and will provide you with the software you want to run. For example, a simple Windows-based intranet for a small company or department could function adequately running Web server software on a PC with at least 16MB of memory, a 486 or Pentium CPU, a 500MB to 2GB hard disk, and at least VGA graphics (As noted earlier in this chapter, a Web server serves the same purpose as any other server on a network: it stores and "serves up" all the programs and documents you place on it).

The client machines, those that will be on your employees' desktops or factory worktables, can be almost anything as long as they have network interface cards. If, however, you want your employees to be able to access Java applets, sound and video files, and multimedia files, they need fast machines: A 486 with at least 8MB of RAM is the minimum requirement, but a Pentium with 16MB is better. They'll also need sound boards, speakers, video cards, high-resolution monitors, and so on. (After all, when you click on a sound link, you feel cheated if you don't hear it.)

For example, Electronic Arts develops interactive entertainment software and is known for producing some of the best-selling computer games in the world. Because its intranet maximizes the multimedia capabilities of the World Wide Web, its 1300 employees need machines that can play movies and sound.

This is a brief, simplistic answer to a question that can have important implications for your company's bottom line. For all the details about hardware options, see Chapter 7, "Choosing Intranet Hardware and Software."

What about Software?

The software you choose will affect every aspect of your intranet. From the browser to the server, you'll want to make sure that your software has the functionality you need, the ease-of-use your users will want, and the affordability that your CFO will demand. Chapter 7, "Choosing Intranet Hardware and Software," helps you sort out the issues regarding software availability and functionality for Windows, Mac, and Unix.

How Do I Secure My Intranet?

As with most questions, the answer depends on who you ask and how you ask it. For most intranets that don't connect to the Internet, your security issues will be the same as the security issues your current network administrator faces. Remember that many security problems are not break-ins but the distribution of confidential information outside the company from within. Disgruntled employees, gossips, and careless remote users can pose greater security threats than an intranet.

If you decide to connect your internal users to the Internet, you'll need to ensure that your intranet security isn't compromised. This means you'll probably need to install a *firewall* to insulate your internal network and intranet from unauthorized users outside your company. Chapter 6, "Planning Your Intranet's Security," gets you started setting up security and discusses firewall products.

How Much Programming Will I Need To Do?

Count on some programming if you plan a top-end intranet that has full human resources and help desk support with an interface to a database and e-mail. Also HTML is a kind of programming in its own right with special issues that you'll need to solve. Chapters 9 and 10 discuss HTML and other content-programming issues.

Java, a platform-independent programming environment that's suited for creating applications for the Internet, intranets, and other types of networks, can be used to create small programs, called *applets,* that can be run on any machine using a browser that supports Java, including Netscape Navigator and Microsoft Internet Explorer. That means the same program you wrote on a Windows NT machine can work equally well on a Macintosh or Unix machine.

> **TIP**
>
> The more interactivity you want your site to have, the larger the programming effort to build that site. A good compromise is to start with the basics and add the advanced functionality in modules. This technique will shorten your development time and spread the costs and programming effort over time.

If you're not a programmer and can't afford one, you may be able to get by using some fancy HTML tricks, some add-in shareware programs, and JavaScript. JavaScript is a scripting language based on Java that is much quicker and simpler to code, and HTML can do some remarkable things by using tables, graphics, links, and style sheets in unconventional ways.

> **WARNING** If you start experimenting with HTML, remember to test any nonstandard coding using any possible browser your user may have. Some HTML functionality may not be available to the browser your users have on their desktops.

Many low-cost programs are available to help you use HTML forms, access databases, create simple animations and imagemaps, and create other useful or interesting effects. Part III, "Constructing Your Intranet," goes into detail on how you can get by when you need to keep the budget down and do it yourself.

Who Should Manage My Intranet?

If your company is small, it may be the same person who manages your Internet Web site. If your intranet is large, you may have to devote several employees to manage the servers and the firewall, to code HTML pages, to write Java applets, and to monitor site traffic. Part II, "Planning Your Intranet," discusses the many hats that intranet builders might wear.

How Much Will an Intranet Cost?

While cost is a factor—in some cases the driving force—behind implementing an intranet, costs alone shouldn't determine your intranet plan. Your plan should include requirements, functionality, construction, implementation, training, and management. Once you've developed a plan to satisfy your corporate intranet needs, you can then estimate the costs. To guess the cost without an idea of the overall plan will surely start your intranet on the road to failure.

Many people make the mistake of only adding the hardware and software costs to arrive at a total cost. Much of your intranet's costs will come from the people who write the programs, code the pages, create the graphics, and write the stories. Another mistake is to only think about costs without including return in the equation. Your intranet can be a valuable tool that allows your company to communicate more effectively and efficiently. When you can do that, you'll be more productive and save money.

Intranet or Internet: Which Is Right for My Business?

The major difference between the Internet and an intranet is focus: An Internet site looks outward from the company, and an intranet site is usually for internal use. You can establish an Internet site without having an intranet, and you can certainly implement an intranet site without connecting to the Internet. Whether you choose to implement one or the other or both, depends on the nature of your business and what you hope to accomplish with this emerging technology.

Here are some questions to help you decide:

- Are you primarily interested in improving communication among your employees, or do you need a better way to get customer feedback?
- Do you want to move in the direction of a paperless office, or do you want to take advantage of the newest way to get your company name in front of millions of consumers?
- Do you want to establish partnerships with suppliers, or do you want to reduce the number of phone calls to your Customer Service department?
- Which would make your business more efficient: getting the most up-to-date information to your employees in the field or making your catalog of products available online?
- How would you profile your corporate culture? Are employees computer literate? Is management comfortable with the security issues involved in connecting with the outside world?
- What are your budgetary requirements? Does your company have deep pockets, or is it a startup?
- What kind of technical resources does your company have? Is your Information Systems group one person or a whole department?

Regardless of which direction your company takes, starting with an intranet has one distinct advantage: You can start small and grow. With an intranet, you don't need to have massive amounts of content done all at once, and you are not presenting your company to the world. You can get your feet wet with the technology; you can get a feel for what's involved in choosing content and designing documents; and you can change your mind.

If you're leaning toward building an intranet, here's one more question to ponder.

Who Is Your Customer?

A corporation that establishes an Internet Web site usually does so with one purpose in mind: to serve the needs of its customers. Likewise, a corporation that establishes an intranet does so for its "customers"—the people within the corporation. If the intranet does not meet their needs, it will fail.

What are your customers' needs? In our experience, people in a corporation have two primary needs: to communicate with one another and to have access to all the information they need to do their jobs well.

For example, everybody in a corporation relies on the Human Resources department for everything from finding out how many vacation days they've accrued to adding a new family member to their health plan. And a beeper has become part of the dress code for employees in the Technical Support group. In addition, new employees and experienced ones need training, and people in Sales and Marketing gobble up new product descriptions faster than Research and Development can generate them.

The samples in Chapter 12, "Setting Up Specific Intranet Sites," were designed to show you how to meet these needs. If you are in the process of setting up an intranet or even if you already have one, take a look at these example sites. You might want to use them as a springboard for thinking through how you want to configure your intranet so it serves your "customers" better.

Many extremely successful (and large) intranets originated as proof-of-concept pilot projects, something you might want to consider. The intranet at Levi Strauss, for example, began as a pilot project with 25 users and six sites. Now the jeans people are well on their way to their goal of connecting 37,500 employees in 60 countries, and they expect the Levi intranet to eventually support full-motion video.

What we are seeing and hearing over and over is that word gets around. An individual department or a small group within a company implements an intranet for a special project or to solve some thorny problem, and the response from users is so enthusiastic that, like the man said, a thousand flowers begin to bloom.

Cultivating an intranet garden has become big business, and it may be what your business needs to come out smelling like a rose.

Our next chapter will show you how to use a browser to access your intranet's functionality. After we've done a high-level run-through on browsers, we'll give you some specific information on two of the most popular browsers around—Netscape Navigator and Microsoft Internet Explorer.

Chapter 2

USING A WEB BROWSER TO ACCESS AN INTRANET

FEATURING

- **Web browser basics**
- **A quick guide to Netscape Navigator**
- **A quick guide to Microsoft Internet Explorer**

In this chapter, we'll cover using a Web browser to interact with your intranet. Along the way, you'll pick up some more intranet basics, including a bit more about HTML. We'll start by giving you an overview of browser features and how to use them, and then we'll show you some specific tips for the two most popular browsers: Netscape Navigator and Microsoft Internet Explorer. Some tips will make using the browser easier, and others can be used as you plan and implement your intranet. Most of the intranet techniques we'll demonstrate will be familiar to World Wide Web users. If you're totally unfamiliar with the Internet and the Web, you may want to check out Christian Crumlish's excellent, practical guide, *The ABCs of the Internet*, from Sybex.

If you're already using the Internet a lot, particularly the Web, you already know how to use a Web browser. You may wish to skim this chapter for now, keeping it in mind as a training tool when you're ready to roll out your completed intranet. By using information from this chapter in your training sessions, you can reduce the amount of work needed to set up your intranet's training program.

TIP   Remember that when you encounter an unfamiliar word or phrase and you want more information than the brief definitions the text provides, check the glossary.

A Little More about HTML

Before we get started on browsers, let's revisit hypertext and HTML or Hypertext Markup Language. As you learned in Chapter 1, HTML is the format used to define pages that your browser can interpret and display. Hypertext allows information to be connected, or *linked*, in a nonlinear way. First, let's look at what it means to link information in a linear way. Using a phone book to look up a phone number is linear; you find the person or business you want listed in alphabetical order, although some other linear structures could be in numerical or time sequence. This book is an example of information presented in a linear, numerical format. You start with Chapter 1 and continue to the end of the book.

As long as there have been linear structures imposed on information, there probably have been attempts to get around the linear system and use something more intuitive. Think about how you might use a reference book on grizzly bears. First, you might look up some information by name or number to get started. For example, you might look in the contents and find a chapter on the physical characteristics of grizzlies. However, once you've begun, you would follow the logical connections in the information. If the book is well written, the chapters should have a structure that reinforces those connections. Sometimes the material may be too interconnected or diverse, and the writer may refer you to other parts of a book or even to other books. Let's say you're reading about grizzly bears in California. The book compares the interactions between the Native Americans in California and the grizzly to the relationship between Europeans and brown bears. At that point, the text might refer you to additional sources, so you might drop grizzlies altogether and pick up a book on pre-Columbian Native

American culture in California or a book on middle-European Gypsy dancing bears. References like those are the beginnings of hypertext. Using HTML, however, instead of flipping to a new section of the book or getting an entirely new book off the shelf, you simply click on the reference and open the new material.

In the computer world, the most familiar hypertext examples are Windows Help files, Macintosh hypercard stacks, and Adobe Acrobat files. These systems allow you to move through information in a nonlinear way by using jumps, or links, that work much like HTML links. Just click on one of these links and you move to the new material.

> **TIP**
>
> **Adobe Acrobat files can be used on your intranet to display information where the formatting and look of the document is important. You can even link Acrobat files to intranet files to extend the hypertext capabilities of your intranet. We'll show you how to use Acrobat files on your intranet in Chapter 10, "Adding Other Content to Your Intranet."**

Now you should have a good understanding of how HTML works. Later in Chapter 9, "Creating Intranet Pages with HTML," we'll get into actual HTML coding. As we get further into intranets, you'll become more familiar with the terminology and pick up some Net slang, as well. We'll start with Web browsers.

Most users call Netscape's Navigator browser simply Netscape; even though it's a bit confusing as Netscape's browser is only one of the software applications they produce. Netscape also makes server software. Microsoft's Internet Explorer is also a mouthful and is sometimes abbreviated MSIE or just IE. Even more confusing, sometimes it's called Explorer, which is also the name of the Microsoft Windows 95's and Windows NT 4's file manager utility. We'll frequently use *Netscape* and *IE* in the rest of this book when discussing browsers.

Web Browser Basics

As we discussed in Chapter 1, a Web browser—usually just called a *browser*—is the application you use to access any HTML-based information. That information—usually called *pages*—can be on the Internet or on an intranet. A browser is able to interpret HTML coding, called *styles* or *tags*, and use those codes to format and lay out the information in a window for you to see. In addition to HTML, browsers can interpret and display information stored in other formats, including sounds, graphics, Adobe Acrobat files, and Shockwave files. Some file types are readable by the browser itself. Others rely on a helper application. Some helper applications run alongside the browser and some inside the main browser window. Those that run inside the browser are called *plug-ins*.

> **TIP**
>
> Plug-ins extend the capabilities of your browser and are usually available for free. Most plug-ins only allow you to read files—to modify them or create your own, you'll probably need to buy the plug-in vendor's authoring software. You'll learn more about plug-ins in Chapter 10, "Adding Other Content to Your Intranet."

If you're familiar with a word processor, page layout program, or graphics program, you'll quickly be able to understand how most browser functions work. One important difference between browser software and most other software is how you obtain and pay for it. Both Netscape and IE are primarily obtained by downloading the software from the Net. Currently IE is available free of charge from the Microsoft Web site. Netscape is also available in a trial version that you may download and use for free for up to 90 days, after which you pay a nominal charge.

> **NOTE**
>
> Besides viewing Web pages, you can use your browser to access FTP, Telnet, Gopher, and e-mail and to read Usenet newsgroups. See *Mastering Intranets* from Sybex or your browser's documentation for the exact procedures.

Both the Netscape and Microsoft browser software have some common features and functionality. First, we'll cover some of these common browser elements including:

- Toolbars
- Icons
- Menus and dialog boxes

More advanced or specialized functionality is covered in the Quick Guide sections on Netscape and IE.

As we cover each browser, you may notice that it's slightly different than the browser you're using. The differences are probably because of two things: You're using a different kind of computer, so your version of the browser is slightly different, or your browser is a different version. At the time we wrote this book, we used the most current versions of each browser, in this case Netscape Navigator 3.01 and Microsoft Internet Explorer 3. Web browser technology changes rapidly, and newer versions are being released as frequently as three times a year. Don't worry—this chapter covers the basics and the newer versions should function much the same as the version you are learning about today.

Toolbars

Like your word processor, browsers use toolbars to make using the software easier. Unlike your word processor, the toolbar functionality used by your browser controls navigation and not formatting. Here is an example of Netscape Navigator's default toolbar:

You can customize it to show icons, text, or icons and text on the toolbar buttons. You can also turn parts of the toolbar on and off.

Microsoft's Internet Explorer also uses a toolbar for easy navigation. Here's an example of its toolbar:

Both browsers' toolbars have one common feature that you don't see on other toolbars—a URL location box. As you'll recall from Chapter 1, URLs (Uniform Resource Locators) are, in plain English, Web addresses. Here's what a URL location box looks like:

You can type your destination URL in the box, and then press Enter to access that page. If you follow links to other sites, you can check the URL of your current page in the location box.

Icons

Icons (or *buttons*) on the toolbar function like most toolbar icons you use in your other software programs; you click on the icons to perform menu functions. The most common icon on both browser toolbars and HTML pages alike is the Home icon. The Home icon is almost universally pictured as a small frame cottage, sometimes with a curl of smoke coming out of the chimney. When you click the Home icon, you return to the Home, or *primary*, page of either the browser or the site.

By default, if you click on the Home icon, most browsers take you to the software vendor's Web site home page. The same thing happens if you click on the browser icon on the right side of the toolbar. Your site will most likely have its own Home icon that will take users to your intranet's home page. You can also use the location or URL of your intranet's home page so it's your browser's default home page. In other words, when you open your browser, you'll see your intranet's home page, instead of the browser's. We'll see how to do this later in this chapter.

> **TIP**
>
> **Once you've installed browsers on your corporate desktops, you can change the default home URL so it accesses your intranet's home page, instead of the browser's.**

Icons are also used on HTML pages to represent links. These icons are sometimes obviously linked to another page or activity, but sometimes not. When we discuss planning your intranet content later in this book, we'll talk about using icons effectively to simplify your site and how to use icons to make the site useful for users with less technical knowledge.

WARNING Icon symbols are seldom universal. If your intranet audience has a wide cultural or regional makeup, you should include some descriptive text in your icon. This will allow users to more quickly grasp the meaning of an icon. After all, the idea of an intranet is to get information to your users quickly, not have them waste time deciphering the meaning of some cryptic icon.

Menus and Dialog Boxes

The menus allow you to access the toolbar functionality using the keyboard as well as the mouse. Menus also provide advanced features or options that aren't used as frequently, such as configuration information. When you select an item from a menu, a dialog box appears that allows you to change settings. Here's an example of a Netscape menu containing some advanced configuration options. And here's a dialog box that appears when you choose the Network Preferences option from the menu.

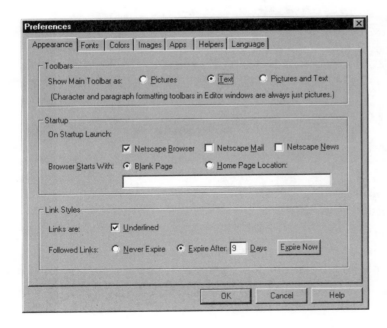

IE works very much the same way. Here's an example of a similar menu in IE:

And the dialog box that appears when you select the Options option:

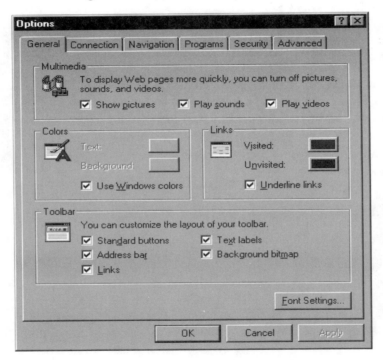

Where Can I Learn More?

The next two sections will cover the two most popular browsers in more detail and will give you a good idea of how to get started using either browser to access your intranet. While you'll find this information useful, this section can't be an in-depth tutorial on using browsers—or we'll never have time to build our intranet! Instead, if you need more information on using browsers, we'll give you some URLs on the Web that you can use to learn more.

> **TIP** If you don't already have a browser, you can get the latest version of Netscape from `http://www.netscape.com/` and IE is available from `http://www.microsoft.com/IE/`. This way you can learn how to use a browser as you read along.

Both Netscape and IE are available in a variety of versions for many operating systems. For example, you can get small, medium, and large versions of both Netscape and IE for Windows 95. The larger the version, the more features available in the browser. If your intranet plan doesn't call for the functionality in a larger version of the software, why take up more space with a full installation?

Because your intranet isn't set up yet, the following two Quick Guide sections will use Internet Web sites to help you learn how to use your specific browser. To follow the examples, you'll need a copy of your browser software installed and an Internet connection. The screen shots for this chapter will feature Netscape and IE on both Windows 95 and Windows NT versions. Your version may look slightly different if you use Macintosh or Unix versions.

A Quick Guide to Netscape Navigator

Start Navigator by double-clicking your Netscape icon. You'll then see the basic Netscape window, shown in Figure 2.1 with the main items labeled. Once the browser loads, you'll need to tell it where you want to go. You do this by specifying a URL. You can simply type one in the Location text box and press enter.

For example, type `www.adobe.com` in the URL box and press Enter. You'll see the Adobe Systems Web site. Click on the Get Acrobat icon, and you'll move to the Acrobat page.

Location or URL

Netscape icon—click
to go to Netscape's
Web site

Menu

Toolbar

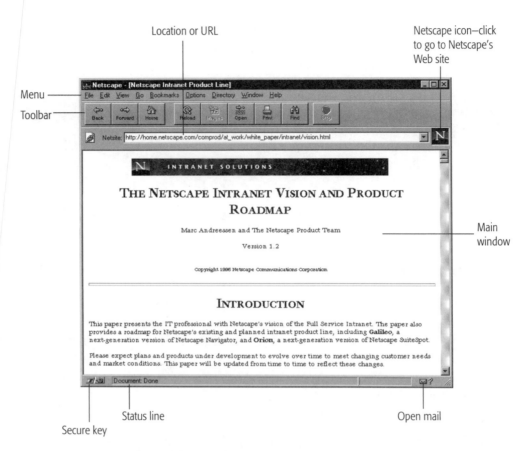

Main
window

Status line

Open mail

Secure key

FIGURE 2.1:   Main features of Netscape Navigator

TIP

Netscape adds the HTTP:// to the front of your URL
automatically.

If you're still a bit confused about Internet and intranet addressing schemes, refer back to Chapter 1 where e-mail, Web, and Usenet addresses are explained.

Later, we'll discuss how to distribute information on your intranet in other formats. Acrobat is a format that is widely used, both on intranets and the Web. You'll want to be able to easily return to this page without having to remember the URL. To save your address, you can *bookmark* it. A bookmark is just an entry in a list that stores information about the Web sites you want to remember. When you're ready to revisit a bookmarked site, you can simply click the name in your bookmark list rather than typing in a URL. To bookmark the Adobe Acrobat site:

1. Click the Bookmarks menu.
2. Click Add Bookmark.

That's it! Now click the Home icon to leave the Adobe site.

To go to a bookmarked URL:

1. Click the Bookmarks menu, and drag your mouse to the title of the Web site you'd like to visit.
2. When you've highlighted the desired URL, release the mouse button, and Navigator will attempt to access the site.

Using the Netscape Toolbar

Now we'll quickly cover the nine buttons at the top of the toolbar. Here's a description of each button's function, as shown in Figure 2.2.

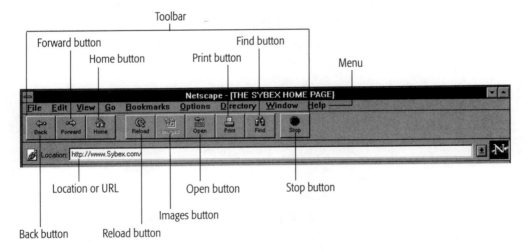

FIGURE 2.2: The default Navigator toolbar

> **Back**   Moves you to the previous document in your *history list*. A history list is a record of all the URLs that you've visited in your current Netscape session. If you exit Netscape, your history list will not be saved. To save a URL, use a bookmark.

Forward   Moves you to the next document in your history list.

Home   Takes you to the home page defined in your browser's configuration. The default home page for Netscape is `home.netscape.com`.

Reload   Reloads the current document. You can reload a document to ensure you have the most current version and not a copy stored on your hard drive. This option is useful for pages that are frequently updated, such as stock quote or sports score pages.

Images   Shows the images on the current page if you have turned off image display. This button will be grayed out for most users.

Open   Brings up the Open Location dialog box. This dialog box functions like the Location window, allowing you to type or paste in a URL to visit.

Print   Prints the current document.

Find   Searches for a word or phrase in the current document.

Stop   Stops loading the current document. Use this button if a page is taking longer to load than you'd like. Once you click the Stop button, any part of the document that can be displayed will appear.

Now we'll go a little bit further behind the scenes and look at some options you can choose when customizing your copy of Netscape.

Customizing Netscape

To customize Netscape, click the Options menu, and then click General Preferences. You'll see the Preferences dialog box. This dialog box has seven option tabs that allow you to choose which area you'd like to customize. We'll just cover the first three tabs: Appearance, Fonts, and Colors.

- The *Appearance tab* lets you change the type and size of your toolbar icons, your default startup window, your default startup URL, and your link options.
- From the *Fonts tab*, you can change your character encoding, proportional font attributes, and fixed font attributes.
- The *Colors tab* lets you modify the colors used for links, followed links, text, and background.

Let's start with the Appearance tab. On this tab, you can choose the size and appearance of your toolbar icons. If your users have smaller 14" or 15" monitors, you'll want to maximize the amount of useful window space they have to display information from your intranet. To do that, you'll want to minimize the space the toolbar takes up by using the Appearance tab, shown in Figure 2.3.

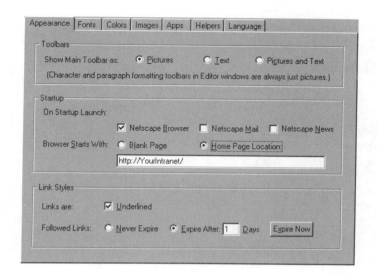

FIGURE 2.3:
Use the Appearance tab to modify the way Netscape looks on your screen.

Click on Text or Pictures to use the smallest icons available. We recommend choosing Text icons if you're less familiar with computers; if your users are more computer-literate, choose Pictures. If you have a larger 17" or 21" monitor, then you can use the Pictures and Text option because you'll have plenty of screen space.

> **TIP**
>
> **Your monitor's resolution, as much as its screen size, determines how much of each document you'll see on each screen. For most intranets, 15" monitors running a 256 color driver at 800 x 600 resolution should produce acceptable results for most users.**

Now click the Fonts tab, shown in Figure 2.4. This tab has very few options, but if you have a small monitor, your choices can affect your intranet usability.

You'll may want to change the default font to something you feel is easier to read on the screen. For intranet usage on an average-sized monitor, try changing the point size to 11 point to get more text in each screen. If you have a larger monitor, 10 point might allow even more text on screen without sacrificing legibility.

> **TIP**
>
> **For easiest readability, your fixed font size should be the same size as your proportional font point size or one point smaller.**

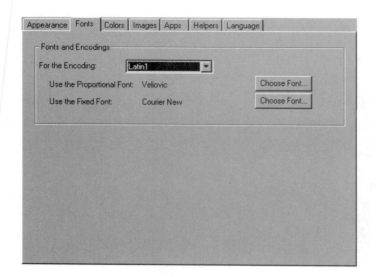

FIGURE 2.4:
Use the Fonts tab to choose which fonts and what size fonts your browser uses.

Next, click the Colors tab, shown in Figure 2.5. You can use this tab to specify the colors you'll see when you open a document. Part of your intranet's goal is presentation. For that reason, we recommend choosing the default colors and backgrounds that are defined in the HTML documents for your intranet installation.

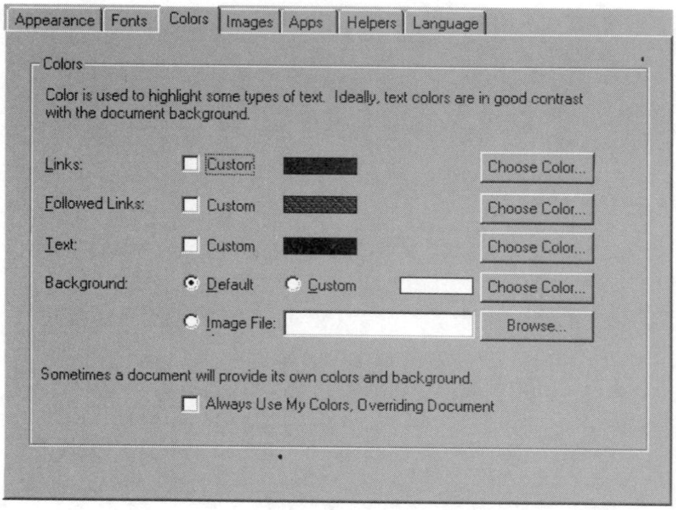

FIGURE 2.5:
The Colors tab

Now that you have a basic understanding of how to use Navigator to access your intranet, we'll move on to Internet Explorer.

A Quick Guide to Microsoft Internet Explorer

Start Internet Explorer by double-clicking on your IE icon. We'll use a Windows 95 version of the software for this Quick Guide to Internet Explorer. If you are using a different version, your screens and options may vary slightly. Figure 2.6 shows you an example of the Internet Explorer browser.

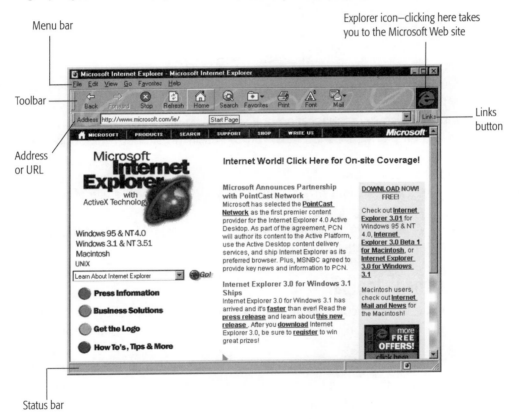

FIGURE 2.6: The main screen in Microsoft Internet Explorer

Returning to the example we used in the previous section, type www.adobe.com in the Address box and press Enter. You'll see the Adobe Systems Web site. Click on the Get Acrobat icon, and you'll move to the Acrobat page.

TIP   IE will add the HTTP:// to the front of your URL automatically.

As we discussed in the Netscape Quick Guide section, Acrobat is a format that is widely used, both on intranets and the Web. You'll want to be able to easily return to this page without having to remember the URL. To save your address, you can add it to your *Favorites list.* The IE Favorites list is like a bookmark in Navigator—an entry in a list that stores information about the Web sites you want to remember.

To add the Adobe Acrobat site to your Favorites list:

1.   Click the Favorites menu.
2.   Click Add to Favorites.

You're done!

You could have also clicked the Favorites icon and then Add to Favorites to accomplish the same task.

You may also save the location of a site you've previously visited in your Favorites list. If you have any saved favorites, you can easily revisit them without having to type in a URL.

To go to a saved URL:

1.   Click the Favorites menu, and drag your mouse to the title of the Web site you'd like to visit.
2.   When you've highlighted the desired location, release the mouse button, and IE will attempt to access the site.

Using the IE Toolbar

Now we'll quickly cover the ten buttons on the toolbar, as shown in Figure 2.7.

Here's a description of what happens when you click each of the buttons on the IE toolbar:

Back   Moves you to the previous document in your *history list.* A history list is a record of all the URLs that you've visited in your current IE session. If you exit IE, your history list will not be saved. To save a URL, save it in your Favorites list.

Forward   Moves you to the next document in your history list.

Stop   Stops loading the current document. Use this button if a page is taking longer to load than you'd like. Once you click the Stop button, any part of the document that can be displayed will appear.

Refresh   Reloads the current document.

Home   Takes you to the home page defined in your browser's configuration. The default home page for IE is www.microsoft.com.

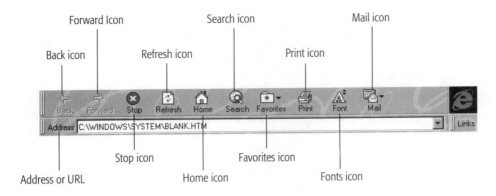

FIGURE 2.7:   The basic features of the default IE toolbar

Search   Attempts to connect you to your default Internet search engine. The default search engine for IE is `home.microsoft.com/access/allinone.asp`.

Favorites   Brings up the Open Location dialog box. This dialog box functions like the Location window, allowing you to type or paste in a URL to visit.

Print   Prints the current document.

Font   Allows you to increase or decrease the font size.

Mail   Allows you to read mail, send mail, or send a link to the current location via e-mail, as well as read news.

Now we'll go a little bit further behind the scenes and look at some options you can choose when customizing your copy of IE.

Customizing Internet Explorer

To customize IE, click the View menu and then click Options. You'll see the Options dialog box. This dialog box has six option tabs that allow you to choose which area you'd like to customize. We'll cover the first three tabs as well as the sixth tab: General, Connection, Navigation, and Advanced.

- The *General tab* lets you change the type and size of your toolbar icons, your default startup toolbar, options on what type of items to display, and your link color options. You can also change your proportional and fixed-width font attributes using the Font Settings button.
- The *Connection tab* allows you customize your Internet connection.

- The *Navigation tab* controls the way you access your intranet.
- Under the *Advanced tab* you can configure your cache, your temporary files, cache size, and other advanced settings.

Let's start with the General tab. On this tab, you can choose the appearance of text, links, visited links, and page backgrounds (see Figure 2.8). You can make sure links and visited links have different appearances, so you'll have a visual clue that you've previously been to a site or page. You can also decide to allow different types of multimedia files to be displayed. For most intranet uses, you'll want to use the defaults, so we won't change those settings yet.

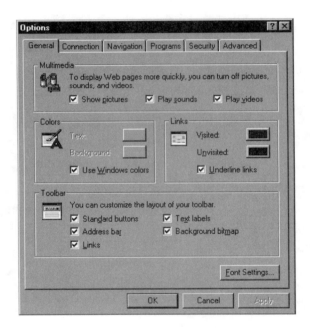

FIGURE 2.8:
You can specify basic options on the General tab, including toolbar icon size, link colors, text, and background colors.

You may also want to change the size and appearance of your toolbar icons. If you have a smaller 14" or 15" monitor, you'll want to maximize the amount of useful window space you have to display information on your intranet. To do that, you'll want to minimize the space the toolbar takes up. You can easily do this by dragging the bottom of the toolbar up until only the portion you need to display is showing. For intranets, you probably won't need the Links icons, so drag up until those aren't visible anymore and release the mouse button.

TIP You can change the amount of "real estate" IE uses by clicking and dragging the bottom of the toolbar up until the text disappears and you're left with just icons.

To further customize the toolbar, in the Toolbar area on the General tab, deselect Text labels and Links to use the smallest amount of screen space. However, we

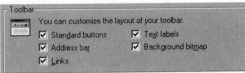

recommend icons with text labels if your users are less familiar with computers; if they're more computer-literate, you can deselect the Text labels options to display icons without the labels. If you have a larger 17" or 21" monitor, then you can use the icons with text labels because there will be plenty of screen space.

You can also change the appearance of the toolbar on the fly by moving the Address area or the Links area. Click the mouse button on the area you want to move, and then holding the mouse button down, drag it to a new position.

Now click the Font Settings button. Figure 2.9 shows you the Fonts dialog box.

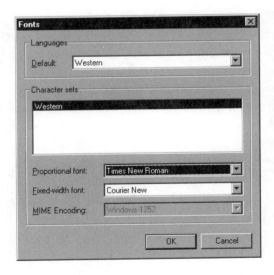

FIGURE 2.9:
The Fonts dialog box allows you to change your browser's default font.

The Fonts dialog box has only three options that affect font size, but if you have a small monitor, your choices here and on the font size menu can affect your intranet usability.

You'll probably want to change the default font. You may have something you feel is easier on the eye. You can also change the proportional and fixed-width fonts. Now you'll want to change the size of those fonts. You must do this from another menu option, so click OK to close the Fonts dialog, and then OK again to close the Options dialog. Now choose Fonts from the View menu.

You'll see a flyout menu that gives you some basic choices. For an average-sized monitor, try changing the point size to medium or small to get more text on each screen. If you have a larger monitor, small or smallest might allow even more text on the screen without sacrificing legibility. Your fixed font size will be the same size as your proportional font point size.

NOTE Remember that different browser versions running on different operating systems may not look the same or have the same settings tabs.

Now you have a basic knowledge of how to configure the appearance of your browser. Next we'll cover the Connection options. Let's start by clicking the Connection tab on the Options dialog box. You should see the Connections tab similar to the one shown in Figure 2.10.

The Connection tab allows you to configure how you connect to your intranet and, if you decide to enable it, how you connect to the Internet. Your first option is available in the Dialing section of the tab and allows you to enable the Connect to the Internet as Needed check box. If you click this option, you will be able to choose any dial-up connections you've made. If you haven't made any connections, you can add a new one by clicking on the Add button and following the Make New Connection Wizard. When you choose to connect to the Internet, your computer will dial and log in to your chosen Internet service when you access any Web URL.

You have two other dialing options: Disconnect If Idle and Perform System Security Check before Dialing. Checking the first option will ensure that your computer disconnects from your dial-up connection if you don't use your computer for a period of time. You can choose between 1 and 99 minutes. Use this option if your Internet provider charges by the minute.

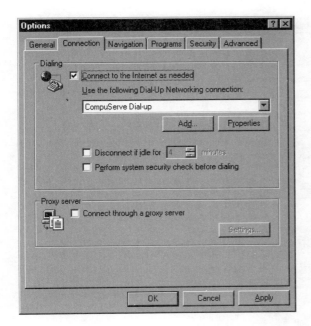

FIGURE 2.10:
The IE Connection tab allows you to specify how your browser connects to the Internet.

The bottom section of the Connection tab allows you to set a *proxy server.* As a security precaution, proxy servers allow your computer to be screened from any Internet connections. That means that your computer first connects to the proxy server. The proxy server then sends your request out to the Internet and receives the information. The proxy server then passes the information back to you. By using this system individual computers on your network are hidden from the Internet and the only public address is that of the proxy server. If your intranet uses a proxy server, you can configure it here.

Let's assume that your intranet users will also be connecting to the Internet. Now we'll go through the steps to configure a proxy server.

1. Click the Connect through a Proxy Server check box to select it.
2. Click the Settings button. You'll see the Proxy Settings dialog box, as shown in Figure 2.11.
3. Enter the name of your proxy. For this example, the proxy sever is named PROXY, and you want HTTP requests to be processed by that server.

Next, we'll cover your options on the Navigation tab. First we'll show you how to change your default Start page to your intranet's home page.

1. Click the Navigation tab. Figure 2.12 shows you the Navigation tab.
2. Make sure you've chosen Start Page from the Page drop-down list.
3. In the Address field, type the URL of your intranet.

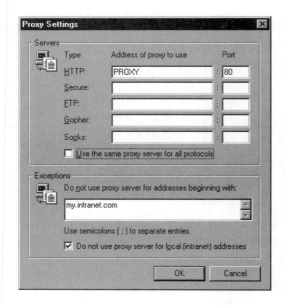

FIGURE 2.11:
The IE Proxy settings dialog box allows you to define a proxy, if your network requires one.

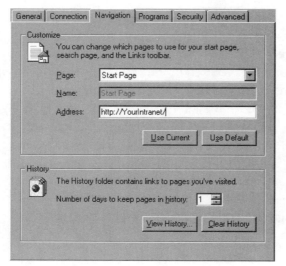

FIGURE 2.12:
The IE Navigation tab allows you to configure your start and search page options. You can also set the number of days to mark links as visited.

Alternately, you can open your intranet home page, and then click the Use Current button on the Navigation tab. To switch back to the Microsoft IE home page click on the Use Default button.

To see all pages you've visited within a specified period of time, use the View History button. If you see a page you'd like to revisit, just double-click it. Click the Clear History box to remove all the visited pages from your History list.

The Advanced tab, shown in Figure 2.13, controls security, cache, Java, and cryptography settings. We'll only discuss Advanced options that most intranet users will need to know. Let's start with the Temporary Internet Files section. This section controls how you access pages on your intranet as well as on the Internet. Instead of downloading frequently viewed pages every time you want to see them, you can save the files on your hard drive in a reserved area called a *cache*. IE lets you adjust the amount of reserved space to save for cached files.

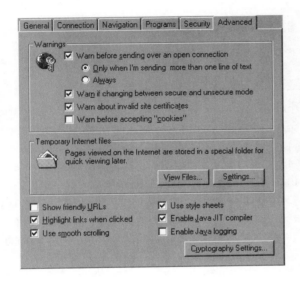

FIGURE 2.13:
The IE Advance tab allows you to set options, such as cache size, Java settings, and cryptography settings.

The first button, View Files, functions a lot like the View History button. It displays a list of temporary files that you can double-click to open.

Of more use to you as you view your intranet is the Settings button. You can use the Settings button to adjust the amount of space reserved for your temporary files. Click the Settings button, and you'll see the Settings dialog box, shown in Figure 2.14.

As you access your intranet you want to be able to get the pages quickly. Since graphics and repeating elements are used frequently and may not change much between visits, you'll want to have those items in your cache for quicker loading. For most users, the option Every Time You Start Internet Explorer will give them the best balance between speedy loading and the most current version of a page. If you choose to check for newer versions on Every Visit to the Page, your load times will be slower on all but the fastest machines with the fastest connections. That's because IE will go check every page every time you load the page. The third option will never check for a newer version. Since you want your users to see newer versions of pages and updated information, this option isn't recommended for your intranet.

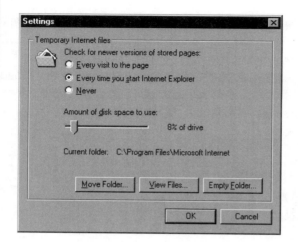

FIGURE 2.14:
Adjust the space reserved for temporary files in the Settings dialog box.

Next you'll see a slider bar that allows you to control the amount of disk space reserved for temporary storage space. The amount reserved is expressed in a percentage of your total disk space. Ten percent of a 500MB drive is a good starting point for intranet usage. If you have a gigabyte drive, try 5 percent and adjust up as needed.

Below the slider is the folder that your temporary files are stored in. You can change that directory, for example, to a second drive with more available space, by clicking the Move Folder button. You'll see a listing of the drives and directories available for your temporary files. Click the new folder in which you want to store your temporary files, and then click OK.

The next button lets you view the cached files. It functions exactly like the View Files button on the Advanced tab. The Empty Folder button removes all the temporary files you've saved. Use this option occasionally to make sure you're not saving unused information that takes up space needed for useful information in your cache.

That covers the basics of IE. Microsoft is rapidly improving their browser and by the time this book is published, a newer, improved version called a *beta*, will probably be in testing, preparing for release. Often you can download beta software to try it out before it's released.

Now you have a good understanding of intranet basics, similarities and differences between the Web and an intranet, and some basic information on how to access your intranet using a Web browser.

Along the way you've picked up some terminology and concepts that will help you as you move through the planning stages of your intranet. Our next chapter will get you started on the planning process.

Part 2

Planning Your Intranet

Chapter 3

INTRANET PLANNING BASICS

- **A planning overview**
- **Comparing an intranet to the Internet, groupware, and LANs**
- **Looking at costs**
- **Examining security issues**
- **Asking the big questions—what software and hardware do you need?**

Now we'll ease into the planning of an intranet project. This chapter will start you off with some basics, and the rest of Part 2 will go into detail on what to plan for and how to present the plan to those who'll need to approve, fund, construct, and maintain the intranet. Building on the basic intranet and browser information we covered in Chapters 1 and 2, this chapter will get you thinking about your overall goals. As you read this chapter then, think about why your company needs an intranet. You don't need to have all the answers yet. After you've thought about this in the context of your company's needs, you can move through the rest of the planning process with a clearer idea of what you'll need to have a successful intranet.

The remaining chapters in this part present an ordered way to set out your intranet's plan. First, you need to establish the business needs and goals for your intranet. Chapter 4, "Creating Your Intranet Business Plan," will show you how to do that. Once you've established your needs and your goals, you can begin to plan content that meets those needs and helps you achieve your goals. Chapter 5, "Planning Your Intranet's Content," helps you define your content in the context of your plan. Once you know what will be on your intranet, its mission and goals, and its users, you can decide on an appropriate security policy. Chapter 6, "Planning Your Intranet's Security," explains some security concepts and the information you'll need to make sure the intranet's content is available to your users without compromising it. After you've put all the pieces into the plan—mission, goals, audience, content, and security—you'll be able to use the material in Chapter 7, "Choosing Intranet Hardware and Software," to make informed decisions on your hardware and software needs.

WARNING	The four basic steps of your intranet project are planning, constructing, implementing, and maintaining. Each step relies on the preceding step, so don't jump to construction yet!

By breaking these tasks into separate areas, we'll be able to keep the focus on planning each part as it relates to the needs of your intranet and avoid the easy trap of confusing intranet planning with developing content. Planning your content is much more work than you might expect it to be. If you start mixing in content creation, you'll end up continually revising the content as you modify your plan. Resist "the fun stuff"—content creation—until you've completed the plan and all team members are satisfied with each individual area as well as with the plan as a whole. We'll cover each area of the plan later in more detail, but for now, we want you to ask yourself some basic questions that are likely to come up repeatedly in the planning process:

- Is an intranet right for my business?
- What can I do with an intranet that I can't do with groupware or on a LAN?
- Will an intranet save my company money? How much will it cost?
- How secure is the information on an intranet?
- What kinds of software and hardware do I need?

You shouldn't try to answer these questions right away. Instead, use this chapter to start thinking about these issues so you'll be ready to apply your ideas when we complete the plan.

Intranet versus Internet Revisited

In Chapter 1, we gave you an overview of the difference between an intranet site and an Internet site. While the difference between the two can be confusing, it is essential that you understand the difference to plan a successful intranet. Let's briefly revisit the differences here. You must be clear on the purpose and function of each and also know when the two can safely overlap. Creating an intranet and creating an Internet presence for your company require different focuses. Because the whole world can access your Internet site, it must be seen as a marketing tool, a way to educate people about your products and services. An intranet, on the other hand, is linked to your company's internal ideas and goals. The Internet site presents the company's external face to the world; the intranet contains the core of its being. Creating the Internet site has more to do with look and feel; data and the flow of internal information are the dominant forces on an intranet site.

Really the differences between an intranet and the Internet are questions of semantics and of scale. Both use the same techniques and tools, the same networking protocols, and the same server products. Internet content is by definition available worldwide and includes everything from a six-year-old's home page to statistics from the U.S. Census Bureau. Most company data is not intended for outside consumption; indeed, some data, such as sales figures and client and legal correspondence, should be protected very carefully. DEC's intranet, for example, is protected from unauthorized access by authentication and encryption schemes. (More on these in Chapter 6.) And from the point of view of scale, the Internet is global; an intranet is contained within a small group, department, or corporate organization. At the extreme is an intranet that is global, but still retains the private nature of a smaller intranet.

The Internet and the Web are famous, and rightly so, for being a chaotic jumble of useful and irrelevant information; the meteoric rise in popularity of Web sites devoted to indexes and to search engines is a measure of the need for an organized approach. An intranet harnesses the usefulness of the Internet and the Web in a controlled, secure environment.

An Intranet versus a Local Area Network

A *local area network* (LAN) is a group of computers and associated peripheral devices, such as hard drives and printers, connected by a communications channel. In such a setup, applications (for example, word processors and spreadsheets) are typically located on the hard drive attached to your desktop computer (although they can also be stored on the server), and document or data files are located on the server's hard drive so they can be accessed by people in the group.

Providing a local area network with the functionality of an intranet, in addition to being difficult, requires a great deal of programming, which is costly both in time and in money. Such systems are frequently described as *closed*—their proprietary specifications make it almost impossible for third-party vendors to create software that works correctly for them. They are also hard to maintain and are not easy to use.

> **WARNING** Even though intranets offer advantages over proprietary networks, don't expect an intranet to replace your LAN completely.

In contrast to a LAN, an intranet can be an inexpensive investment, is easily updated and maintained, and is inherently easy to use. What makes this possible? The open nature of the Web server and browser and TCP/IP allow you to set up a basic intranet. Using more sophisticated Internet utilities can enhance your intranet's functionality more easily and quickly than traditional LAN-based groupware. An intranet can be the whole of the Internet's functionality on your private network or just a subset. Unlike a LAN, where you have to take the whole NetWare or NT package and then buy specialized software that only runs on that platform, an intranet lets you choose the components you want to enable in your company, in many cases, across operating and networking systems and Web browsers are available for virtually all operating system and hardware combinations.

Genentech, the biotechnology pioneer based in San Francisco, discovers, develops, manufactures, and markets pharmaceuticals, such as a human growth hormone and a blood clot–dissolving drug for heart patients. The Genentech computing environment consists of about 2,000 Macintosh computers, 1,000 Windows-based PCs, and hundreds of Unix workstations. The only software that runs on all of them is the Web browser—in this case, Netscape—which, along with TCP/IP, make it possible for anybody working at any of those machines to run any Genentech-specific proprietary application on the server, whether it was developed for the Mac, the PC, or a Unix system. For details and many more questions and answers, see Appendix B, "Intranet Protocols—TCP/IP," and Chapter 7, "Choosing Intranet Hardware and Software."

The primary disadvantage of intranet technology is its new, ever-changing nature. Because intranets are so new, there isn't a lot of collaborative software, or *groupware*, that's been developed for intranet use. Investing heavily in complex group-enabled software before the industry is mature may leave you stuck with a system that's obsolete in six months.

> **NOTE** LAN-based groupware technology has been around much longer than commercial, business-oriented intranet technology and has had time to stabilize and develop a sense of the marketplace. Don't expect your intranet to duplicate the functionality of some high-end groupware applications exactly—yet.

That's rapidly changing as companies expand their traditional markets to include Web-based (Internet and intranet) applications. Currently you can get resource scheduling software, calendar-tracking applications, bulletin board and chat systems, and other groupware applications for your intranet. As the market continues its rapid growth, software application developers will write software to take advantage of the cross-platform nature of Web-based technologies.

How Can an Intranet Save Money/Make Money for My Company?

Before you implement an intranet, you will, of course, want—or perhaps be required—to do a cost/benefits analysis (for more on this, see the next chapter, "Creating Your Intranet Business Plan"). You'll want to figure out how much your intranet will cost and how soon you can expect to recoup that cost in intranet-derived benefits. All this depends on what kind of business you have, the breadth of your intranet implementation, your current procedures, and your ability to recast those procedures in ways that save time and money—in other words, in ways that affect the bottom line and thus make your business more profitable.

Here are some examples of how several companies are using an intranet to distribute information in faster and less expensive ways, to communicate with employees in a more timely manner, and in general, to run their businesses more effectively:

- Cargill International employs more than 70,000 people engaged in commodities trading around the world. Even with only 25 percent of company materials on its intranet, Cargill estimates it saves tens of thousands of dollars annually by posting electronic updates rather than printing, binding, and distributing them through traditional means.

- John Deere, the company whose tractors plow farms and fields everywhere, is repurposing obsolete equipment as Web clients. At its Waterloo Works division in Iowa, several hundred six-year-old Macintosh IIcx computers were converted to dedicated Web browsers.

- For the 30,700 employees of Eli Lilly, the pharmaceutical firm, the ability to easily access timely information provides a significant competitive advantage. By using Lilly's internal Web site, employees can now find more information in one day than they could previously find in several days in the library.

- McDonnell Douglas distributes some 4 million pages of documentation every year and estimates that distributing this information in paper form costs twice as much as disseminating it via a Web. Because manuals for an aircraft can run from 45,000 to 50,000 pages, McDonnell Douglas is experimenting with placing this information on its intranet so it can be accessed by maintenance crews and onboard by pilots using Pentium PCs.

- Through its intranet, the Merrill Lynch Private Group makes research information available to 15,000 consultants and clients. When the system is fully developed, Merrill Lynch expects to cut its need for paper by 90 percent—currently 7 million pounds annually.

- Sandia National Laboratories, in Albuquerque, New Mexico, manages research programs focused on national security, energy, and the environment for the U.S. Department of Energy. The lab's intranet is helping to save taxpayer dollars by reducing its reliance on mainframe resources, lowering application development costs, reducing printing and distribution costs, and making employees more productive by giving them direct access to the information they need to do their jobs.

What about Security?

Whether you own a small craft shop or manage the mutual fund distributions for a multimillion-dollar corporation, securing your resources is a top priority, as you install a LAN for the first time, implement an intranet, or connect to the Internet.

If you're thinking about an Internet site for your company or an intranet that will be connected to the Internet, you need to establish policies and procedures that will protect you against external intrusion. It's been estimated that intruders cost big business more than $800 million in 1995. Although you can never assume your system is 100 percent secure, many practical and technical solutions are available, and you should know about them and consider them in your decision-making processes. These are discussed in depth in *Mastering Microsoft's Internet Information Server* by Peter Dyson, available from Sybex. In particular, take a look at Chapter 10, "Windows NT Server Operating System Security," and at Chapter 11, "External Security and Firewalls." In this book, we'll just stick to the basics of intranet security.

WARNING Security is a hot-button issue. Expect management to be extremely concerned about how your security is set up and administered. By planning your security policy in advance, you'll be better able to address security concerns.

If you're thinking about only an intranet for your company, your security concerns change considerably and focus on internal issues. (Although some corporate intranets do connect to the outside world, most are for employees only and are off-limits to outsiders—the "barbarians" mentioned earlier in this book.)

WARNING Most security problems come from internal sources. This doesn't mean you can ignore the potential threat of a break in; it does mean you must think about security in new ways to solve intranet-related issues.

Unfortunately, internal security problems are the most common. With the proper access, a disgruntled employee can wreak havoc with a file system, and without proper procedures in place, your intranet could catch a virus. You'll find ways to deal with these and other intranet security problems, both accidental and malicious, in Chapter 6. You may also want to place information that is available only to one department on your intranet. For example, you would probably want only designated people in Human Resources and Payroll to have access to information about employee salaries.

What Software Do I Need?

To get started, you need three basic tools:
- Web server software
- HTML authoring tool
- Browser
- TCP/IP-based network

As your intranet grows, you will most likely want to add a search engine to help your users quickly find information. You may also discover you need to build intranet applications, such as bulletin boards, chat areas, or employee benefits enrollment forms. If so, you'll need one or more programming tools or languages, such as C++, Java, or ActiveX. You may also choose to add software that interacts with a database, monitors and analyzes your log files, or controls access to your intranet.

> **TIP**
>
> **Don't spend too much time thinking about software at this point. Remember that software is only one piece of an intranet plan. You need to start with your business needs, and then move on to content and security before you can decide what software you need. We'll get to software and hardware in Chapter 7.**

If you're already familiar with technology issues or if you check out the intranet resources available on the Internet, you'll frequently encounter the phrase *cross-platform compatibility* and hear its praises touted. Cross-platform compatibility is techie talk for describing one of the intranet's most-valued features—its ability to connect all kinds of hardware running all kinds of software.

For example, the intranet installed at Electronic Arts (described in Chapter 1) brings together Windows-based personal computers, Macintosh computers, Unix clients, and

Novel, Unix, and Windows NT servers. We're talking about three operating systems here (an *operating system* is a set of programs that control hardware allocation; it's the foundation on which applications are built).

As we discussed in Part 1, the parts of an intranet that make this cross-platform compatibility possible are TCP/IP, HTTP, HTML, and Web browsers. As we continue through the planning stages, you'll learn even more about how those technologies fit together to make your intranet work. Chapter 7, "Choosing Intranet Hardware and Software," explains all this in down-to-earth terms by giving you lots of practical examples. When you finish, you'll know what software you have that you can use, what software you need that you can get for free, and what software you'll need to buy.

And What about Hardware?

Your hardware needs must wait until you complete most of your intranet plan—defining intranet goals, making content and audience decisions, and establishing a security policy. Once you have an idea of the scope of all those factors, you can decide how much hardware your intranet will need.

> **TIP**
>
> Hardware is more than just a machine that acts as a server. You may need special adapter cards, routers, ISDN or T1 service for intranet-to-Internet connections, or other specialized hardware. You may also need special expertise to set up and configure that hardware. Make sure to include everything in your intranet plan.

If you're a small startup with simple information-sharing needs, you may be able to have an existing server do double-duty, running Web server software alongside other server software. At the other end of the hardware scale, if you expect several hundred or thousand employees to use your intranet to run collaborative software applications, use remote login to connect from the road, e-mail, distribute software, or serve multimedia, video, or sound files to users, then your hardware will need to be sophisticated and powerful enough to meet the peak-time demands that your users will put on the system. The surest way to kill your intranet project is to build a slow intranet that frustrates users.

TIP

Even though your hardware can be simple, if your plan calls for moderate to large intranet growth in a short period of time, you may want to invest in more than the minimum required hardware. If you spend a bit more money now, you might save a significant amount of time when it becomes necessary to expand your intranet.

Now you have some idea of the issues you'll need to address in your intranet's business plan. You have thought about some of the common planning questions and the high-level answers to those questions. As your plan takes shape, we'll expand on these issues in the following chapters.

Chapter 4

CREATING YOUR INTRANET BUSINESS PLAN

FEATURING

- **Understanding intranet planning**
- **Creating an intranet plan**
- **Identifying business needs**
- **Identifying planning-related issues**
- **Identifying user-related issues**
- **Examining costs**

In the last chapter, you started thinking about some big intranet planning issues: intranet goals, scope, security, hardware, and software. This chapter helps you begin to deal with those issues as you flesh out your intranet plan. To help you get your intranet off the ground, we'll go step-by-step through the planning process. We'll look at the choices you will have to make along the way, and we'll point out how you can avoid some of the pitfalls. We'll also look at the issues you will have to address before, during, and after you bring your intranet online.

Intranet Planning is More than Money

When you start planning your intranet, the first question you'll probably hear is "How much will this cost?" While costs are a major factor in deciding both the scope of your intranet and even whether or not to have one, the bottom-line setup costs aren't as important as deciding your overall return from your intranet. Your overall return factors in several cost elements including:

- Cost of setup, including hardware and software
- Cost of converting existing information for use on your intranet
- Cost of creating new information
- Cost of designing and programming for intranet applications
- Cost of training

And while that can quickly add up to a significant sum, you'll see that costs are reduced in other areas including:

Printing   Materials will still need to be printed, but users will only have to print the relevant information as needed. For example, if your current HR manual is 300 pages, the printing and binding costs can be very high because this type of manual is often frequently revised. By storing this information on your intranet, you can quickly produce updated sections at a much lower cost. When an employee needs to print a form from that manual or a section on a particular policy, they only print the pages they need—a significant savings over printing and binding the entire manual.

Communication   Communication is improved. The way an organization communicates its message is vital to the success of the organization. Communicating with both the public and staff can change the way people see your company and your product. Employees often complain about poor communication; they feel left out of the loop or like they're working on a project that has no focus or purpose. Using an intranet, people can share information in an easy-to-use format that removes many organizational constraints.

Technology   Skills are enhanced. Your staff and organization benefit by keeping employees' skills current. Intranets are an easy way to teach new skills or upgrade existing skills. The Web and the Internet are hot topics in the newspaper and on television and your employees have a natural curiosity to see what the hype is about. You can use this natural curiosity to encourage your users do some simple self-training.

As you plan your intranet, keep in mind the costs are only one aspect of the plan and that costs will change as you assess your audience, intranet goals, content requirements, resources (hardware, software, and human), and security issues.

Creating a Realistic Intranet Plan

You can now begin creating your intranet business plan. The business plan should include information on why you need an intranet, what your goals are, what resources you'll need, and how much it will cost. You'll also use the business plan to begin thinking about content and security.

A little planning now will smooth over problems later. You've heard it before, and now we're telling you again: intranets have a way of growing quickly in new, exciting ways. If you've done the planning up front, you'll be able to harness the positive growth of your intranet.

WARNING If you haven't created a plan, your intranet will grow out of control without direction, potentially dragging down the processes you were hoping to improve.

Crafting Your Intranet Plan

An intranet is the perfect solution for any organization with anywhere from twenty to several thousand people who either all work at the corporate headquarters or are scattered over a wide geographical area and will access the system from a remote location. It's also an ideal fit for any situation in which a large amount of constantly changing information must be made available to all these users simultaneously and as cost-effectively as possible.

Most companies do not want to put documents on their intranet that are considered sensitive in either a competitive or a legal sense, and most companies avoid putting personnel files and payroll information on an intranet unless an effective security system is in place. As you can see, establishing the hardware and software systems for your intranet is the easy part; deciding on the content is much more difficult.

TIP
Don't worry about using a special planning tool, such as Microsoft Project, to create your intranet plan. Because your project will include many different aspects of your intranet, one tool may not be suitable for all the tasks you'll need to include in your plan.

Once your group, department, or corporation has made the initial decision to implement an intranet, several important factors will determine whether the transition from a traditional host-based system to an intranet will be a smooth process or a violent upheaval. Many of these issues are not straightforward technical issues with one correct answer but thorny political issues that will take all your diplomatic skills to resolve. The earlier in the switchover to an intranet that you air and resolve these issues, the smoother the transition process will prove to be.

TIP
Document your planning process. Keep notes from your meetings and e-mails from other members on the team. Your documentation will be helpful when you begin to write your intranet plan.

In the next part of the chapter, we'll look at the planning issues you will have to deal with before you start building your site. These issues fall neatly into two groups: Internal issues that you have some degree of control over, and external issues that are driven by users of your intranet. We'll also suggest ways that you can avoid some of the pitfalls inherent in the intranet planning process.

Internal Issues

Internal issues include the following:
- Forming the project team
- Evaluating in-house expertise
- Setting goals and objectives
- Developing content
- Designing, building, and testing your intranet
- Tracking results and responding to feedback
- Defining success
- Maintaining content

Forming the Project Team

The first step is to form the project team. This team will cross traditional boundaries in your organization and may include members from several departments, including the following:

- Technical Services, sometimes called IS (Information Systems), DP (Data Processing), or MIS (Management Information Services)
- Marketing
- Sales
- Product Research and Development
- Customer Service
- Public Relations
- Publications or Creative Services
- Training or Education Services

Technical Services people will focus on the technical aspects of setting up the Web site and be invaluable as security consultants; however, in most corporations, this is one of the least important aspects. Deciding what the intranet will actually do, defining the appropriate level of system security, and defining rules for maintaining the site will generate much more discussion and will turn out to be much more important issues than which hardware to use in your installation.

First, you'll want to give each member of the team a copy of your corporate Web browser—if you have one—and be sure they all spend some time surfing the Web and looking at all sorts of sites: the good, the bad, and the ugly. And this should be a part of their ongoing education. If you haven't decided on a browser yet, download at least two different browsers and use this part of your planning to evaluate them.

NOTE   **Have your team members review Chapter 2, "Using a Web Browser to Access Your Intranet," if they aren't already familiar with browsers.**

Companies that already have some sort of centrally focused computer system will find that it's relatively easy to adapt their approach to developing an intranet site. FedEx, for example, has more than 10 years experience with its Powership program, which allows customers to use FedEx software to track any individual package. When the people at FedEx decided to develop an intranet, they found it to be a relatively easy process because all key departments were already used to working together, and the usual office politics and turf wars did not surface.

The person or group in charge of an intranet will need all sorts of skills, some technical and some diplomatic. Here's a list of some of the major jobs by category:

Webmaster The Webmaster is the point of contact with users and is responsible for replying to complaints and suggestions and for coordinating with other sites in your company or organization. This person receives all the e-mail sent to your intranet and usually has the overall view of how the site works and is responsible for each area of the intranet. Sometimes the Webmaster address is an e-mail alias set up to forward e-mail to an existing account or set of accounts if a team is responsible for the overall site. Many Webmasters also perform the duties of the Web administrator.

Web administrator This person is responsible for the day-to-day running of the intranet, monitoring the usage logs, adjusting the configuration as needed, and making the backups and system upgrades as needed.

Content authors These people create the content used on the intranet. They are not necessarily technical people, but they must know their subject, be able to prepare an HTML document, and be able to write well. They will also be responsible for submitting new material and updating old material as things change within the organization.

Intranet developer This person develops the scripts and programs needed to do the things that you can't do using HTML. The intranet developer is essentially a programmer who can develop code to make your intranet do new things.

Some companies will find it easier to assign site maintenance responsibilities to the departments that originate the content for the site, rather than having one person or group manage all the Web sites within the company. This approach is useful for large intranets where someone closer to the material may be better off maintaining it. For small intranets, the Webmaster fulfills all of the duties described here.

As well as deciding who has access to what kinds of information, you must also keep tabs on network usage, check usage statistics, and continue efforts to fine-tune the daily operation of your intranet.

Evaluating Existing Expertise

The first step in this evaluation process is to look at the resources you already have within the company. Technical people who have experience with open systems, Unix, the Internet, scripting languages (such as Perl), network protocols (such as TCP/IP), and so on, will simplify the switch to an intranet. If your experience is restricted to the mainframe legacy systems in place, it's time to get some training and upgrade your technical skills.

Someone in the project team has to take the technical lead, establish the Web servers for the intranet, and keep up-to-date on the almost daily advances and developments in areas as diverse as the latest hot Web browser, new networking hardware, and improvements in server and operating system software. You don't have to implement all these improvements on your intranet immediately (just think of the training costs), but it's important that someone in your organization stays abreast of the latest developments.

As new and improved Web site development tools appear from the software vendors, the skill level needed to set up and then run an intranet will fall. Many new HTML editors allow you to create pages in a graphical environment much like a word processor. This can shift some of the emphasis from your project team and technical staff to your users as they gain the knowledge necessary to create pages. But don't expect your users to be able to evaluate and make technical recommendations on the other important intranet issues, such as hardware upgrades and operating system changes. You or someone on your technical staff will continue to perform that function.

Setting Goals and Objectives

Simply having a corporate intranet is not an appropriate goal for your corporation; saying that you want to "offer technical support and education" won't do either. You must establish a set of clearly defined, detailed goals and then get the members of the project team to sign off on them as a group. If you ignore this step, your intranet site will end up unfocused and confusing.

> **TIP**
> Take your high-level goals and use them to develop a mission statement for your intranet. You can adapt this mission statement, so don't worry if it changes as your plan develops.

Before you start slinging HTML pages all over the place, pause for a moment and ask yourself a few fundamental questions about what you want your intranet to do:
- Why is the company creating this intranet?
- What is the purpose of the site? What is its mission statement?
- What does the company want to get out of this site?

Prioritizing Your Goals

You may well find that you end up with a list of several goals, in which case you will have to prioritize them. You can do this by asking these questions:

- What will give the biggest return (depending on how you choose to define this) on the effort invested?
- What will generate tangible results most quickly?

Once you have prioritized the goals, keep them in mind by continually asking questions as you continue through the design process:

- What am I trying to achieve on this page?
- Why is this page here?
- What is the best way to present this information? As a table, as text, or as a graphic?
- How does this page advance our goals?

One or more negative answers indicates that your site is headed toward trouble, and it's time to correct your course before things get too far out of line. Only by establishing appropriate goals will you be able to determine a suitable return on investment for the company.

> **TIP** Beginning an intranet with just a small number of test users is often the best way to start; then, after you iron out the wrinkles, you can bring more and more people online.

Even after you've set up your intranet, you'll need to keep refining your goals. Feedback is likely to be loud and immediate, and some of it might even be useful. Implement the best suggestions as you broaden the scope of your intranet and increase the number of users. As you read the sidebar case studies in Chapter 12, you'll see that several of the most successful intranet sites started as pilot or proof-of-concept projects that later grew into full-fledged intranets.

Defining Success

Once your intranet is online, track results and compare them against your original goals to help in the next step of the process, which is to reach a definition of how you measure your site's success.

Keep this definition to reasonable proportions, and add specific, quantifiable results. Avoid general statements, such as, "I want our site to be used a lot," and instead use a statement containing elements that you can actually measure, such as, "Our intranet is successful when we cut policy manual publication costs by 30 percent in the first year."

To evaluate your success, you can measure two main areas of operation:

- Raw data
- Internal benefits

The applicability of these categories will depend on your organization and the original goals you set. Let's look at each one in turn.

Raw Data

Raw data are based on variables that can be measured easily, including the number of hits each day and other usage statistics. It's relatively easy to generate some big numbers that sound impressive when budget-review time rolls around. You can also use fluctuations in these raw data over time to measure the success of changes you've made in your intranet-site structure, page layout, and content.

Internal Benefits

Internal results show the effect that your intranet is having on your own organization. These results might appear as fewer telephone calls to the Technical Support, Human Resources, or Legal departments. These are real benefits that you can measure and, perhaps more important, can quantify and express as dollars and cents.

For example, companies have cut the printing and mailing costs associated with publishing their sales and marketing materials by offering the same information on their intranets—and that is a real benefit they can measure precisely.

Maintaining Content

One of the intranet's most attractive features is the ease with which you can change content and revise your site. Some of the tasks associated with maintaining an intranet include the following:

- Adding new information to existing pages. You should preserve and reuse as much of the original material as possible to keep costs down.
- Analyzing user hit patterns to decide which intranet pages are working and which are not and then revising those pages that are not working.
- Automating the production of new pages or revisions to existing pages, perhaps using output from a database to create new price lists every month or using automatic document-conversion software.
- Developing templates to establish the look and feel of your intranet, particularly in terms of choosing background colors and placing major elements on the page.

Depending on the sources you're using to process your company data into a form suitable for display on your Web site, you may be able to save time and effort by automating data preparation. For example, if you routinely calculate new prices at the end of each month, be sure this data is in a form that you can convert easily to HTML. If you're a parts distributor and you add several hundred new parts to your inventory each month, be sure your suppliers give you the information you need in the right format. And if you're presenting training material or policies and procedures materials, buy one of the converters available to process this material into the right form for your Web site. Do you want your employees to have access to a corporate database? If so, what sort of database support is needed—Microsoft's ODBC or SQL? Can your server and some simple CGI programs take care of your needs? Later in this book, we'll look at applications you might want to use for some of these tasks; see Chapter 7, "Choosing Intranet Hardware and Software," for details.

External Issues

External issues include the following:
- Deciding what your "customers" want to see on your Web site
- Setting up access to your Web site
- Providing intranet access to third parties
- Providing user training
- Managing browser-support issues
- Using TCP/IP in the enterprise

Deciding What "Customers" Want to See?

What do your "customers," the people within the company who use the intranet, want to see? According to a recent survey, people want to see several things when they access an intranet site:
- Applications to help them find and download software updates, service packs, and bug fixes
- Specific, factual information, including technical information of all kinds, HR information, and sales and marketing information
- Technical support, including online bulletin boards that are monitored or staffed by tech support personnel

When choosing content, here are some of the questions you should be asking:
- Is every person in the company a potential user, or only a specific group or department?
- What do you think your users want to see on your intranet?
- How often do you expect "customers" to use your intranet?
- What will keep users coming back to your intranet site?

- Do you have to attract new users, or do you have an existing captive audience? Is your intranet purely for internal consumption, or will customers or suppliers also access your intranet?
- How does the typical user access your site—by direct network connection, by dial-up modem, by ISDN link, or by some other means?

In planning your site, look for ways to reduce the volume of material presented to each user, and increase the value of content they do see. If you don't address users' needs, they won't stay long, and your intranet will fall into disuse—a real waste of a potentially invaluable resource.

Providing Access to Your Intranet

People will access your site directly once word starts to spread about how useful the information is and how much time they can save, but you'll have to help get the word out. You can do so via traditional methods, such as memos and e-mail, but you can also use one intranet to advertise another if you include a *What's New* section on the original intranet.

People in another division may also access your intranet via links from their intranet. This might be a site run by a different part of your corporation or a site concerned with a similar product or service. The creators of the other site have added a link to your site because they think you have something on it that their users will value, and it makes them look pretty good to be associated with you in this way.

NOTE   Users may also dial in to your network, and then once connected, access your intranet from there. If you decide to allow dial-in access, you'll need to include it in your security, hardware, and software planning.

Providing Intranet Access to Third Parties

One of the larger questions that will come up sooner or later in your company is whether to allow third parties access to your intranet. Third parties can include vendors, partners, clients, or just about anyone who is outside your organization. Even former employees accessing their pension information are technically third-party users. Giving access to others can raise certain security warning flags, so be sure you have a good business reason for allowing it.

A recent survey from Forrester Research indicates that of the Fortune 1000 companies polled, 46 percent allowed some kind of third-party access and 26 percent did not. A substantial number, however, almost 30 percent, were planning to add third-party access in the near future.

The same survey asked companies to describe who had access to the intranet. All responded that their employees had access, 49 percent allowed their business partners and members of strategic alliances access, and 14 percent allowed their customers to access their intranet.

Providing User Training

Training your users is one of the most important parts of any software rollout. Yet, training is often overlooked in the planning process. If it's included, funding and time constraints can bump training to a secondary role. Saving money and time by not including appropriate training is a false savings. Your technical support costs will escalate as you try to support 100 or more users one at a time. If you properly train employees, they'll start with a solid intranet knowledge base and be able to use the intranet itself to learn more.

There are some things to keep in mind in regards to training, as you plan which software to use and as you develop content. One of the greatest attractions of an intranet is that all users need learn and use only one application, the Web browser. Unfortunately, new versions of the two most popular Web browsers seem to appear every few months, and version control, distribution, and user training can be a nightmare.

First, you have to decide if the new version of the browser will actually bring any benefit to your users; perhaps it offers new features your users want or fixes an annoying bug. Once you decide that you need the new version, you have to figure out how to distribute it in a reasonable and cost-effective way; for example, you could create a Web page that has a link to a local copy of the new browser in a special self-extracting archive that installs the software on the workstation. You also have to ascertain if your users will need additional training as a result of the new features.

TIP Plan a series of lunchtime training sessions to kick off your intranet. Your first session should include highlights of your intranet plan, including your mission and goals, as well as who to contact for more information. Other sessions should be more hands-on, explaining the functionality of your intranet.

As you plan your content, think about incorporating training materials, tutorials, and informational links to your site to help users answer their own questions and train themselves. A form that users can fill out to ask questions and make suggestions can give you useful feedback on what your users want and need to know. Basic HTML information is always useful to have on your site if you allow or expect employees to maintain some of their own pages.

Remember your intranet is only useful if it's used. If your company's employees can't understand how to use your intranet, they won't use it and the project will fail.

Managing Browser-Support Issues

The last section pointed out the need for user training as browsers change, but what should technical support staff do in the face of constantly changing browsers? Here are a few tips:

- Be sure your users know your policy and understand which browsers you support and which ones you do not. Publish this policy on your intranet.
- Most browser problems appear when you try to use the latest and greatest additions or extensions to HTML. By staying just behind the browser curve, you can minimize these problems.
- Offer training classes to new users. Not everyone spends the evening surfing the Web and, therefore, intuitively knows how to use a Web browser.
- Stay current with the problems reported about the browser you chose as the main interface to the intranet.
- If the company currently uses several browsers and you want to support only one, be sure to set a reasonable deadline for when you will stop supporting those other browsers, and be sure everyone knows about your deadline and understands what it means.
- If you plan to support multiple browsers, you should also provide optimized HTML pages for each of them. This means you may have to create a different page for Netscape and IE, using tags specific to that browser on each page.
- If you plan to support multiple browsers, be sure you test your Web pages with each of them to see how colors and graphics are displayed.
- If your site relies on a plug-in, distribute it with the browser so users do not have to wait for it to download from the intranet.

TIP   Keep costs down by choosing one browser and then ensuring that everyone has access to and training on it. Supporting two or more browsers can increase costs 30 to 50 percent, which is not a viable option for most companies. For more on browsers and browser-related issues, see Chapter 7, "Choosing Intranet Hardware and Software."

How Will You Use TCP/IP in the Enterprise?

One of the thorniest problems in crafting your intranet plan has to do with networking protocols and how any new additions fit into the overall corporate picture. The TCP/IP set of protocols is at the center of the intranet and must be at the center of yours. In some corporations, several protocols will be in use at the same time, and staff and machine resources will be needed to support each protocol. Many corporations will use Novell NetWare products with IPX/SPX protocols; others will use older, mainframe-based systems.

The recent releases of Microsoft's Windows 95, Windows NT Workstation, and Windows NT Server all contain TCP/IP, so upgrading to one of these systems can help make TCP/IP easier to deploy. These operating systems can also easily handle multiple protocols on the desktop and on the server.

Unfortunately, the cost of buying a TCP/IP package for every computer in an organization that has a large number of DOS/Windows 3.1 client computers can be quite significant, not to mention the costs of implementing the package on a slow computer that may already be at its memory and hard-disk capacity limits.

The Layers of TCP/IP

The TCP/IP set of networking protocols exists as four layers of software built on top of the fifth layer—the network hardware itself. The four layers are as follows:

1. The *Application* layer consists of applications that use the network.
2. The *Host-to-Host Transport* layer provides end-to-end data delivery.
3. The *Internet* layer defines the datagram and manages the routing.
4. The *Network Access* layer consists of software capable of accessing the network hardware.

Below these theoretical layers, you'll find the actual network hardware, the *network interface card* (NIC). When data is received from the network, it travels up through these layers from the NIC to the application; and when data is sent to the network, it travels the other way.

Another approach is to use a NetWare-to-TCP/IP gateway server. A gateway server allows the PCs on your network to continue to run their Novell IPX/SPX protocols and allows you to run TCP/IP on the server.

TIP	If you run large legacy systems over SNA (IBM's proprietary *Systems Network Architecture*) 3270 systems, adding TCP/IP may mean utilizing a product such as Attachmate's TCP Server. TCP Server can run IP to each desktop, provide access to the SNA host, and run individual sessions to each desktop. Microsoft's SNA Server for Windows NT is another possible solution. SNA Server is included as a part of Microsoft's BackOffice suite.

We'll look at TCP/IP networking–protocol basics in Appendix B, but for more in-depth information, see *Mastering Intranets* or even a book devoted exclusively to the TCP/IP protocol.

How Much Does an Intranet Cost?

It all depends. An intranet is an ideal environment for a group of 200 or so people, which is the case at Sony Display Tube Co. in San Diego. This business unit, which produces all of Sony's 32-inch CRT tubes, created an intranet to communicate key numbers (good output quantity, reject costs, inventory discrepancies, and full profit-and-loss financials) to its 230 employees. Every manager and coach had a computer on his or her desk, and several touch-screen workstations were on the shop floor. Sony hired an outside company to build the intranet and develop graph-generating software, reportedly at a cost of about $11,000. Keeping these figures up-to-date takes one person a couple of hours each day.

In a series of articles for *Internet Advisor* (http://www.advisor.com/), Paul Youngworth "built" a corporate intranet. Getting to the prototype stage (a full-scale example of how the eventual implementation will function) took him three months and about $5000. The costs were broken down as follows:

Server (120MHz Pentium, 32MB RAM, two 1GB hard drives)	$3,300
Network server	$700
Communications server	$495
HTML editor	$195
Graphics editor	$69
Search engine	0
Imagemap editor	0
Total Cost	**$4,759**

The zeros in the second column are not a mistake. A lot of current Web software is free and can be downloaded from the Internet. One thing missing from Paul's list is the client browser. He's considering Netscape Navigator, which goes for $49, or Microsoft Internet Explorer, which is available for free. His costs also don't include a network card, routers and cabling, and TCP/IP software for every client machine that will be on the intranet.

> **TIP**
>
> Check out `http://www.shareware.com` for imagemap editors, HTML editors, and other Internet utilities that you can use to create your intranet. You can get a free search engine from Excite at `http://www.excite.com.`

He is also making the assumption that a LAN that supports TCP/IP is already in place. Another thing that's missing is the cost to convert paper files to HTML files, a cost that's measured primarily in terms of human resources. Finally, he didn't include the three month's salary paid to his Webmaster to set up and configure the intranet.

> **TIP**
>
> When Simon & Schuster, the publishing house, first decided to build an intranet, document conversion loomed as a daunting prospect. The developers discovered, however, that although an HTML tagger could convert a 30-page Microsoft Word document in a day, a non-techie could do the same job in an hour with one of the Microsoft Internet Assistant tools. Check out Part III, "Constructing Your Intranet," for extensive information about creating, maintaining, and converting documents for your intranet.

Obviously, as you start to add hundreds or even thousands of users to an intranet, costs will mount. And costs will also vary, depending on whether you must make major server and/or user hardware purchases and whether you plan to connect your intranet to the Internet. In general though, intranets are inexpensive systems that employees can access using their PCs and workstations and a TCP/IP network.

NOTE   Useful information on costs and *ROI*s, return on investments, can be found at `http://www.netscape.com/comprod/columns/intranet/index.html`, `http://www.microsoft.com/intranet/` and `http://www.microsoft.com/backoffice/article/nscpresp.htm`.

As you begin planning, you'll no doubt discover you have to make trade-offs. Some planning and design decisions are closely related, and in some areas, it's hard to separate them precisely. You'll find yourself having to make compromises to reach your final goal.

This chapter is primarily about abstract issues like management, training, mission statements, and team planning. Now, however, let's look at some of the specific issues you'll face as you craft your intranet plan. The next chapter, "Planning Your Intranet's Content," lets you have some fun and be creative with the kinds of materials you can put on the intranet, from the corporate handbook to a video of your CEO skydiving.

Chapter 5

PLANNING YOUR INTRANET'S CONTENT

FEATURING

- **Planning your intranet's content**
- **Looking at different types of intranet sites**
- **Taking advantage of your intranet**

Now that you've decided on your intranet business plan, you can begin to plan how to implement the ideas you've decided to use for your site. In this chapter, we'll show you how to think about content planning—don't worry about construction yet, we'll get to that in Chapter 9. We'll discuss overall content issues, site structure issues, and a method for getting your content created once your plan is in place. Don't forget that creativity isn't impossible when achieving a corporate mission. You can design an entirely successful corporate intranet and still make it fun to use.

Planning Your Content

Just as you planned the function and mission of your intranet, you need to plan your content before you create it. Many companies rush to constructing sites without first deciding what the goals are and what needs to be constructed to meet those goals.

> **NOTE** Remember that planning and designing your intranet content isn't the same as designing the pages. You'll want to wait to design the look of the pages after you've decided on the functionality.

We'll cover a lot of ground in this section. We'll help you decide on how to develop your content, how to plan your intranet's design, your intranet's pages, and give you some examples of different types of pages you can consider for your site. We'll start with developing content that fits your intranet's mission.

Developing Content

Your intranet's content should reflect the business planning you've done so far. You'll need to decide what kind of content to put on your intranet and where you'll get that content. A good starting point is to examine existing electronic and print-based information within your company. You may already have lots of corporate information that is useful, but inaccessible to your employees. The information may be in binders spread around different departments or in word processing files on your LAN. As you think about the information already available, keep in mind that the content you offer will be determined, at least in part, by the business strategy that you adopt. You should also identify external sources, including other pages on other intranets within your company, to which you want to link. If your company has an Internet Web site, you may reuse some of this information on your intranet. Review everything before it is put up on the Web server; be sure that only good, solid information gets the distribution that the intranet brings.

For example, if your goal is to give your employees better access to information, then your site might include links to corporate information, press releases, employee forums, links to project plans, internal documentation, procedures, or methodologies.

> **TIP**
>
> Throughout this chapter, keep in mind that your content must serve a purpose. Always reevaluate your content with your intranet's mission in mind.

Just tracking the changes needed to keep your site's content up-to-date can be a full-time job. If you find that you're providing access to hundreds or thousands of constantly changing documents as part of your system administration duties, consider using a document-management package.

Designing Your Intranet

In this section, we'll also review the various ways you can organize and link information. Let's say you're creating a training manual or a tutorial. A simple linear design will work well where each page will link to the one before and the one that follows. Applications that impose a hierarchy on your data, such as a table of contents, require more careful design. A Web-based design, in which one page links to many and each of these new pages also contains many links, is another difficult design task. Be sure you understand all the intricate dependencies before you start to code the HTML.

> **TIP**
>
> Design your intranet's structure and functionality with the same care you'd give to the look of the individual pages. Remember that good design includes structure and content as well as appearance.

It sometimes helps to use a model from the print world as a guide. Does your material resemble a printed catalog, with lots of part number listings? Or is it a technical support bulletin that has separated, self-contained sections? Or does it resemble a book in which one chapter leads into the next? Once you've decided on your model, lay out the basic design on paper.

For example, let's say you've decided on a home page that has links to four major areas: Product Information, Corporate Information, HR Information, and a search page. As shown in Figure 5.1, each of the four secondary pages contains a link back to the home page and to the search page. The Corporate Information page contains links to the Product and HR Information pages. Finally, the Corporate and HR pages contain links to each other. Start by drawing a rectangle representing the home page and label it. Below that, draw more rectangles, one for each of the other pages, and label them. Draw a line from the home page to each page and insert arrows that point both ways.

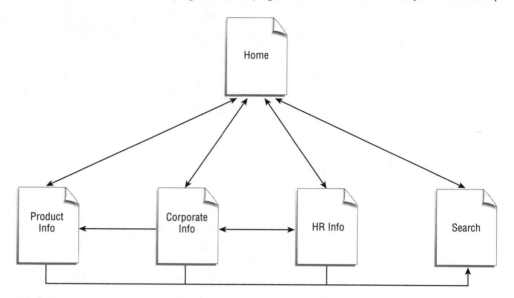

FIGURE 5.1: Drawing your pages and links before you start helps you plan your site.

This type of design, which is more difficult to create, more closely resembles a magazine or newspaper than a book because users can navigate through the pages in a different order every time they use them. The design you choose should reflect the mission you've defined in your intranet plan from the previous chapters.

Let's say you've decided that communication is your goal. Emphasize communication in the way you define areas of your intranet and the graphics that you use. For example, use terms like *talking* and *feedback* and graphics of people talking, meeting, or communicating in some way.

As you continue to add to your intranet's design, you can use your sketches to keep track of your content as well as the structure.

Creating Each Page

Once you have the content in place, what remains is the task of converting the material to a form suitable for display on your intranet. Anything you can do to automate that process should be given serious consideration, particularly if your content is likely to be volatile and to change frequently. Take an incremental approach when making changes; this allows you to retain material that can be reused, and it minimizes the amount of discarded material.

You need to decide what percentage of existing material can be used on your Web and who will be responsible for converting that information. You'll also need someone to create the pages. You should include that person in your plan and outline their duties.

In Part 3 of this book, we'll delve into some of the tools that you can use to create your sites. In Chapter 9, "Creating Intranet Pages with HTML," we'll look at HTML in detail; in Chapter 10, "Adding Other Content to Your Intranet," we'll describe how you can write scripts and use the Java programming language to enhance your sites. And in Chapter 11, "Using Intranet Authoring and Management Tools," we'll take a look at some of the Windows-based tools you can use to speed up Web-page creation and to help you to manage your intranet site.

> **TIP** Tools may make the job easier, but they're not a substitute for planning and expertise. You can create excellent HTML pages for your intranet with a simple text editor and a shareware graphics program.

Testing, Testing, Testing

You'll hear us say this more than once: Test your pages, and then test them again, and then test them some more. A background in software development has given us a healthy respect for careful testing of any kind of software. You should make absolutely sure the people who do the testing are not the same people who developed the content or who programmed the pages. These people will be too close to the original material, and they'll see exactly what they expect to see; if you use someone who has no such preconceived notions as your tester, you'll create an intranet of a much higher quality.

Part of your content plan should include a test plan detailing

- What should be tested
- Who will perform the tests
- What to do if there are problems
- When to retest

Once you've established a written plan and done some testing, you'll need to revise it to fit the way your intranet is used.

WARNING Testing is almost universally overlooked or understaffed. Make sure it's in your plan and is a required step in delivering your intranet.

Tracking Results and Responding to Feedback

Once your intranet site is up and running, you'll start to get e-mail and comments from people, as well as network statistics telling you who is accessing your intranet and what they are doing once they get there.

You must be ready to deal with these comments in an effective manner. With the speed of electronic communications these days, you should have a mechanism in place to provide a reply to queries within one working day at the outside, and faster is better in this case.

You can also use HTML forms to collect data. Forms have the advantage of allowing you to control the format of the data collected. Figure 5.2 shows you a sample form.

Users can simply fill in the form and click the Send Feedback button. A small program or script then reads the form's data and converts it to a format you can more easily use. The program may even e-mail a copy to your Webmaster and also write the info to a log file.

Looking at Different Intranet Functions

There are as many kinds of intranet sites as there are individuals and corporations. You can certainly categorize the sites by size, but a more useful breakdown is to look at the kinds of sites by function. When planning your intranet, you'll need to determine the sorts of pages that are appropriate for the kind of information you want to publish and are also appropriate for your audience.

The best way to do this is to take a look at the whole range of functions now being performed on corporate intranets; along the way, we'll discuss a number of specific tips for actually building these pages to help you start thinking about the kinds of issues that you might encounter. You may find that you can use all of the following examples, or you may find that you only use one. Let's take a look.

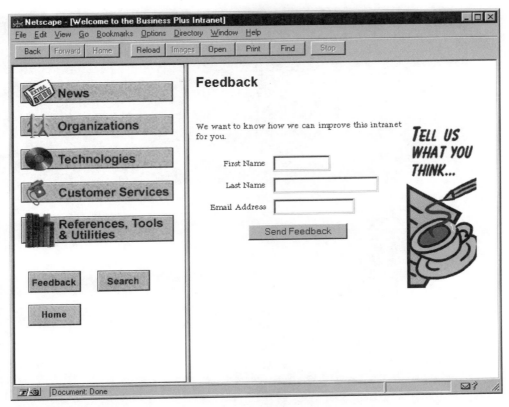

FIGURE 5.2:   A form used to gather input and suggestions from users

A Typical Home Page

The home page is often the starting point for any exploration of your intranet site. Your home page sets the tone for the rest of your site, both by way of an introduction and as a gateway; it acts as a combination magazine cover, billboard, and front page headline.

A small intranet may have just one home page where everyone starts their explorations, but as soon as more departments begin adding their own material, the concept of a single home page doesn't fit very well, and you'll find that there will be lots of them—one for each department or subject on the intranet. For example, Figure 5.3 shows links to some of the many home pages on Silicon Junction, the Silicon Graphics intranet site.

FIGURE 5.3: The Silicon Graphics intranet links branches around the world and departments and groups within the company. (Copyright Silicon Graphics, 1996)

The home page reflects the personality of the sponsoring organization or department. Some are flashy and attention grabbing; others are subdued. You should try to keep the initial home page short and to the point; users don't want to scroll down to see material that was initially hidden from view. One of the first elements users should see is a collection of navigation buttons they can use to jump to other pages.

What each button actually does depends on the needs of your site, but some common applications might include the following:

Contents button	Displays an organized view of your whole site.
Map button	Displays a graphical overview of your site. Be careful when using large graphics, and remember that they take time to download to a browser.
Search button	Opens a search engine that allows users to specify a word or a phrase in which they're interested.
Previous and Next buttons	Allow a user to move around your site quickly and easily, even on an initial visit.
Icon buttons	Site-specific buttons that give users access to the main content of your site.

Your home page should always indicate the main focus of your intranet and indicate who is in charge. For example, if your intranet's primary purpose is to provide technical support, make sure your images and text convey that purpose. At the bottom of your home page, you can add a signature that includes a copyright statement, the date when the page was last revised, an e-mail address, your extension, and the physical address of your department.

A Table of Contents or Index Page

Another popular function offered on many sites is a table of contents or an index page. A table of contents is similar to the table of contents in a book; it indicates the kind of information your site provides and how it is organized.

> **TIP**
>
> On a contents page, be sure the Next and Previous buttons operate in the order suggested by the table of contents.

However, if the terminology used for your intranet page titles is particularly technical or complex, making it difficult for the average person to use a table of contents, an index can be especially useful.

The items in an index are arranged in strict alphabetic order. Even if you don't have entries for all the letters in the alphabet, leave all the letters in place. Just think how disorienting an alphabet that only contains 12 letters will appear to most of your users.

And always remember the indexer's golden rule: Use entries that the reader will recognize. If your site contains many graphical elements or icons, consider adding them to your index. If your index grows too long and becomes unwieldy, place the entries for a single letter or for a group of letters on a new page and provide links from these pages back to the main index page.

A Glossary or Dictionary Page

If you have a glossary or dictionary page, users can look up the meaning of specific technical words or jargon. A company glossary can be just the thing to orient newcomers quickly and easily. For example, a software developer might use a glossary page to describe the functions performed by the software libraries developed in-house. You could also use a glossary-type structure to describe the separate elements that make up your company's product line. You can even let users jump from an intranet page into the glossary and right to the definition of any term you've linked to the glossary. Again, even if you don't have entries for all the letters of the alphabet, be sure all the letters remain in place.

A Technical Support Page

A technical support page might include instructions on how to perform a specific operation, such as an upgrade, or it might contain a troubleshooting chart designed to help users identify and then fix specific problems. Some companies are using an intranet as a help desk, where employees with technical problems complete online forms detailing the kinds of problems they are experiencing. Figure 5.4 shows you an example technical support page.

For a how-to operation, you might include an initial summary of the operation and then list all the items and tools that will be needed during the upgrade. The content in this case will consist of the steps of the procedure; describe what each specific step will accomplish and include photographs or other illustrations where appropriate. If you need to include warnings, be sure to place them immediately before the related step. And be sure to provide information or a short test that lets users evaluate whether they have performed the operation correctly.

When providing troubleshooting information, be sure each step in the process is well thought-out, well written, and at the right technical level for the majority of your users. After all, they're accessing your page because they have a problem; if your Web pages are badly laid out and are difficult to follow, you're compounding their problem and increasing their irritation at the same time.

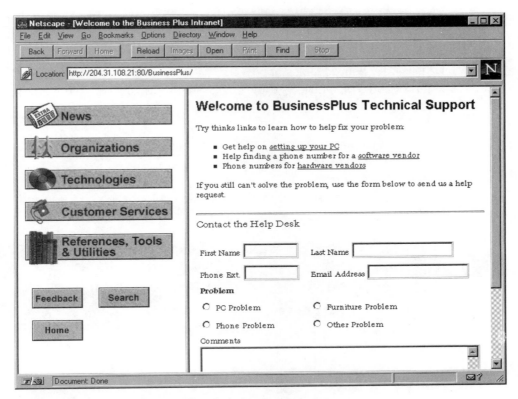

FIGURE 5.4: An example of a simple technical support page

A Technical Report Page

Many companies use their Web sites to present new or updated technical information to interested parties throughout the company. Sun Microsystems, the inventors of the Java scripting language, is a good example of a company using this approach. For those interested in Java, Sun engineers prepared technical information papers.

A technical report page is one instance in which you can violate the rule about only using short pages. Generally speaking, long Web pages are considered a bad idea; they require a user to scroll through the document several times to go from beginning to end. Users might want to print out a technical report, however; and if it is a self-contained document (all on one long page), they don't have to chase down related pages to see the whole thing.

You can also provide many kinds of links on a technical report page, including the following:

- Original raw data, from which your conclusions are drawn
- Statistically derived tables of data
- Text or audio of interviews with subjects in the study or with other experts in your field
- Audio and video clips
- Text of other papers by the same author or authors
- Reference works cited and the bibliography
- The author's biography
- Web sites and newsgroups that provide more information on these and related topics

> **TIP**
>
> You can also provide technical reports or *white papers* in two formats—HTML, for online reading and Acrobat for printing. You'll find more info about alternatives and additions to HTML pages in Part III.

An Employee Home Page or Biography Page

A personalized employee home page or biography page is a useful way to introduce people who have recently joined your company or to announce promotions or changes in job responsibilities.

You will find that a biography page gives your site a warm, personal tone and can add to its credibility. Include photographs and audio or video clips, if you can; even a cartoon or a short animation segment adds spice. All these elements can help humanize the subject or subjects. Employee home pages are usually one of the most visited areas of a site for two reasons: it's a good way to find out information about a person, and it's fun to see what your coworkers have put on their pages.

A Press Release Page

A press release can announce new, upgraded, or revised products, new staff, even new research and development projects. Although press releases are aimed at news editors, you'll find it helpful to place press releases on your intranet at the same time you place them on your Internet site. Sometimes this is the only way employees find out what the rest of the world has already learned about the company from the daily newspaper! If your company is high-profile and very newsworthy, you may even have a marketing section or live links to other articles or news services on the Internet, blending the line between inside and outside communications.

A Download Menu Page

A download menu page gives your users a quick and easy way to download documents, readme files, device drivers, technical support bulletins, bug fixes, service packs, software revisions, compressed file archives, such as zipped files, and so on.

Your page can use plain text descriptions of files, or you can use icons to indicate the range of file types available for download, including text files, executable files, PostScript files, Acrobat files, and zipped files. Along with each file name, include the file format, the size of the file in bytes, and the revision level so users know exactly what they're getting themselves into. Figure 5.5 shows a typical download page.

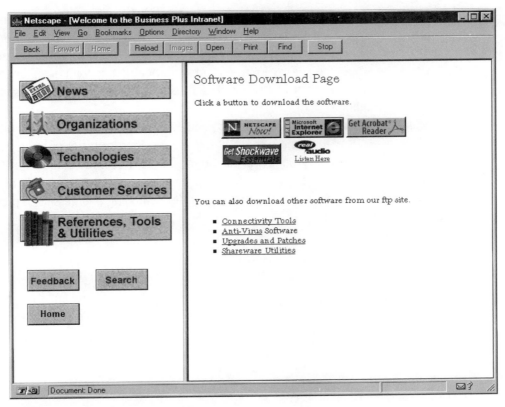

FIGURE 5.5: A software download page

This information helps users make intelligent choices about whether they can run or use the file before they spend the time downloading it, how long the download is likely to take, and whether they will have sufficient hard-disk space to store the file after they have received it from your site.

A Search Engine

A search engine, which uses a keyword to locate specific resources, is a specialized kind of intranet application. Once your intranet grows above a certain size, you'll find that adding some sort of search capability will make your intranet much easier to use. And quite simple searches will find lots of applications; not everyone needs to run complex Boolean searches.

Search engines are also an inexpensive way to boost your intranet's usability. Many search engines are available for under $350, and depending on your needs and server platform, you can even get a good search engine for free.

Schlumberger, the oil-field services company, uses an adaptation of a search engine on its intranet to locate people with specific technical expertise. Schlumberger's field engineers are usually located in its field offices, which are spread all over the world. Using the search engine, employees can look for a person with experience in a specific geological province or for someone with experience in a particular aspect of technical interpretation.

Many large companies incorporate search engines into the online company or telephone directories. This makes it easy to find the telephone number of your man in Rangoon or the name of the managing director of the Buenos Aires office.

An intranet that gives users access to large databases will most certainly need a search engine. Figure 5.6 shows the query page for searching a large site of product and customer information.

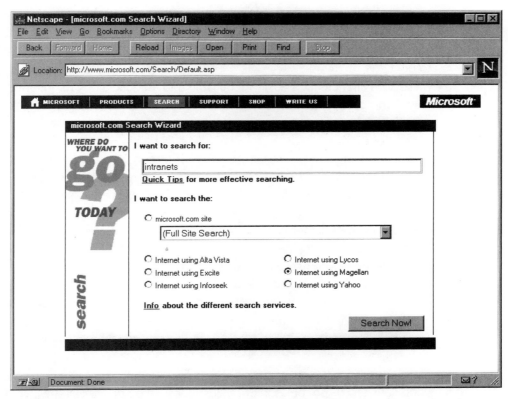

FIGURE 5.6:   If your intranet connects large amounts of data, you'll want to add a search engine.

Making the Most of Your Intranet

As your corporate intranet evolves, you'll have to make many changes and adjustments, but here are some suggestions for getting the most out of this young and emerging technology today:

- Let those people in your company who are most familiar with the content recommend what to post on your intranet site. Management will have to okay their suggestions or provide guidelines in the case of restricted material, but the people on the ground are the ones who know the value of the information they control.

- Prepare a plan of what material will be posted along with a justification for posting it. After all, posting this information on your intranet is supposed to benefit the company in some way, so you need a good solid business reason to do it.
- Make sure all material is easily identifiable and that users of your intranet know who posted what information. Always add a contact name, an e-mail address, and an extension number so people can ask questions or make suggestions.
- Consider adding a *FAQ* (Frequently Asked Questions) section or organizing a question-and-answer forum so experienced group members can share information with people from outside your department and with recent arrivals.
- Help others to help themselves. Post hints and tips that other departments can use when creating their sites. Add examples of how to use HTML effectively or how to use scripts to access a corporate database. Create introductory documents that show others what you did to create the intranet and how you did it. If you have Web access, add links to browser tutorials, HTML information, and other intranet-related sites.
- Apply the appropriate level of security, and restrict certain types of information using passwords.
- Make your site as useful as possible. Add links to other sites when it makes good sense to do so, but don't do it just because other sites exist within the company, and never link to a site still under construction.

The corporate intranet is after all only a tool, and it's only one of many that can be used to improve internal communications. Creating an effective intranet certainly requires careful planning and a clear understanding of the corporate goals involved, but it can make corporate communications across the entire enterprise cost effective and efficient.

Now that you have a good idea of the kinds of things you may put on your intranet, have a meeting with the project team and discuss the possibilities for content as they relate to your business plan. Remember to write everything down since the time between planning and construction may vary, and you'll want to remember all the good ideas you've generated.

The next chapter will discuss security planning. This area is a hot topic, and there are no general answers, only questions. We'll use those questions to develop a security plan and policy for your intranet.

Chapter 6

PLANNING YOUR INTRANET'S SECURITY

FEATURING

- **Understanding security threats**
- **Developing an intranet security policy**
- **"Building" a firewall**
- **Understanding proxy servers**
- **Evaluating your intranet's security**

Many corporate intranets are self-contained and are not connected to the outside world. For these intranets, the important security concerns are those most familiar to all network administrators: access, authentication, file and directory rights, and permissions. Once you connect your intranet to the wider world of the Internet, security issues change dramatically, and you must be prepared to devote a great deal of time and attention to protecting your intranet from external intruders.

In the sections that follow, we'll cover common threats to security, describe how you can set up a reasonable security policy for your intranet, and look at some techniques you can use to protect your intranet from external intruders. Network security is a complex topic, and in this chapter, we can only give you the basics.

For more information, you might want to look at a couple of good books on the subject: *Building Internet Firewalls,* by Brent Chapman and Elizabeth Zwicky (O'Reilly and Associates, Inc.,1993); and *Firewalls and Internet Security,* by Bill Cheswick and Steve Bellovin (Addison-Wesley, 1994.) For a Microsoft NT Server book, see *Mastering NT Server 4,* by Mark Minasi (Sybex, Inc. 1997)

Even though we're only giving you an overview of security issues and options to deploy on your intranet, the material is much more technical that the rest of the book. We'll try to make it as easy as possible by including lots of definitions and throwing in some sidebars to clarify complex techniques or issues. Remember, as you plan your intranet, you only need to know the concepts *behind* intranet security issues—not the step-by-step procedures for installing and configuring a firewall or proxy server. The details come later, for now focus on the concepts that you'll need to understand to create a security plan.

Defining Security Threats

Network security is the aspect of a system administrator's job that has to do with ensuring only authorized persons use the network and that they do so only in authorized ways. The role of security is to make network hardware, software, and data available whenever they're needed by those users who are authorized to use them. This availability may be different for different users at different times; privileges and access permissions may change.

Before establishing a security policy, you must know what threatens your network's security. Network security can be threatened, compromised, or breached from the point of view of hardware, software, company-confidential data, and even network operations. An example here will help. If a disgruntled employee tries to discover a private password, that network is *threatened.* If that employee's successful in discovering the password but doesn't use it, the network is *compromised* and can't be considered secure—even though it may not have suffered any actual damage. And if the employee actually uses the password, network security has been *breached.*

Common network security threats range from complete network infiltration to simple virus contamination. Some threats are accidental, and others are malicious; some affect hardware, and others affect software. We'll look at them all in the following sections. To create an effective security plan, you must look at all the possible threats, along with their consequences, and then develop effective measures against each threat. For information about some specific security measures, see the "RAID Explained," and "Packet Filtering Explained" sidebars, later in this chapter.

Internal Threats

Internal security problems are often the most common. Users entrusted with certain levels of access to systems and hardware can be a major threat if not controlled and monitored carefully. Put simply, you never know what someone is going to do. Even the most loyal employees or workers can change their tune and turn malicious, wreaking havoc on your computing environment.

WARNING   **Employees can walk away with manuals, leak secrets to competitors during a interview, or simply leave a PC unattended at a trade show after it's remotely logged in to your corporate network. None of these problems is directly related to your intranet, but these kinds of security problems should be addressed in your intranet plan.**

Ask your human resources department or hiring managers to check your workers' backgrounds, references, and previous employers carefully. Your security administrator should routinely change and audit your security methods. You don't want to be paranoid, but you should be cautious.

External Threats

External security threats are the most problematic. You never know when an outsider will attempt to breach your systems or who the perpetrator may be. Some people go to great extremes to gain access to your systems and information. There are many documented cases of outsiders easily gaining access to systems that were once assumed to be protected. Even the Department of Defense admits that its computer systems were attacked more than 250,000 times in 1995. That statistic alone should stop you in your tracks and make you think. It has been recently theorized that a well-funded group of computer crackers could bring the entire country to a screeching halt within 90 days with almost no trouble at all.

Therefore, if you decide to connect your intranet to the outside world via the Internet, you'll discover a whole new set of potential problems. Millions of people use the Internet every day, and the numbers are growing; some of those people will try to break into your system just to see if they can do it.

WARNING Think carefully about the security ramifications *before* connecting to the Internet! Too many system administrators connect first and think about security later, and this is the exact opposite of how you should do it. Treat the Internet as the potentially hostile environment that it is.

Administering and installing a security plan can be a complex business, and many excellent training courses are available. Don't be afraid to get some extra training; it will stand you and your company in good stead.

Now that we've talked about the two basic types of threats, let's take a closer look at what some of those internal and external threats are. For convenience, we've broken the material into three groups—threats to computer systems, threats to hardware, and threats to information.

Threats to Your Computer System

Your computer system has three components, all of which can be compromised: hardware, software, data and data files.

Threats to Hardware

The first component of your computer system is the hardware you use. Let's take a look at some of the more common threats to your hardware:

- Theft of a computer, printer, or other resource.
- Tampering by a disgruntled employee who interferes with dip switches or cuts a cable.
- Destruction of resources by fire, flood, or electrical power surges. Don't forget that those sprinklers in the ceiling can put out hundreds of gallons of water a minute; most of the damage to computer systems comes not from fire, but from the water used to put out the fire.

Threats to Software

The second component of your system is software. Threats to software include the following:

- Deletion of a program, either by accident or by malicious intent.
- Theft of a program by one of your users.

- Corruption of a program, caused either by a hardware failure or by a virus. More on virus attacks in a moment.
- Bugs in the software. Yes, they do happen, and their effect may be immediate and catastrophic, or they can be subtle and come to light years later.

Threats to Information

The third component of your system is the data and data files used by the corporation. Threats to information can include:

- Deletion of a file or files. As we'll mention again and again, make and test your backups regularly.
- Corruption, caused either by hardware problems or by a bug in the software.
- Theft of company data files.

Establishing Your Intranet Security Policy

Once you've compiled a list of all the ways in which your network may be threatened, you can begin to formulate an intranet security policy. In many ways today's computing world is radically different from the computing environments of yesteryear. These days many intranets are in private offices and labs and are often managed by someone employed outside the traditional computer data center or IS department—someone who may have little or no understanding or interest in system administration and security-protection techniques.

A connection to the Internet is, of course, a two-way street. Once your intranet is connected to the Internet, you're giving outsiders the means they need to reach *your* internal networks. A major component in planning your intranet is the process of defining a set of *reasonable* security goals and then implementing a security policy based on those goals.

We use the word *reasonable* here because it's extremely difficult to both service your normal users without inconveniencing them and keep out intruders at the same time. And never assume that your system is bulletproof. As soon as you do, you've let your guard down, and someone will surely break in, which could cost you your entire network, your sensitive data, or even your business. Read this section carefully before finalizing and implementing your security policy. Let's take a look.

Defining Security Goals

As you begin to formulate your security policy, consider the following:

- Look at exactly what you are trying to protect—network hardware, software, company-confidential data, and network operations.
- Look at who you need to protect it from—current users, previous employees, and outsiders trying to break into your system.
- Look at what you need to protect it from—fire, smoke, floods, extremes of temperature and humidity, power outages, earthquakes, and theft.
- Determine the likelihood of these potential threats.
- Implement measures that will protect your assets in a way that you or your firm can afford.
- Review your processes and procedures continuously, and improve them every time you find a weakness or a new security mechanism becomes available.

Your security policy should minimize all types of threats and ensure network compromise or security breaches are as infrequent as possible. It should also minimize the effect of any security breach once it occurs.

As you develop your security policy, focus on the following goals:

- Preventing malicious damage to files and systems
- Preventing accidental damage to files and systems
- Limiting the results of any deletions or damage to files that do occur
- Protecting the integrity and confidentiality of data
- Preventing unauthorized access to the system
- Providing appropriate disaster-recovery systems so the server can be restored and be back online again quickly

Establishing Effective Security Measures

Once you've defined your intranet security goals, you can decide which of the many available security techniques make sense for your intranet.

> **TIP**
>
> There are a lot of options and most intranets won't implement all the measures listed on the next few pages so don't worry if they seem complicated or excessive.

Let's look at some of the options:

- Be sure the server is physically secure from theft and damage. Servers are usually kept in locked rooms or cabinets; after all, few people should even need access to the server itself.
- In addition to keeping the server in a physically secure area, you may want to keep it on a separate network with restricted access to enhance the server's security.
- Use power-conditioning devices, such as line conditioners, to clean the electrical power coming into the server or a UPS (*uninterruptible power supply*) to keep the network running long enough so an orderly shutdown can be performed. For other, noncritical network hardware components, such as workstations, a surge suppresser is usually sufficient.
- Implement *fault-tolerant* services on your server, such as *disk mirroring* or *disk duplexing* available in Windows NT Server. *Fault tolerance* is a system design method that includes a certain number of redundant components to ensure the network continues to operate even in the event of individual failures. At the printed circuit board level, fault-tolerant design provides redundant circuits and chips and the capability to bypass faults automatically. At the computer system level, any elements that are likely to fail, such as hard disks and disk controllers, are duplicated. In some extreme cases, the entire computer system is duplicated in a distant location to protect against vandalism, acts of war, or major natural disasters. Two approaches to hard-disk fault tolerance, in which the same information is written to two different hard disks at the same time, are called disk mirroring and disk duplexing. In disk mirroring, both hard disks use the same hard-disk controller; in disk duplexing, each hard disk has its own, separate disk controller.
- Take advantage of RAID and choose the level that makes most sense for your operation. (See the sidebar "RAID Explained" for more details.)

RAID Explained

Windows NT Server includes several levels of *RAID* (Redundant Array of Inexpensive Disks) support. RAID is a technology used instead of the old *SLED* (Single Large Expensive Disk) design, in which a hard-disk failure spelled disaster. Instead of using one enormous disk drive and writing all data to that disk, RAID uses an array of less expensive disks and one of several methods for writing data to ensure redundancy. Each level of RAID is designed for a specific purpose:

RAID 0   Data is written to one or more drives, but there is no redundant drive. RAID 0 provides no fault tolerance because the loss of a hard disk means a complete loss of data. For this reason, some classifications omit this level of RAID.

RAID 1   Two hard disks of equal capacity duplicate or mirror each other's contents. One disk continually and automatically backs up the other disk. This is also known as disk mirroring or disk duplexing, depending on whether one or two independent hard-disk controllers are used.

RAID 2   Each bit is written to a different drive, and then parity and error-correction information is written to additional separate drives. The specific number of error-correction drives depends on the exact allocation algorithm being used.

RAID 3   Same as RAID 2, except a single parity bit is written to a parity drive instead of checksums to checksum drives. A parity bit is just extra information that is written at the end of a file used for error checking. Checksum is an error-detection scheme where each transmitted message is accompanied by a numerical value based on the number of set bits in the file to make sure the message isn't garbled.

RAID 4   Data is written across drives by sector rather than by the individual bit, and a separate drive is used as a parity drive for error detection. Reads and writes data independently.

RAID 5   Data is written across drives in sectors, and parity information is added as another sector, just as if it were ordinary data. RAID 5 allows overlapping writes, and a disk is only accessed when necessary. This level of RAID is faster and may be more reliable than some of the other methods.

In terms of speed, there is not much to choose from among these RAID levels—the appropriate level of RAID protection depends on how you use your network. Levels 1, 3, and 5 are available commercially, and levels 3 and 5 are used most often. Level 2 is generally considered too expensive for commercial use and Level 4 is comparable to Level 5 but isn't used because of the poor performance.

- Schedule and make frequent backups and test them to ensure they contain what you think they do. Store your backups at a secure off-site location, preferably one that can provide temperature, humidity, and access controls, as well as fire protection.

- Install callback modems to prevent unauthorized logon attempts from remote locations. This type of modem takes note of the caller's logon information and then breaks the connection. If the telephone number that originated the call and the logon information are both appropriate, the modem dials a predefined number and allows the user access to the network. You can use callback modems with Windows NT Server.
- Use all the audit trail and logging features available in your chosen operating system. The audit trail records details of every user action on the system, whether it was successful or not. You can use this information to look for break-in attempts.
- Control access to sensitive files and directories. Be sure you've appropriately assigned the read, write, and execute permissions on all the content files and directories on your intranet.
- Inform all users about your security policies and about their duties and responsibilities as users.
- Consider using *traffic padding,* a technique that equalizes network traffic and thus makes it more difficult for an eavesdropper to infer what is happening on your network.
- Implement *packet filtering,* which makes eavesdropping almost impossible. See the sidebar "Packet Filtering Explained" for more information.
- Prepare a plan that you can execute when you detect that your network is under attack. Decide the steps you'll take and the order you'll take them in. Decide under what circumstances you'll shut down the intranet service, any connection to the Internet, or the entire internal network.

Packet Filtering Explained

Packet filters either allow or block *data packets* (discrete units of information), often while routing them from one network or network segment to another and most often between a private network and the Internet. Packet filtering can be done in a router (which is often called a *screening router*) or on an individual host computer using special software; both implementations are considered a form of *firewall,* a secure barrier behind which your local area network operates in safety. We'll look at firewalls in more detail later in this chapter.

Packets can be filtered on the basis of
- Packet source address
- Packet destination address
- Source port number
- Destination port number

Packets can also be screened based on whether they're trying to initiate a connection. For example, you might decide to block connections from sites or addresses that you consider untrustworthy, or you might decide to block access from all addresses external to your own network. Here is what this might look like:

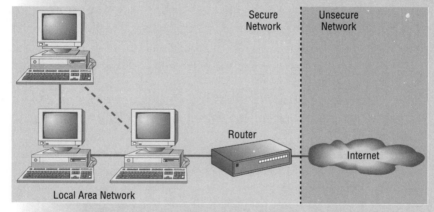

Before a packet can be screened, you must establish a set of rules that the router uses in blocking or allowing packets. These rules are usually stored in the router in a specific order and then applied in that same order once a packet is received—so be sure the order makes sense. Once you've set these rules, test them. In most packet-filtering routers, the packet is automatically blocked if a packet does not satisfy any of the rules you set up, this being the safest course of action for the router to take.

When compared with a software-based firewall system running on a host computer, most routers have very limited reporting functions, but they can maintain internal information about the state of connections passing through them and the contents of various data streams. Packet-filtering routers tend to be fast and invisible to users.

Router vendors such as Cisco, Wellfleet, 3COM, Digital Equipment Corporation (DEC), and many others supply routers that you can program to perform packet-filtering functions.

- Provide virus protection for all users, and scan all file servers and workstations daily. Use virus scanners that stay loaded and run all the time.
- Ensure all operating-system patches are installed immediately when they're distributed. Don't expect the manufacturer to track you down and tell you about them.
- Don't send confidential information in clear text across the network. Instead, encrypt all sensitive messages and files before transmitting them across any network, including an intranet.
- Limit the services offered on your network to those that are necessary. If you're not using one aspect of the server package (for example, if you're using the Web server, but not the Gopher or the FTP servers in Microsoft's Internet Information Server), turn it off or uninstall it.
- Limit the number of logon accounts on the host, and be sure to look for and then remove any inactive accounts that you find.

All these recommendations have their place in your security plan, but the best security plan in the world is worthless unless you carefully and precisely put it in place and then follow up by taking the appropriate steps to keep it working.

Know Your Server

Understanding why you are establishing your intranet should help you define most of your security policies. For example, if your Web site is designed to deliver information internally, don't put it on a place on your network where it's exposed to the entire Internet. Put it behind a firewall, or put it on an isolated part of your network where there's no Internet access.

If your Web site is designed to deliver information and content to people accessing your intranet from remote sites and you want to control access to that information, your security policy should specify guidelines for this kind of access. Decide how you will control access; the most common way is with user IDs and passwords and with procedures that verify users.

Some of the policies that you establish for preventing external threats are the same as those for preventing internal threats. You can, however, use other mechanisms, such as firewalls and proxy servers, to diminish external security threats; more on both subjects in a moment.

A Note about Passwords

Passwords are a low-tech but essential security element. Here are some guidelines you can follow to make your password choices as effective as possible:

- Passwords should always be a mixture of upper- and lowercase letters and numbers.
- Passwords should be a minimum of six characters.
- Keep passwords secret and change them frequently. The worst passwords are the obvious ones: your name, your initials, your telephone number, the name of your city, your birth date, names of your pets or your children, names of TV characters or anyone even remotely associated with *Star Trek*, groups of the same letter or sequences, such as *qwerty*, or complete English words. The English language has a finite number of words, and a computer can run through them quickly.
- Change all passwords at least every 90 days, and change those associated with high-security privileges more often.
- Add expiration dates to user accounts to force password changes and the termination of short-term user accounts, such as those assigned to vendors, contractors, and temporary employees.
- Remove all default passwords from the system. If a service company set up your server, be on the lookout for passwords or accounts such as Guest, Manager, Service, and the like, and remove them immediately.
- Do not allow more than two invalid password attempts before disconnecting.
- Promptly remove the accounts of transferred or terminated employees, as well as all unused accounts.

And you should also remember to review the system log files on a regular basis to look for evidence of password abuse and failed logons.

Securing Intranet Server Configurations

You can securely configure your intranet server in two major ways: One involves physically isolating the server, and the other isolates the server based on the networking protocol in use. Let's take a look.

Physical Isolation

Placing your intranet server on a section of your network where unknown Internet users can't access it is always a great policy. This, in effect, eliminates most of the possibilities for intrusion from an outsider. A potential intruder would have to physically gain access to your premises in order to violate security and gain access to the intranet server. Physical access to your premises is something you can control, and it goes a long way toward securing your Web site.

You should also consider the physical location of the server itself; it should be behind a door with lock and key, even during normal business hours. You can install mechanisms that require the use of card keys on the server for access—before someone can actually sign on to the server using the server's keyboard.

Protocol Isolation

Protocol isolation techniques involve Web servers that do not use TCP/IP as the primary means of network communication. Some Web servers are capable of using other network protocols to communicate with Web clients needing access. For instance, you can opt to use Microsoft's NetBEUI protocol, or perhaps you can use IPX/SPX, which is more performance-oriented than NetBEUI. If your Web server has no way of talking to the rest of the Internet, logic dictates that a potential intruder wouldn't be able to talk to your Web server from across the Internet. Protocols are a very technical subject and way beyond what we can teach you in this book. We'll give you some basics, however, in Appendix B, "The Internet Protocol—TCP/IP." You can also find information about computer terms and concepts on the Internet at `http://www.sandybay.com/pc-web/`.

Controlling Access to Your Intranet

You can control access to your Intranet in three ways, and you can use these methods to restrict access to a single intranet document or to directories containing a large number of documents:

> **By user authentication**   This refers to authentication by username and password and is often provided by the operating system. Some operating systems, such as Windows NT, have robust security systems; some have relatively fragile security, and Windows 3.1 has none to speak of.

> **By IP address or domain name**   Most servers let you exclude specific users or groups of users by their unique IP address. We'll be looking at this in much more detail in Chapter 8, "Installing Intranet Software."

By encryption   Using one of the popular encryption techniques is often recommended to ensure confidentiality of applications. Many popular servers support SSL, and some of them, including those from Microsoft and Netscape, include support for digital certificates. See the following sidebar for a more detailed look at encryption.

Encryption Is the Key

Encryption is the process of encoding information in a special way so it's secure from unauthorized access; the reverse of this process is called *decryption.* Encryption allows you to communicate securely over an unsecure communications channel.

To encrypt a message, you encode it using a *key,* which is a special number—typically 40-, 64-, 80-, or 128-bits long, with the longer keys giving more secure encryption.

The two most common encryption techniques are

Private key schemes   An encryption algorithm based on a private encryption key known to both the sender and the receiver of the message; also known as *symmetrical key encryption*.

Public key schemes   An encryption algorithm based on using the two halves of a long bit sequence as encryption keys. One part of the number is called the public key and is available to anyone who wants a copy. The other part of the number is known as the private key and is always kept secret. Either half of the bit sequence can be used to encrypt data, but the other half is required to decrypt the data. In this system, a person sending a message can encrypt that message using the recipient's public key. Once this is done, the message can only be decrypted using the recipient's private key.

Secure Web servers use public key encryption techniques for a variety of purposes, including user authentication, encryption, and digital certificates. A *digital certificate* is a way of authenticating key holders so you can be sure they are who they say they are.

To set up a secure server, you must first obtain a digital certificate from a security company. The way you go about obtaining such a certificate depends on the server you are using; both Netscape and Microsoft servers use VeriSign as the certifying authority. See VeriSign's Web site for more details:

```
http://www.verisign.com
```

Once you have the digital certificate and the encryption keys from your security company, you can use SSL (*Secure Sockets Layer*) to add security to your intranet. (SSL is an interface developed by Netscape that provides for encrypted data transfer.) Once SSL is in place, you can use *Secure HTTP* (an extension of HTTP used for authentication and encryption) to make sure all your documents and forms are fully encrypted.

The configuration procedures you have to use for each of these methods depends on the operating system and server software you're using. The Microsoft Internet Information Server package integrates closely with the native security elements available in Windows NT Server; other server software packages add their own security layer to that provided by the underlying operating system. The Microsoft Internet Information Server and the Netscape servers all support SSL and the use of digital certificates.

External Security

Now that you've started to formulate a security policy for your intranet, it's time to take a look at some of the methods you can use to stop malicious intruders from gaining unauthorized access to your network. We looked at using a packet-filtering or screening router earlier in the chapter in the sidebar, "Packet Filtering Explained." In this next section, we'll look at the strengths and weaknesses of *firewalls* and *proxy servers*, which are security systems used to restrict access between a protected private network and a public network, such as the Internet. We'll look at firewalls first. Once again, this is fairly complex material, and you may need to go over it twice.

Understanding Firewalls

Firewalls are becoming an increasingly popular way to control access to network systems; in fact, well over one-third of all Web sites on the Internet are protected by some form of firewall. According to a recent survey, 10,000 firewall units were shipped during the whole of 1995, and this figure is expected to grow to 1.5 million by the year 2000.

The firewall sits between your private local area network and the Internet, and all traffic from one to the other must flow through the firewall; nothing is allowed to go around the firewall. Although the firewall monitors all the traffic that flows between the two networks, it's able to block certain kinds of traffic completely. If the firewall does its job, an intruder will never reach your protected internal network. The firewall also performs several other important tasks, including authenticating users, logging traffic information, and producing reports.

> **NOTE**
>
> Some firewalls permit only certain types of network traffic access; other firewalls are less restrictive and block only network services that are known to be problems, such as FTP (File Transfer Protocol). For various historical reasons that we don't need to worry about here, the FTP protocol requires that the remote host initiate an *incoming* connection in order to transmit data. This is a well-known problem, and most firewalls are well equipped to handle it.

The Benefits of Using a Firewall

Let's take a look at some of the major benefits you might expect from adding a firewall to your armory of security tools:

- Controlled access to sensitive systems
- Protection for vulnerable intranet services
- Centralized security administration
- Logging and statistics on network usage
- Sophisticated packet-filtering schemes
- Configuration from stand-alone hardware systems, which aren't dependent on other hardware and software systems

A firewall can act as an efficient choke mechanism, allowing you to control the point at which your network connects to the Internet. You can use it as the main component of your security plan.

Some Reasons for Not Using a Firewall

The increased security a firewall brings to your network carries a penalty in the form of loss of convenience. Unless you take special steps, it may no longer be possible for users on the protected network to access sites on the Internet directly. Having looked at the benefits of using a firewall, let's look at some of the drawbacks, which include the following:

- Access to desirable services can be more restricted than you'd like or more complex than normal. One way to solve this problem is to use a proxy server, a program that deals with external servers on behalf of internal browsers. We'll look at proxy servers in a moment.
- The potential for backdoor access increases if it isn't strictly controlled. Once one user establishes a separate connection to the Internet that does not go through the firewall, the network is compromised, and the firewall can no longer protect your system.
- Additional system administration and training are required.
- The cost can be prohibitive.
- The configuration can be too complex to implement correctly.

And then there are the threats that no firewall, no matter how capable, can protect you against, including viruses, malicious staff with access to the secure portion of your network, and new, undefined threats from outside your system.

WARNING   Firewalls are only as good as the security information that existed when the software was developed. A firewall, just like a virus scanner, can't fight threats it isn't aware of and new threats appear every day. To ensure that your firewall "knows" about all potential security problems, keep your software up-to-date.

Firewalls and Your Security Policy

It's probably obvious, but it never hurts to say it: a firewall can't protect your network against an attack that doesn't come through the firewall. Many companies that connect to the Internet are concerned about proprietary data leaking out through their Internet link but have no coherent policy about how to manage dial-in access via modems or how to handle and secure backup tapes. For a firewall to be successful in protecting your network systems, it must be one element of a consistent overall security policy.

When implementing a firewall, ask these questions:

- What do you want the firewall to do?
- What level of control do you want?
- How much can you spend to get it done right?
- What will maintaining it cost?

As with many aspects of network security, there is no single right answer when it comes to firewalls. What you'll need for your intranet depends on the nature of the problems you're trying to solve, the types of services you want to offer to users, and the level of risk that you and your company are willing to take. The techniques you use will also depend on the amount of time, money, and expertise that you can bring to bear on the problem.

Configuring Your Firewall

Where you locate your firewall depends on the design of your network and exactly what you want to protect. Figure 6.1 shows a simple configuration in which the firewall sits between your intranet and the Internet. The firewall blocks access from the Internet for everything except incoming e-mail.

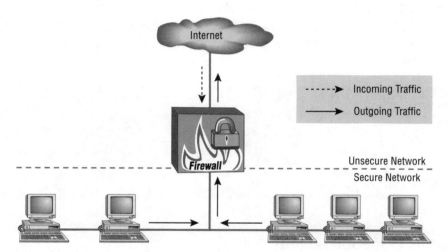

FIGURE 6.1: Simple firewall configuration

Figure 6.2 illustrates a slightly more complex example of what's usually called a *dual-homed firewall,* a common configuration that's currently used by companies that have Web servers. This type of firewall has two network connections: the first to the secure internal network, and the second to the Internet. Network traffic originating in the secure network can pass out to the Internet, to the bastion host, or to the server that contains the firewall; incoming traffic from the Internet can only access the bastion host and the services it offers.

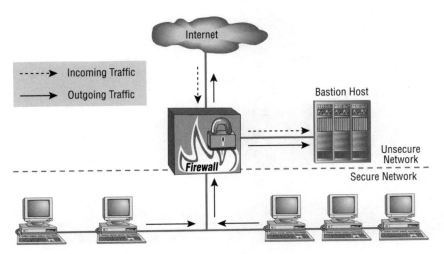

FIGURE 6.2: Dual-homed firewall configuration

The *bastion host* (the name comes from the highly fortified projections on the outside walls of medieval castles in Europe) is your public presence on the Internet and therefore is exposed to possibly hostile elements. But even if the bastion host is compromised (and you should plan on it), your internal network is isolated and remains secure.

Don't allow user accounts on the bastion host if you can avoid it; they make the host more susceptible to attack while at the same time making it more difficult to detect those attacks when they do occur.

Figure 6.3 illustrates a variation on the dual-homed firewall configuration that brings the bastion host inside the secure area.

Here the firewall has three network interface cards:

1. An external connection to the Internet
2. A connection to the secure internal network
3. A connection for the bastion host

WARNING IP routing must be turned off on the bastion host machine, which prevents IP packets from getting to the rest of the network.

Although this arrangement brings the bastion host inside the secure area, it's still isolated from the secure internal network.

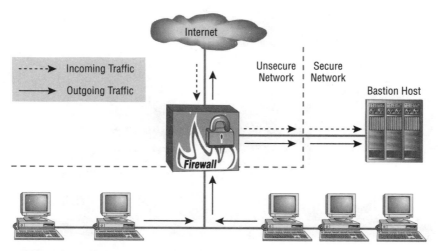

FIGURE 6.3: Extending the firewall configuration

Finding Firewall Products

The National Computer Security Association (NCSA) recently announced the results of its tests on firewalls. Products were subjected to a veritable barrage of attacks from outside the firewall, while a set of fairly typical business applications—including e-mail, FTP, and Web servers—ran on the secure side of the firewall.

The 15 vendors whose products passed these tests can label these products NCSA certified, so when you're looking for firewall software, try a product from one of these companies:

Atlantic Systems Group	Milkyway Networks, Inc.
Border Network Technologies, Inc.	On Technology, Inc.
Digital Equipment Corporation	Technologic, Inc.
CheckPoint Software Technologies, Inc.	Trusted Information Systems, Inc.
Global Technology Associates, Inc.	Radguard, Ltd.
Harris Computer Systems, Inc.	Raptor Systems, Inc.
IBM	Sun Microsystems
Livermore Software Laboratories International	

Understanding Proxy Servers

A proxy server offers another solution to several of the problems associated with connecting your intranet to the outside world and to the Internet. A proxy server is a program that handles traffic to external host systems on behalf of client software running on the protected network; this means that users of your intranet can access the Internet through the firewall. It's like a one-way mirror—you can see out but a potential intruder can't see in.

A proxy server sits between a user on your intranet and a server on the Internet. Instead of communicating with each other directly, each talks to a proxy (in other words, to a "stand-in.") From the user's point of view, the proxy server presents the illusion that the user is dealing with a genuine Internet server. To the real server on the Internet, the proxy server gives the illusion that the real server is dealing directly with a user on the proxy host. So depending on which way you're facing, a proxy server is both a client and a server. This transparency is one of the major benefits of using a proxy.

Proxy clients communicate with proxy servers, which relay approved requests on to the genuine external servers. When replies are received from those external servers, the replies are passed back to the clients. The browser itself is never in direct contact with the Internet server. Figure 6.4 illustrates this concept. A proxy server can run on a dual-homed server or on a bastion server; the only requirement is that the proxy server be a computer that your users can reach, which in turn can talk to the outside world of the Internet.

However, the proxy server doesn't just forward requests from your users to the Internet. It also looks at the requests that it processes, so it can control what your users can do. Depending on the details of your security policy, these requests can be approved and forwarded, or they can be denied. Rather than requiring the same restrictions be enforced for all users, advanced proxy servers can give different users different capabilities.

Proxy servers are usually paired with some mechanism that can be used to restrict IP-level traffic between the Web browsers running on your network and the real Internet servers. With IP-level connectivity between the browser and the real servers on the Internet, users may be able to bypass the proxy server. This could pose a security problem on your network.

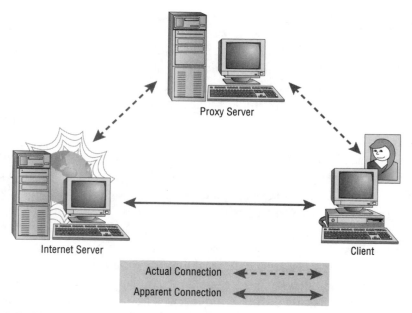

Proxy Server

Internet Server

Client

Actual Connection ◄ - - - - - - ►

Apparent Connection ◄———————►

FIGURE 6.4: How proxy servers work

IP Addressing Explained

An *IP address* is a unique 32-bit number used to identify a computer or a workstation. It's usually written as four numbers separated by dots or periods (this format is often referred to as *dotted decimal*). Such an address might look like this:

```
198.15.170.10
```

This IP address can be divided into two parts. The network address is made up from the high-order bits (normally the leftmost bits in any byte that are most significant) of the address, and the host address comprises the rest. For more information on how IP addresses fit into the whole intranet scheme of things, see Appendix B, "Intranet Protocols—TCP/IP."

Benefits of Using a Proxy Server

As always, there are arguments for and against using proxy server technology. Here are some benefits of using a proxy server:

- It blocks access to services on the Internet that you don't want your users to be able to access.
- It protects vulnerable intranet services.
- It hides the real IP address of the user from the rest of the Internet. This is another way to avoid the attentions of an unwelcome intruder.
- It provides logging and statistics on network usage.
- It's relatively easy to configure and manage.
- It doesn't require the use of valid Internet IP addresses, and this again can increase your system security.
- It's often distributed as part of a Web server package.

Having listed the reasons why you should consider using a proxy server, it's only appropriate to list some of the reasons why a proxy server might not be the answer you are looking for.

Some Reasons for Not Using a Proxy Server

Here are some of the drawbacks to using a proxy server on your network:

- It requires client software that can "talk" to a proxy server.
- It provides no protection from inside intruder attacks.
- It requires additional administration and training for both administrators and users.
- It can degrade application performance.
- It doesn't provide packet filtering.
- It may not support all TCP/IP application protocols yet.

Configuring Your Proxy Server

Proxy servers can be configured with what are commonly referred to as *bad addresses*. A bad address is not really "bad"— it's one of the special IP addresses that aren't routable through the Internet. These addresses are commonly used to configure networks behind a proxy firewall server. One common set of bad addresses is the 10.0.0.0 class A network. *InterNIC* (the organization that licenses domain names and maintains unique addresses for all computers connected to the Internet) has set aside this entire block of addresses for testing purposes, which you could certainly use behind a proxy server. Here is an example of how to do this:

1. Set up your proxy server hardware with two network cards. One network card has a real, routable Internet address of something like 204.176.47.2, and the other uses a bad address of 10.0.0.1.

2. Plug the 204.176.47.2 network card into your Internet router connection, and plug the 10.0.0.1 network card into your local network. This is the first step in creating the isolated barrier between the Internet and your network.

3. Now, configure each workstation with a unique address on the 10.0.0.0 network, using a gateway address of 10.0.0.1 or the server's bad address.

4. Configure each application that understands and uses a proxy server with the proxy server address of the server, 10.0.0.1.

That's it! Now when the client software needs to access the Internet, the requests are sent to the network card in the server that has the address 10.0.0.1, at which point the proxy server actually forwards the request to the destination after including its own valid address of 204.176.47.2. When the request is returned to the server, the proxy server returns it to the originating workstation.

For a workstation to use a proxy server, however, it must have software that knows how to talk to a proxy server. The Netscape Navigator and Microsoft Internet Explorer Web browsers can both use a proxy server, as can many other e-mail, news, FTP, Web, and Telnet software packages. We'll look at how to set up both of these browsers with a proxy server in Chapter 8, "Installing Intranet Software."

Firewalls, proxy servers, and packet-filtering routers are emerging solutions to some of the security problems associated with connecting your intranet to the Internet. Keep in mind your own circumstances as you consider and weigh the advantages and dis-advantages of each solution, but remember that your first line of defense against unwelcome intruders is the security systems built into the underlying operating system. For example, Windows NT Server has an extensive set of security features, including rights and permissions based on individual accounts and group membership.

Once you've put all the different security elements into place, the next step is rigor-ously testing it for cracks and weaknesses. Several tools exist for this purpose, and we'll look some of them next.

Testing Your Own Security

For several years now, administrators in the Unix world have been using a set of programs collectively known as *SATAN* (Security Administrator Tool for Analyzing

Networks) to test the effectiveness of the security established at their sites. Now users of Windows NT Server can use a package called Kane Security Analyst (KSA) from Intrusion Detection, Inc., for this same purpose. Let's look at both of them here.

SATAN

SATAN is available free on the Internet, and for this reason, many critics have argued that SATAN lets potential intruders take advantage of the information it contains to learn how to infiltrate systems more effectively.

> **TIP**
> You can use SATAN to your advantage. Run it against your own site to check for security holes before outsiders try to break in.

Nevertheless, the program has been a wake-up call to network administrators. SATAN collects data from each host in the specified network and creates reports for each host by type, service, vulnerability, and trust relationship. SATAN also offers several tutorials that explain the system security weaknesses and how a system administrator can eliminate them; the package also includes a FAQ.

KSA

KSA is an extensive and well-supported commercial package that runs on Windows NT Server.

> **NOTE**
> Future versions of KSA will be available for Unix systems, Novell NetWare versions 3.*x* and 4.*x*, and networks using Lotus Notes. Check out the Web site at http://www.intrusion.com for more details.

KSA examines your server system and then presents you with three-dimensional bar charts in the following six major categories:

Account Restrictions   Assesses password controls, use of logon scripts, and password-expiration dates.

Password Strength   Rates your password policies. A future version will include a password-cracking dictionary to show you how easily your passwords can be guessed.

Access Control Checks user rights and removable drive allocations.

System Monitoring Collects together a miscellaneous set of security-related concerns.

Data Integrity Checks the UPS installation and configuration.

Data Confidentiality Tests to see if passwords are stored in clear text or in encrypted form.

KSA's Report Manager is easy to use and offers almost 30 reports; data can be exported in the usual database formats.

KSA creates no accounts or services, however. To use it, you must be logged in as the administrator; although once the analysis is complete, the results can be shared with all users who have access to the system. KSA takes an instant snapshot of the state of your system; as you follow its recommendations and make improvements in your security policies, rerun the program to see how you're doing.

Software packages such as KSA can do little to actually catch intruders; that's up to the appropriate law-enforcement agencies. What they can do is highlight the security weaknesses in your system in a way that is just about impossible to ignore.

This chapter went much further into technical issues than the rest of this book—for good reasons. Security is an important, complex issue that requires a lot of thought and planning to implement properly. If you've made it this far, you're ready to put it all together and decide on the hardware and software you'll need to start building your intranet. The next chapter helps you decide what to use based on your intranet's mission and purpose, content, and security policy.

Chapter 7

CHOOSING INTRANET HARDWARE AND SOFTWARE

FEATURING

- **Looking at the big picture for hardware and software**
- **Choosing an intranet browser**
- **Selecting the right intranet server software**
- **Choosing hardware for your intranet**

We'll start this last chapter in Part 2 by taking a look at Web server software and how it works together with your Web browser to create a basic intranet. We'll also delve further into client-server architecture as it relates to intranets. Although we've touched on these elements in earlier chapters, we're going to examine these concepts in much greater detail. We'll then look at the Windows family of operating systems and evaluate them as potential platforms for both intranet server and browser software.

> **NOTE**
> One kind of specialized intranet software that we won't cover in this chapter is authoring software. Authoring software is just another name for the HTML editing tools you'll use to create intranet pages. For information about authoring tools, see Chapter 11, "Using Intranet Authoring and Management Tools."

The world of intranets is rapidly changing, so quickly that we can't cover everything because the production time of a book can eclipse new intranet software arrivals. Many Web server packages are available—we'll give you the product names and company contact information (including individual URLs) for scores of other, perhaps less popular, Web server packages and concentrate on the major software packages. We'll discuss how you can choose exactly the right Web server software package to meet your intranet needs.

Finally, we'll bring this chapter to a close with a discussion of how you can select the right Web server hardware systems, including several systems you can buy off the shelf as complete intranet solutions, called *turnkey* systems.

So How Does It All Work?

We looked at the basic components that make up an intranet in the earlier chapters; now it's time to revisit the topic and add a little more detail to those bare bones. For the software side of the story, we need to go back to 1989, when Tim Berners-Lee, a researcher at the European Particle Research Center (CERN) in Switzerland, and his coworkers proposed a way of formatting documents so they could be easily transmitted, displayed, and printed on almost any kind of network computer. Berners-Lee also invented the term *World Wide Web* to describe the results of his work, although we usually shorten this to just *the Web*.

The World Wide Web was released for internal use at CERN in 1991, where it was used for publishing scientific research papers and the results of experiments. In 1992, the system and the software were made available to the rest of the world.

Berners-Lee's proposal consisted of two separate but closely related parts:

- *Hypertext Markup Language* (HTML) for formatting the documents
- *Hypertext Transfer Protocol* (HTTP) for transmitting the documents from one computer to another

Not only did HTML format attractive documents that you could either look at online or print, but these documents could also contain hypertext links to other documents on other computers on the Web.

> **NOTE**
>
> **Remember our discussion of hypertext in Chapters 1 and 2? Hypertext is a way of presenting information so you can look at it in a nonsequential way, regardless of how the original topics are organized in the document. Hypertext was designed to allow the computer to respond to the nonlinear way that humans think and access information—in other words, by association, rather than by the linear arrangement of most films or books.**

In a hypertext application, you can browse through the information with a great deal of flexibility; you can even choose to follow a different path through the information each time you look at a specific document—something you can't do with video or recorded speech.

As mentioned previously, a hypertext document can contain a hypertext link to any other document or resource on the Web, and this link is managed by HTTP. When you select a link, the associated document is displayed, even though it may be on a different computer system thousands of miles from your location.

Now we'll take another look at the client-server model and see how it fits into your intranet's design.

Client-Server Revisited

We briefly mentioned client-server technology earlier in this book, but let's revisit the concepts before we get into the more technical side of the software and hardware. The computer that requests the document is known as a *client*, and the computer that makes the document available is known as a *server*. Put the two together, and you have the fundamentals of the client-server model for distributed computing. Clients request information from the servers, and the servers store data and programs and provide network-wide services to clients.

This arrangement exploits the available computing power by dividing an application into two distinct components: the client (sometimes called a *front end*) and the server (sometimes called a *back end*). Client-server computing lightens the processing load for the network server, but tends to increase the load on the PCs attached to the network.

Server computers tend to have larger and faster hard-disk drives and much more memory installed than conventional PC file servers. In some cases, the server may not be a PC but a minicomputer or a mainframe computer. So how does this fit into your intranet plan? Let's look at the role of the intranet server.

The Role of the Intranet Server

On an intranet, as on the Internet, the client software is called a *browser*, and the server software is called a *Web server*. You use the browser to look at the HTML content files located on the Web server. The software running on the server ranges from very simple (in the case of some of the free public-domain Web servers) to extraordinarily complex (in the case of some of the high-end commercial servers). The server receives a request for information from the browser, locates and retrieves the file, sends it to the browser, and then closes the connection. Any graphics on the page are processed in the same way, and the browser displays the results.

Web servers usually store text and graphics files, but they can also serve files of other types, including word-processing documents, audio, video, and animation. We've mentioned some of these; we'll discuss them in more detail in Chapter 10, "Adding Other Content to Your Intranet."

Most of the traffic processed by the Web server is one way, from the browser to the server, although the increasing use of HTML elements, such as forms that send data back to the server for processing, is starting to change this. The number of two-way transactions is definitely on the rise.

A intranet or Web server can also run other programs, such as database-related applications or search engines, and several standard interfaces have emerged to manage these functions, including CGI (Common Gateway Interface), Microsoft's ISAPI (Internet Server API), and Netscape's NSAPI (Netscape Server API). Linking programs can be written in C or C++ or even in Visual Basic, and recently Sun Microsystems' Java Programming Language has seen a huge wave of interest due to its platform-independent nature. Java is also popular because it allows fairly sophisticated programs to be run on the client's CPU cycles rather than the server's.

We'll look at Java in much more detail Chapter 10, "Adding Other Content to Web Pages." Single-purpose Web server software may become a thing of the past as the functions it performs are absorbed into the underlying operating system.

Having said that a Web server is perfectly capable of running other programs, you should not come away from this section with the idea that you can use a Windows 95 system both as a Web server and as someone's personal workstation; that won't work. Users of an intranet set up in this way would see very poor performance, and the person whose workstation this is would never get any computer time to get any work done. Likewise, Windows 3.1 is only suitable as a browser platform for intranet use. Windows

NT Workstation can run a small to intermediate intranet without any difficulty, and NT Server can run large intranets with ease.

Servers and Security

As intranets become more widespread and as more intranets connect to the Internet, network security will become more important. In many servers available today, you can easily and conveniently restrict access to specific pages in a variety of ways, including:

- User name and password access
- Secure Sockets Layer (SSL) encryption
- Specific IP addresses

Many servers access user or group security management information from the underlying operating system. Although it's obviously convenient to be able to manage users and groups from a central location, it can also be a potential security risk if too much information (such as a password) is passed around the network without some form of encryption. Look back at Chapter 6, "Planning Your Intranet's Security," for more details on this important topic.

Selecting an Operating System Platform

In selecting normal business or scientific applications, the choice of operating system can be paramount and, in some cases, may actually be determined by the availability of a specific application or group of applications. In the intranet world, this is no longer true.

One of the biggest benefits of an intranet is that the operating system choices for the Web server and for the PCs or workstations running browsers on your network are almost unlimited. The TCP/IP networking protocol can connect anything to anything else, and as we will see in a moment, browser software is available for every conceivable hardware and software platform. You can mix and match components to the delight of your system administrator or Webmaster. In the rest of this short section, we'll look at the strengths and weaknesses of the various Windows operating system platforms in relation to running Web server software and then go on to look at Web browsers.

Windows 3.1

Windows 3.1 (and Windows for Workgroups, also known as Windows 3.1.1) may be the world's most popular operating environment, but it has several important shortcomings when considered as a Web server platform, particularly in the areas of basic stability, resource allocation, and networking support. It doesn't include a TCP/IP package, so you must buy one separately, and then you've got to make sure the package actually works with the Web server software you choose. Windows 3.1 has limited multitasking features and under high loads will perform poorly. We don't recommend setting up your intranet server on a Windows 3.1 system.

Windows 95

The built-in networking support in Windows 95 is extensive and is easy to set up and use. Windows 95 is much more robust than Windows 3.1, and it has better multitasking features. Because TCP/IP support is bundled with the operating system, you don't have to buy it as a separate product. This reduces the overall costs compared to using Windows 3.1. For a small intranet serving a modest number of users, Windows 95 is a good choice for a server platform, as long as you're not trying to use it as a workstation at the same time. And, of course, Windows 95 makes a great workstation.

Windows NT

Windows NT is a big step up from Windows 95 both in terms of price and in terms of capabilities. NT Server is a well-built, fully functional, multi-user, multitasking operating system, capable of supporting a major intranet.

The release of NT Server 4 adds the popular Windows 95 user interface, the Internet Information Server (IIS)—capable of running Web, FTP, and Gopher services—a search engine called Index Server, the FrontPage HTML authoring package, and the Internet Explorer, all of which make Windows NT Server 4 a tough act to beat as a robust, capable Web server.

NOTE We'll take a detailed look at installing and configuring IIS in Chapter 8, and we'll look at the latest version of FrontPage in Chapter 11.

Windows NT Workstation 4 also has the Windows 95 user interface, and it includes a slightly restricted version of the Internet Information Server called the Peer Web Services. This package is also capable of running a small-to-medium-sized intranet without difficulty. Currently Peer Web Services restricts you to 10 simultaneous connections.

Look for Windows NT 5 to further support and integrate both intranet and Internet functionality into the operating system.

Macintosh and Unix

Macintosh offers the great, easy-to-use, 32-bit operating system that is its hallmark. You won't find as much available server and intranet software for the Mac, but if you're already using Macintoshes for graphics or page layout, you can easily use those tools when creating your intranet. If you decide to base your intranet on the Macintosh, we'll discuss your server options a little later in this chapter.

Unix is the classic Web server operating system. You can easily use a Unix-based Web server as part of your intranet configuration. You can run any of the different "flavors" of Unix—HP-UX, Linux, Sun, and so on—and be certain to find software you can use. Different versions of Unix are available to run on everything from a 486/Intel machine to a high-end Hewlett-Packard machine. Unix offers a stable, time-tested operating system that offers 32-bit preemptive multitasking—just the environment you need to run a successful medium to large intranet. The primary drawback to Unix is the difficulty in managing any Unix environment. The technical knowledge required to administer and tune a Unix-based intranet is much greater than for a Windows- or Macintosh-based intranet.

Next, let's take a look at your intranet browser options. Just because Netscape and IE are the biggest, don't think they're your only choices.

Choosing a Browser

For most people, the most visible element of their intranet is the Web browser. In this section, we'll look at some of the more popular choices available for the Windows family of operating systems. The basic features that seem to be driving recent browser developments in the two most popular browsers, Netscape Navigator and Microsoft's Internet Explorer include the following:

Navigation Moving around on the Internet or on your local intranet has never been easier. Internet Explorer has a larger number of customizable features, but Navigator has better options for users dialing in from remote locations.

HTML   Navigator is very fast at the fundamental browser task of rendering HTML pages; however, Internet Explorer supports cascading style sheets, which give intranet designers much more precise typographical control than they have ever had before.

Java, Plug-ins, and ActiveX   Java and plug-ins are still the standard ways to add features to the basic browser, and both browsers support them. Microsoft's alternative, ActiveX, is a powerful response to the challenge.

Built-in support   Both browsers support VRML (*Virtual Reality Modeling Language*) and in-line audio. Microsoft has gone a step further with ActiveMovie, a native video playback mode capable of handling several formats. Both browsers also feature integrated Mail and News functionality.

Collaboration tools   Internet telephone, remote whiteboard, and chat are standard features of both these browsers. A whiteboard allows you to draw, scribble, and write just as if you were in a conference room at work. The whiteboard applications are likely to see the most use in the corporate world, which will have little use for Internet telephones until they can boast the clarity, flexibility, and feature set of internal telephone systems.

You'll find much more information on cascading style sheets, the pros and cons of both Java and ActiveX, and information to get you started with VRML in Chapter 10.

Both Navigator and Internet Explorer offer a basic set of features that conform to the HTML 3 standard. You can use either product to view HTML-text content, headlines, graphics, lists, tables, and links to other sites. Both browsers use helper applications to display or play back data contained in a wide variety of special file types, including the audio, video, and animation used on many intranets. Both are easy to get and easy to install. Internet Explorer is free, and Netscape Navigator costs about $49. Let's take a look.

Browser Wars: Microsoft versus Netscape

Not long ago, it seemed that every software company involved with the Internet was busy creating a browser, but over the last year or so, a series of technical and marketing maneuvers have resulted in only two browsers emerging as the clear leaders: Navigator from Netscape and the Internet Explorer from Microsoft. Other browser vendors just can't seem to keep up with the breakneck pace of development set by these two leaders.

Netscape Navigator

For many people, Netscape Navigator from Netscape Communications is still the browser to beat. Version 3 increases the capabilities of this market leader in almost every direction and effectively defines the industry de facto standards for many important features, including HTML, graphics, plug-ins, and JavaScript support. JavaScript gives HTML content developers a mechanism they can use to embed small but useful programs into their Web pages; they can also use JavaScript to manipulate programmable elements of the Netscape browser and the document that it displays.

In theory, the World Wide Web is based on open standards accessible to all; the facts, as you might reasonably expect, are somewhat different. It turns out that much of the material you see on the Web is actually quite craftily tailored to take advantage of little known and often poorly documented features of the Netscape Navigator.

One area in which Navigator can easily hold its own against Microsoft's Internet Explorer is in terms of speed. Navigator 3 is faster at rendering HTML pages in almost all cases than is Internet Explorer, and the difference is not only apparent over dial-up connections but also over local area networks and intranets. Navigator is also faster at reloading a page from its cache.

Because of Netscape's platform-independent philosophy, you can find a version for almost all the popular operating systems, including Unix and the Macintosh. If your company is interested in linking several of these systems together using an intranet, Netscape Navigator is still the best choice; Microsoft cannot match this range, at least not yet.

Microsoft Internet Explorer

With Internet Explorer, Microsoft finds itself in the somewhat unusual position of challenger rather than champion. Netscape Navigator has a huge lead in terms of market share, and Microsoft is pulling out all the stops in an attempt to catch up.

Internet Explorer version 3, included with any new Microsoft operating system, goes a long way toward catching up with Netscape Navigator. Microsoft has done a good job of cloning all the important features found in Navigator, including support for Netscape plug-ins, support for JavaScript (which Microsoft insists on calling Jscript), and support for Navigator objects.

But Internet Explorer is much more than a simple-minded clone, and some people will say that the IE—the first truly competitive version of Microsoft's browser—has passed Navigator in one or two crucial areas, including operating system integration and support for both ActiveX as well as Java.

Some of the ground-breaking new features from Microsoft include ActiveX, a direct descendant of Microsoft's OCX control standard that is based on Microsoft's

Component Object Model (COM). ActiveX began life as a 32-bit Windows-only project, but recent developments to reach out to the Unix and Macintosh communities reflect Microsoft's attempts to broaden its appeal; we'll see exactly what those developments are in Chapter 10, "Adding Other Content to Your Intranet." Currently, between 1000 and 1500 ActiveX controls are available, and many third-party programming tools also support the ActiveX standard.

What's on the Horizon

Netscape Navigator has the greatest market share with an astonishing 75 percent; Microsoft can lay claim to about 10 percent, and the remainder is spread among several much smaller companies. Because Microsoft ignored both the Internet and intranets, Netscape had a distinct head start on the market for quite a while (which explains its lead in market share).

Where will the "browser wars" take us? Netscape's plans for the future will concentrate on improving the browser as a mechanism for communicating and collaborating. Expect to see improvements brought over from its Collabra Share line of products, including group discussion, scheduling, and calendaring features. The goal seems to be to produce a Notes-like feature set in the browser, aimed at the corporate world of intranet users.

On the HTML front, Netscape will likely support style sheets, but at this point it is not yet clear which implementation it will adopt. Microsoft emphasizes a version of cascading style sheets; if Netscape elects to support a different specification, confusion will be inevitable. Look for additional HTML tags from Netscape in the near future, some designed to support object embedding and others aimed at improved page layout. And to go up against the functions provided by Microsoft's ActiveX controls and VBScript, you'll see new Java classes and improvements to JavaScript.

Although Microsoft was late in joining the browser game, it's now firmly committed to the race and is releasing improved versions of the Internet Explorer at an astonishing rate. A series of upgrade releases is planned for the immediate future. Internet Explorer version 3 runs only on Windows 3.x, Windows 95, and Windows NT 4, but version 4 should run on these platforms plus the Macintosh.

Eventually Microsoft plans to integrate its browser into the Windows 95 Explorer. It will then make no difference whether you want to access files on your own local hard disk, on your intranet, or on the Internet; you'll use the same tool for all these tasks. Forward and Back buttons will let you use Web-like navigation to find your way around an HTML page or around your hard disk; indeed, even the Windows desktop will become an ActiveX element and be called the Active Desktop.

Web browsers are currently changing so fast that they definitely give you the feeling of the *browser du jour*. Upgrades are appearing at the rate of four or more a year from both major vendors; any organization of substantial size must be prepared to do some major planning just to keep up with it all. All this version trauma can lead to some large and unexpected support costs, but the way to cope seems to be to recognize that the rate of change is not going to slow any time soon. Plan your strategy accordingly.

The only thing that is certain in the browser wars is that the changes and the hype will continue to pour out of both Microsoft and Netscape; may the best browser win.

Other Intranet Browsers

About a year ago, it seemed that everyone was pushing their own browser; now we're down to only two major players. What happened to the rest? Some have disappeared, and others have merely languished, having failed to keep up with the leaders. Let's take a look.

Mosaic in a Box

Mosaic in a Box for Windows 95 from CompuServe Internet Division (previously known as Spry) has unfortunately not kept up with the changes made in the other popular browsers and lacks support for elements such as tables and frames. Currently Spry offers a replacement based on Microsoft's Internet Explorer called SpryNet Starter Kit. For more information, see

```
http://www.spry.com/softcenter/nettools/internet/browsers/index.html
```

NCSA Mosaic

Mosaic from the National Center for Supercomputing Applications (NCSA) tends to lag slightly behind the leading browsers. The NCSA likes to wait until a proposed new feature becomes well established before implementing it. The original Mosaic browser is now at version 3, and you can find out more at

```
http://www.ncsa.uiuc.edu/SDG/SDGIntro.html
```

Netcom

Formerly called NetCruiser, NETCOMplete, a customized software system containing Navigator or IE, is only available to owners of a Netcom Internet account. For details, see

```
http://www.netcom.com/software/index.html
```

Spyglass Mosaic

Known previously as Spyglass Enhanced Mosaic, this capable browser is only sold directly to other companies for use in their products; you can't buy it directly. Companies such as O'Reilly & Associates, OpenText, AB Software, and Datastorm all bundle this browser with their products. For information, see

```
http://www.spyglass.com/products/smosaic/
```

How to Select the Best Browser for Your Organization

The inevitable question arises: Do you *need* the latest version of any of these browsers? And what kind of support and training issues are involved in supporting more than one browser in your corporation? The answers to these questions depend on how you use your intranet within your organization and the technical level of the people involved. If you use all the latest technology on your intranet, you'll need browsers that support that technology. If you stay a little behind the crest, you'll find that you have many more choices available.

As soon as users gain easy access to the Internet, you'll be faced with people downloading beta versions, trying to run unstable software, not to mention the incompatibilities between systems and a host of other configuration problems. Surveys have shown that costs increase substantially when more than one browser is supported within an organization. Here's what you should do:

1. Evaluate the technical needs of your intranet.
2. Evaluate the technical knowledge of your users.
3. Evaluate those browsers that meet the technical needs of your intranet.
4. Choose the browser that best meets these needs.
5. Make that browser available, along with any necessary helper applications or plug-ins, to all your users.
6. Publish your policy on your intranet so your users will understand the reasons for the choice.
7. Go back to the beginning of this list of steps and repeat the process as often as necessary.

In developing content for an intranet, chances are you'll be familiar with your user base, and you can encourage standardization. If all your users have the same browser, network bandwidth, and viewing capabilities, you can develop your content to take advantage of this environment much more easily. Because there are just so many choices to be made, staying current with both browser and Web server software can be a full-time job in some organizations. Speaking of Web server software, let's look at some of the choices available.

Choosing Intranet Server Software

Web server software is available for all the popular operating systems, including all varieties of Unix, Windows NT Server and NT Workstation, Windows 95, OS/2, the Macintosh, and even Windows 3.1. We can't cover all possibilities in this book, so we'll concentrate on the Windows products. If you need detailed information on a specific server product, first check that server's Web site. Once you've decided on a server you can get more detailed information from books like *Mastering Intranets* or *Mastering Netscape FastTrack Server*.

The Web server software runs on the hardware and operating system combination that you have chosen as your server platform. A basic server doesn't actually do much work from a computational point of view. The software runs all the time, waiting to make connections and serve documents to users on the intranet when they ask for them.

> **TIP**
>
> In the Unix world, a program that runs unattended and is invisible to most users of the system is known as a *daemon*, usually pronounced "dee-mon." Daemons manage all sorts of tasks, including mail, networking, and Internet services. Some daemons are automatically triggered by events to perform their work; others operate at set time intervals. Because they spend most of their time inactive, just waiting for something to do, daemons do not usually consume large amounts of computational power. You'll often find that when a program name ends in the letter *d,* the program is a daemon. That is why some of the earliest Unix-based Web servers all have *d* as the last letter of their names, as in NCSA httpd.

In the sections that follow, we'll provide a short description of each of the server products, along with an Internet address or URL for the vendor where you can find more information. Prices range from free for some of the public-domain servers, to thousands of dollars for the high-end servers with all the bells and whistles. And because Web server prices are constantly changing, we only include approximate prices, if any. For the most accurate information, consult the individual Web sites if you want to know more about the price of a specific product.

Now let's take a look at some of the most popular server software packages.

Windows-Based Web Servers

We'll now run through the range of Windows-based servers, from the very simple to the complex and from freeware to very expensive servers. Along the way we'll give you some information about each and try to point you in the right direction if you need more detail.

Commerce Builder

The Commerce Builder server from The Internet Factory, Inc., is a modestly priced, fully featured Web server, with good security and proxy-server features. It runs as an application on Windows 95 or as a service on Windows NT.

On both platforms, you control the server using a Control Panel applet, and you can set configuration parameters at a global level for all Commerce Builder servers, at a class level for all Commerce Builder servers of the same type, or at a local level for each individual server.

Integration with NT's user database is excellent, which means you don't have to re-create every user and group on your system; all the information comes from NT, an important consideration when creating your intranet. You can then control access to various parts of the system using these user and group accounts. You can also create access-control filters and restrict access based on IP address or domain name; you can even control access down to the individual page level. Commerce Builder also supports SSL 2 for encrypted data exchanges between client and server and for server identity authentication. You can also host as many as 16 virtual servers on one physical system, each with its own domain name and individual IP addresses.

Commerce Builder's proprietary macro language (*Server Macro Expansion,* or SMX) allows you to connect to any ODBC data source, including Microsoft Access, SQL Server, and FoxPro databases. And in addition to HTTP services, the Commerce Builder package also includes a Chat Room feature and a caching proxy server.

A new version of the product, called Merchant Builder, will be available soon. For more details, see

```
http://www.ifact.com/
```

EMWAC https

This basic server from EMWAC (European Microsoft Windows NT Academic Center at Edinburgh University Computing Services in Scotland) runs on both Microsoft's Windows NT Server and NT Workstation. This may be the advantage you need as Microsoft's Internet Information Server will only run on NT Server. Also, if you want to stage an intranet pilot test and do not plan to connect to the Internet (or at least not in the early stages), this server has one major benefit: it's free.

A major drawback, however, is little security of any kind; there aren't any user accounts, passwords, or file or directory access controls, which means that the whole site is public. The server runs as a service under the System account.

EMWAC supports CGI 1.1 scripts and imagemaps and allows for the execution of Perl scripts and many executable files. All configuration is done through a Control Panel applet. For more information, see

```
http://emwac.ed.ac.uk/html/internet_toolchest/https/
contents.htm
```

Microsoft Internet Information Server

Released in early 1996 and now bundled with Microsoft's NT Server 4, the Internet Information Server (IIS) is a powerful Web server that is closely integrated with NT Server's operating system security controls, including user and group accounts and file and directory permissions. You can also allow or deny access based on a specific IP address or based on a range of IP addresses. At the time of writing this chapter, a new beta version of IIS is about to be released.

IIS creates a generic user account on NT Server that has read-only rights to the files in the IIS server directory; if you don't need any security controls, you can simply put your HTML content files in the appropriate directory, and that's it, you're done. In addition to the Web server, IIS also includes a Gopher server and an FTP server.

NT Server 4 also includes FrontPage, which we'll look at in Chapter 11, "Using Web Authoring and Management Tools," a search engine called Index Server, and Microsoft's Internet Explorer Web browser. All this makes it a powerful and capable all-in-one package. Although IIS is advertised as being free, you must first purchase a copy of Windows NT Server 4, which with a 10-user license costs $999.

IIS also supports SSL 2 security and virtual servers, CGI and Perl scripts, server-side Java, and Microsoft's Internet Server API (ISAPI) for creating more complex Web-based applications.

Java support is conspicuous by its complete absence; however, you'll find Microsoft's Database Connector included in the package. Database Connector lets you link to ODBC-compliant databases including Microsoft Access and SQL Server as well as databases from other vendors, including Oracle, Sybase, and Informix.

System logging features are weaker than those found in some other top-of-the-line servers; you won't find anything like the complex series of reports created by Netscape's Enterprise Server.

For more information, see one of these URLs on Microsoft's Web site:

```
http://www.microsoft.com/infoserv/

http://www.microsoft.com/intranet/

http://www.microsoft.com/ntserver/

http://www.microsoft.com/ntworkstation/
```

Microsoft Windows NT Workstation, Peer Web Services

The Peer Web Services included with Windows NT 4 Workstation is a slightly cutdown version of the Internet Information Server released with NT Server 4. Some of the logging functions have been removed, but Peer Web Services will comfortably run a small intranet without any problems. The Internet Explorer Web browser is included in this package, but the FrontPage HTML authoring program and the search engine aren't included.

Netscape FastTrack Server

Netscape Communications Corporation was founded by many of the original members of the NCSA and CERN programming and technical teams. According to Netscape, more than 80 percent of the company's revenue comes from providing the software to run corporate intranets, and more than 70 percent of Fortune 1000 companies use Netscape software.

Netscape originally released two products, Netscape Communications Server and Netscape Commerce Server, which were followed by the top-selling Netscape Enterprise Server and Netscape FastTrack Server. Recently this product line was revised again to include the extensive SuiteSpot intranet package.

Netscape's FastTrack Server is a popular server you can use to get your intranet up and running fast. With SSL 3 support, Navigator Gold page–authoring tool, extensive server-level access control, and excellent performance, this server is hard to beat and has the sales history to prove it.

You configure the FastTrack Server (and also the Enterprise Server) itself or from the Netscape Web browser. You can, therefore, manage your Web remotely if you wish; all you need to know is the administration screen's URL and password for the server you want to configure or manage. The normal HTTP port number (80) is not used for administration; instead, the new port number is assigned by the installation program. You can change this number if you wish, but not to port number 80.

Logging features are adequate. The server creates the usual access logs and error logs as separate files, and you can look at the contents of these files from within the administration program.

You can create virtual servers, specify a common footer entry for each Web page, and tune server performance. You can grant or deny access to the server or to single pages based on IP addresses or host computer name, and you can control users' read and write permissions for specific files and directories. For more information, see

```
http://www.netscape.com/comprod/server_central/product/
fast_track/index.html
```

Netscape Enterprise Server

Netscape's Enterprise Server builds on the foundation of the FastTrack server and offers additional features of interest to those departments or corporations in which many people share content preparation and management tasks. It includes the MKS Integrity Engine for HTML–document check-in, check-out, and revision control. Once someone checks out a document, no one else is able to modify that document until it's checked in again, and the MKS system maintains copies of all previous versions of documents on the server. Your administrator can view a list of these different versions, which includes the names of the users who made the changes, and he or she can even go as far as editing a previous version of a document for future use.

This server features

- Enhanced monitoring and logging features
- Server-side digital certificate authentication in tandem with third-party companies, such as VeriSign
- Authentication for client-side public-key certificates
- An integrated full-text search engine from Verity Topic, which supports simple and Boolean searches
- Simple Network Management Protocol (SNMP) support
- HTML content-management using Netscape's LiveWire package

NetWare Server API (NSAPI), CGI, and WinCGI interfaces are all supported along with Java and JavaScript, allowing the easy addition of features using C++, Perl, or even Visual Basic. The FastTrack and the Enterprise servers both include Netscape Navigator Gold, a program that combines HTML-authoring features with the standard Web browser. The Enterprise Server is also at the heart of the SuiteSpot collection of intranet building blocks.

Netscape SuiteSpot

Netscape's SuiteSpot is a large modular collection of server software for building and maintaining an intranet; it includes several major server components, some of which are available now and some of which are still in the planning stages:

Catalog Server   Provides indexing, browsing, and searching of the intranet's content based on open standards, such as the Summary Object Interface Format (SOIF) for catalog and metadata exchange.

Certificate Server   Issues and manages both client- and server-side public-key digital certificates based on the ITU (International Telecommunications Union) X.509 standard.

Directory Server   Provides a universal directory service based on the Lightweight Directory Access Protocol (LDAP) and Internet RFC 1777, a subset of the X.500 ITU directory standard.

Enterprise Server   Supports all the popular programming APIs, which we looked at in the previous section; Enterprise Server is a fully featured–Web server package.

LiveWire Pro   Allows the creation of online applications and provides a graphical site manager used to create and manage intranet sites and content, including applications connected to corporate databases.

Mail Server   Provides e-mail services based on RFC 1730 and the Internet Mail Access Protocol (IMAP) version 4.

News Server   Allows NNTP-based discussion groups and accepts news feeds from Usenet.

Proxy Server   Adds a caching proxy server for secure Internet/intranet networks. SuiteSpot also takes advantage of any relational database system you choose, including those from CA/Ingres, Informix, Microsoft, Oracle, and Sybase. To find out more, check out

```
http://home.netscape.com/
```

Netscape also offers a wide range of products you can use to extend your intranet to customers, suppliers, and business partners.

Open Market Secure WebServer

The Open Market Secure WebServer from Open Market, Inc., competes with the servers from Netscape.

Secure WebServer is a secure server based on WebServer, but it also supports SSL and S-HTTP (secure HTTP), which allows the server to communicate with compatible browsers using encryption.

The Open Market server runs on Windows 95 and Windows NT, as well as on all popular versions of Unix. You will find information on WebServer at

    http://www.openmarket.com/servers/

Purveyor IntraServer

Purveyor IntraServer from Process Software is another powerful, fully featured Web server, this time squarely aimed at the intranet market. IntraServer bundles Purveyor's Encrypt WebServer with InfoAccess's HTML Transit (a program that converts documents from word processing formats to HTML) and Nomad Development Corporation's WebDBC database connectivity tool, which supports both CGI and ISAPI access.

Purveyor's Encrypt WebServer installs as a service under Windows NT and starts automatically when the server boots up. Once it's running, you can access the NT user database, so you don't have to re-create existing users and groups. The tabbed administration window makes configuration easy. You can create virtual servers and configure a proxy server; you can also perform these tasks remotely using a Web browser with Purveyor's Remote Server Management.

The Link Viewer lets you look at your site in a tree structure of linked documents, and it can find broken URLs to local or external HTML pages. Purveyor, codeveloper of the ISAPI also used in Microsoft's Internet Information Server, also supports CGI.

Process Software also provides several strong Internet products available for Windows NT and Windows 95 systems, NetWare, and openVMS. Find out more at

    www.process.com/purveyor.htp

WebSite

WebSite from O'Reilly and Associates (yes, the same O'Reilly and Associates that brings you the Unix, C programming, and X Window System books) is similar to the original CERN server, but it runs as a service on Windows NT Server and NT Workstation and as an application on Windows 95.

The package also includes WebView, which gives you a graphical representation of your site; HotDog, an HTML authoring tool; and the Spyglass Enhanced Mosaic Web browser.

WebSite Professional adds several features to the basic WebSite package, including SSL and S-HTTP support, a WebSite API (WSAPI), and Cold Fusion Standard for ODBC database connectivity and application development. To find out more, check out

```
http://website.ora.com
```

Other Windows-based Web Servers

In the previous section, we looked at some of the most popular Web server-software packages. There are, of course, many more Web servers on the market; a new product seems to be announced every day. Table 7.1 lists as much information as we have been able to collect at the time of writing on the other Windows-based Web servers and their vendors.

Many of the vendors may have more than one Web server product available while others are busy establishing strategic alliances with other software companies and so the names of their products change; there just was not room in the table to list them all. Check out the URLs in the table if you need more details. These servers almost all run on either Windows 95, Windows NT Server, or Windows NT Workstation, although a couple can run on Novell's NetWare, and at least one of them runs on DOS.

Table 7.1: Web server software

Server Name	URL	Vendor
Alibaba	`http://alibaba.austria.eu.net/`	Computer Software Manufaktur
Basis	`http://www.idi.oclc.org/`	Basis
CyberPresence	`http://www.cyberpi.com`	CyberPresence
Esplanade	`http://www.ftp.com/`	FTP Software
ExpressO	`http://www.peak-media .inter.net/`	Peak Technologies, Inc.
FolkWeb	`http://www.ilar.com/ folkweb.htm/`	ILAR Concepts
GLACI-HTTPD	`http://www.glaci.com/`	Great Lakes Area Commercial Internet
Hype-It	`http://cykic.com/`	Cykic Software, Inc.

Table 7.1: Web server software (continued)

Server Name	URL	Vendor
IBM Internet Connection Server	`http://www.ics.raleigh.ibm.com/`	IBM
Jigsaw	`http://www.w3.org/pub/WWW/Jigsaw/`	W3 Consortium
LanWeb	`http://www.wonloo.com/`	WonLoo Technologies, Inc.
NetBasic WebPro	`http://www.toolsthatwork.com`	Tools that Work
NetManage IntraNet	`http://www.netmanage.com`	NetManage
NetWare Web Server	`http://www.novell.com/`	Novell
Skylight Web Server	`http://www.fireants.com/web.shtml`	Network Engineering Technologies
Oracle WebServer	`http://www.oracle.com/`	Oracle
SAIC-HTTP	`http://www.server.itl.saic.com/`	Science Applications International
Sitebuilder	`http://www.american.com/`	American Internet Corp.
SoftNet WebServ Enterprise	`http://www.puzzle.com/prodinfo.htm-tech`	Puzzle Systems
Spinnaker Web Server	`http://www.searchlight.com/`	Searchlight
SuperWeb Server	`http://www.fonrtiertech.com/Products/product.htm`	Frontier Technologies
VBServer	`http://www.dev.com/products/vbserver/vbserve.htm`	VB
WebQuest	`http://www.questar.com/product/p_wq-95.sht`	Questar Microsystems, Inc.
Webware Commercial	`http://www.edime.com.au/webware/`	Edime
YAWN	`http://www.cpu.lublin.pl/tawn/`	CPU s.c
ZBServer	`http://www.zbserver.com/`	ZBSoft

Mac Intranet Servers

In addition to Netscape, you have some choices for a Macintosh-based server. We've included WebSTAR and Web Server 4D. For more information, see

```
http://www.yahoo.com/Computers_and_Internet/Software/Internet/
World_Wide_Web/Servers/Macintosh/
```

WebSTAR

WebSTAR, from Quarterdeck Corporation, is a capable, low-cost Web server that runs on Macintosh and is suitable for use with a small- to medium-sized intranet. WebStar does not include any of the advanced security features you might need when conducting business over the Internet, but then you won't need those features on your intranet.

WebSTAR requires a full TCP/IP connection (or Open Transport) to the Internet and/or a Local Area Network. StarNine recommends a Macintosh with 8 or more MB of RAM, running 7.0.1 or greater, and MacTCP. StarNine also recommends a full TCP/IP connection, such as a T1, fractional T1, ISDN, or a 56k line. A 28.8bps modem connected via PPP or SLIP will work as well, although it's not recommended. For more information, see

```
http://www.starnine.com/
```

Web Server 4D

According to MGD, Web Server 4D for Macintosh has been shipping since November 10, 1995; the Windows version will ship February 14, 1997. A download purchase of Web Server 4D from MDG Computer Services is available from

```
http://www.mdg.com/
```

The 4D can track new versus repeat users via cookies as well as by referring URL, has increased security features, and enhanced e-mail, logging, and CGI support.

Unix Servers

Many Unix servers are available, including servers from Netscape. You can find out about other Unix intranet servers by checking

```
http://www.yahoo.com/Computers_and_Internet/Software/Internet/
World_Wide_Web/Servers/Unix/
```

This book discusses only the Apache and Sun servers, but depending on corporate needs as outlined in your intranet plan, a shareware or freeware server may work just fine. The Netscape offerings are already described in the Windows section; refer to that section and the Netscape Web site at `http://www.netscape.com` for more information. Now let's look at Apache and Sun.

Apache

For more than six months now, Apache has been the most popular web server in the world. The November WWW server–site survey by Netcraft found that Apache is run on over 40 percent of all web servers. The Apache project has been organized in an attempt to answer some of the concerns regarding active development of a public-domain HTTP server for Unix. The goal of this project is to provide a secure, efficient, and extensible server that provides HTTP services in sync with the current HTTP standards. For more information, see

```
http://www.apache.org/
```

Sun

Sun has Solstice, not really an intranet server, but an intranet management product that provides integrated intranet functionality, including e-mail, security, server, and system management. For more information, see

```
http://www.sun.com/solstice/index.html
```

How to Select the Right Server Software

The Web server–software packages we have just looked at are like other kinds of software in that the packages all do pretty much the same thing, but some do it faster, and others do it with more security or with a different user interface. So how do you choose which package is right for you? Each will have advantages and disadvantages. Here are some questions you should be asking:

- Does the Web server software have to run on hardware you already own?
- Does the Web server software have to run on a specific operating system; perhaps one with which you have a great deal of experience, either personally or within your company?
- What level of performance will you need? Many of the public-domain servers are not as optimized for performance as the commercially available servers.
- Is price a major issue? If so, it may make the difference between a public-domain server and one of the commercial offerings.

- Do you plan to connect to the Internet? If so, you may need proxy services. Several of the commercial and a few of the public-domain servers offer proxy services.
- How do you plan to use your intranet? Depending on how you plan to use it, you may have no other choice than to go with a commercial package to get the security features you need in your organization.
- How much technical support do you need and what will it cost? Modifying the public-domain Unix-based servers is not a task for the faint-hearted or the inexperienced; if you need to be able to call on outside technical support, then you automatically select one of the commercially available Web server packages.

Many of the Web servers are available from the Web sites listed in the earlier sections for a free trial period; make up a few dummy test pages of HTML and try them out for a while.

When it's time to make your final choice, list your priorities by answering the suggested questions, and narrow the selection down to two or three servers. Then, make a feature-by-feature comparison of the remaining servers, and pick the one that has the largest number of ticks in the boxes that are most important to you and your corporation. That is the one you should choose for your intranet.

Choosing Server Hardware

In this section, we'll take a look at some of the more important hardware-related issues you'll need to address when choosing the hardware system for your intranet. We'll begin by looking at the network requirements and then at a selection of custom Web servers available on the market today.

Estimating Your Network Requirements

The network requirements for setting up your intranet are not complex. You must have TCP/IP installed, but how fast a network do you need? As always, this depends; it's often a trade-off between the size of the HTML documents you will be serving to your users and the length of time you think they will be willing to wait to receive those documents.

And, if any of your users connect over a communications link from a remote site, the performance they see depends on the speed of the communications circuit as well as the speed of your network. Over a T1 connection, a 150K-HTML file will take just about a second to transmit, but over a 64Kbps-ISDN connection, that same file will take more than 20 seconds to transfer. These are theoretical numbers, and as your network services more users, these time estimates will grow, and users will have to wait longer and longer to receive their document.

When requests arrive faster than the server can process them, the number of active sessions increases and server response time falls. So the balancing act now becomes a trade-off between the size of the documents you'll be serving, the rate of incoming requests, and the speed of the network connection.

There are many published formulae you can use to estimate how these factors interact, but the following simple formula gives a good rule of thumb calculation of the size file you can transmit without degrading network performance:

```
S = N / 1000 C
```

where:

S is the average size of the document

N is the network speed in bits per second

C is the number of connections per minute

Looking at All the Options

Unless you want to run lots of intensive scripts or make a lot of database accesses, you don't need powerful hardware to run a small- to medium-sized intranet. Systems in the middle of the computational range, such as Intel 486 or Pentium systems running NT or NT Server, or a mid-range Macintosh, such as XXXX, will all be able to handle modest numbers of users—just don't run the Web server on a PC that is someone's everyday desktop machine.

With higher numbers of users or if you want to add complex CGI scripts, database access, or other processor-intensive tasks, you'll find that the more powerful systems will definitely give better performance.

One thing you certainly will need is plenty of hard-disk space to hold both the HTML content you prepare and the extensive logging files that some of the servers produce. Be generous, 1GB hard disks are cheap these days; plan ahead for the growth that your intranet will inevitably undergo.

Choosing Turnkey Web Servers

Several vendors have put together turnkey Web server systems, based on Intel Pentium processors with lots of memory and large hard-disk systems. They select and configure the hardware and then install an operating system and an intranet package on top. Using one of these systems can save you a great deal of time because you know right from the start that the components are going to work together, and the amount of research that you have to do is greatly reduced. If you do not have extensive experience in selecting, installing, and maintaining hardware and software, these turnkey systems could be just the ticket.

Compaq ProSignia and Proliant

The Compaq ProSignia is based on a 133MHz Pentium processor and is available on several different operating-system configurations, including Windows NT Server, NetWare, OS/2 Warp Server, or SCO Open Server. The Web server software is either Netscape's FastTrack Server or Microsoft's Internet Information Server.

Based on a 133MHz Pentium with 16MB of RAM and a 2GB hard disk, the Compaq Proliant 1500 is also available in the same operating-system configurations as the Compaq ProSignia, and it runs the same Web server–software packages.

Compaq's new, dual-Pentium server system, the Compaq Proliant 2500, is aimed squarely at the intranet market and is intended to replace the aging Proliant 1500. Rackmountable, the Proliant 2500 supports several SCSI options, as well as 2.1 or 4.3GB SCSI hard-disk systems and up to 1GB of memory, and it's based on 200MHz Pentium Pro processors. As is the quad speed CD-ROM drive, 10/100Mbps Ethernet support is built-in.

You can also use the 6/200 FlexSMP dual-processor board as a two-processor upgrade to the Compaq Proliant 1500 to protect your current hardware investment; this board can also manage a maximum of 512MB of memory.

If you add a modem, you can configure Compaq's Automatic Server Recovery software to send an alert to your pager if the system goes down or reboots for any reason. For more details, see

    http://www.compaq.com

Intergraph InterServe Web 30

The InterServe Web 30 from Intergraph is based on a 133MHz Pentium or 150MHz Pentium Pro processor with 32MB of RAM and a 1GB hard disk. Software includes Windows NT Server and Microsoft's Internet Information Server, along with Internet Assistant for Microsoft Word. Unfortunately, there is no room in the case to add a tape backup; you'll have to use an external unit. Other Web products are available. For details, see

```
http://www.intergraph.com/ics/interserve/
```

Pacific Internet WebCube

The WebCube W1050 from Pacific Internet is based on a 180MHz Pentium processor with 32MB of RAM and a 2GB hard disk along with a QIC tape backup. The operating system is the Linux release from Caldera, and the Web server software is the Apache Server; Windows NT Server and Microsoft's Internet Information Server are also available as an alternative. Wsedit, HTML-Edit, and HoTMetaL are also supplied. For information, see:

```
http://www.pacnet.com
```

Now you should have all the information you need to put your intranet plan together. You have a business plan that includes a mission statement and goals, plus a team assembled to implement that mission to achieve those goals. You also have plans for content, security, software, and hardware. Your next step is to revisit each section and tie it to the whole. See how each piece is related to the others and work out some connections. If you've followed our book, your answers should flow smoothly. If not, revisit and make adjustments, as needed.

Rewrite your plan, including everything you've learned. You can now start to assign resources to the project, such as staff, machines, and a budget. Once you've rewritten and agreed to the plan, you can start the next part of the process—actually creating your intranet, the focus of Part 3.

Part 3

Constructing Your Intranet

Chapter 8

INSTALLING INTRANET SOFTWARE

- **Getting started with Netscape Navigator**
- **Getting started with Internet Explorer**
- **Working with helper applications**
- **Setting up Netscape's FastTrack Server**
- **Setting up Microsoft's Internet Information Server**

This is the start of the nuts-and-bolts section of this book. First, we'll cover installing two of the popular Web browsers that we looked at quickly in Part 1, market leader Netscape Navigator and the challenger from Microsoft, the Internet Explorer.

In the second part of the chapter, we'll look at the issues involved in installing and configuring the popular FastTrack server from Netscape and Microsoft's Internet Information Server. Much of what we say about the Internet Information Server also applies to the NT Workstation Peer Web Services product and to the Personal Web Server available with the FrontPage 97 Bonus Pack.

Installing Netscape Navigator

Installing Netscape Navigator is easy enough once you decide which version you want to install: the 32-bit version for users of Windows 95 and Windows NT, or the 16-bit version for users of Windows 3.1.

> **TIP**
>
> **The compressed installation file containing the 32-bit version of Netscape Navigator is called something like N32*xxxxx*.exe, and the compressed file containing the 16-bit version is called N16*xxxxx*.exe. The exact numbers vary based on the most current version. Makes sense, doesn't it?**

Let's assume that you want the 32-bit version because you're using Windows 95 on your client computer. The latest version at the time of this writing is 3.01. Here's how to install it:

1. Choose Start ➤ Run to open the Windows 95 Run dialog box.
2. In the Open field in this dialog box, type the location of the file, in this example C:\N32301, and press Enter. A dialog box opens confirming that you are about to install Netscape Navigator.
3. Click on the Yes button to open the Extracting dialog box and then another dialog box that welcomes you to Netscape's Setup program.
4. Click on Next to open the Choose Destination Location dialog box, which asks you to confirm the name of the directory where Navigator will be installed. The default directory C:\Program Files\Netscape\Navigator is usually a good choice.
5. Click on Next to open a dialog box that asks if you want to install CoolTalk. Choose Yes or No. Setup starts to copy the appropriate files into the directory you specified in step 4.
6. Choose whether to install the CoolTalk Watchdog program in the dialog box that opens after the files have been copied. This program is useful if you're connected to a network or are connected full-time to the Internet.
7. Click on No in the next dialog box that opens, asking if you want to connect to the Netscape World Wide Web site. There is really no need to at this time.
8. When another dialog box opens to tell you that the installation is complete, click on OK to continue.

9. Click on Yes in the next dialog box to view the `Readme.txt` file. The Readme file opens in Notepad. If you don't want to view the Readme file at this time, choose No to return to the Windows 95 Desktop.

And that's it; you're all done. The file `N3230S.exe` is still in its original location. The installation is now done with this file. Make a backup of it if it's located on your own hard disk. If you installed from the network, your network administrator will make the backup.

Installing the 16-Bit Version of Netscape Navigator

The installation process for the 16-bit version of Netscape Navigator is in two parts, and both steps are simple.

The first step is to unpack, or uncompress, the `N16301.exe` file, and the second step is to install the software. The file is actually self-extracting and contains everything it needs to uncompress itself; you do not need a separate program to perform this step for you.

Place the `N16301.exe` file in a temporary directory, and install it from there. The steps you use are similar to those outlined above for the 32-bit version, except that you use File ➢ Run from the Windows 3.1 Program Manager to start the installation.

For more information on using Netscape Navigator, see Chapter 2 of this book or *Surfing the Internet with Netscape Navigator* by Daniel A. Tauber and Brenda Kienan, available from Sybex.

Installing Internet Explorer

Installing Internet Explorer is also straightforward—it may even have been installed as part of your Windows 95 or Windows NT 4 installation. If your system didn't install IE as part of the operating system, we'll give you the steps to install Internet Explorer using Windows 95. The steps for Windows NT 4 or Windows 3.*x* are similar.

1. Copy the distribution file, which is a compressed, self-extracting file, into a temporary directory on your hard disk.

2. Choose Start ➤ Run to open the Run dialog box, and in the Open field, type the name of the distribution file, which is usually some variation on the name **MSIE*nn*.exe**, where *nn* indicates the version number.

   • You can also open the folder or directory that contains the distribution file, and double-click on the icon for that file.

3. If you're installing Internet Explorer for the first time, choose a location for the program files. Most people choose the Program Files folder or directory. If you're installing Internet Explorer as part of the Plus! package or upgrading from an earlier version of the program, the installation program decides where to put the program files.

4. Follow the remaining instructions on the screen to complete the installation; when the installation is complete, you'll find a new icon on the desktop called The Internet.

You can start the Internet Explorer in two ways: You can click on The Internet icon, or you can choose Start ➤ Programs ➤ Internet Explorer. The first time you start the program, the Setup Wizard takes you through several setup steps; some of these steps are aimed at home users of the Internet and may not be appropriate for your situation on an intranet.

TIP   For more information on using Internet Explorer, see *The ABCs of Microsoft Internet Explorer* by John Ross, available from Sybex.

Just like all the other Windows 95 icons, The Internet icon has a Properties command in the menu that opens when you right-click on the icon on your desktop. You can also open this same set of dialog boxes by choosing View ➤ Options from the menu bar inside Internet Explorer. Figure 8.1 shows the Connection tab in the Options dialog box. If you're connected to an intranet, you can clear the checkmark from the Connect to the Internet As Needed option in this dialog box.

Unlike shortcuts to programs and data files in the Windows 95 environment, you can't remove The Internet icon by dragging it to the Recycling Bin, but you can keep it and just use another name. Right-click on the icon on your desktop, and use the Rename command. The current name of the icon is highlighted, and you can use the usual editing keys to change its name to something more meaningful, such as Intranet or Intranet Browser. Press Enter when you've finished editing the name to make your changes permanent.

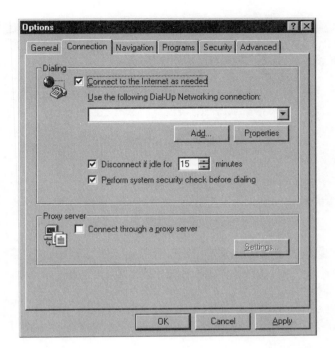

FIGURE 8.1:
Use the Connection tab to control access to your intranet.

Keeping Internet Explorer Up-to-Date

Internet Explorer is available free from Microsoft, and so are the periodic updates that Microsoft makes to fix bugs and add new features. It's a good idea to check Microsoft's Web site from time to time to see if a new version is available.

You can jump directly to the Microsoft Web site from within Internet Explorer. Select the Product News icon from the Links toolbar, or select Help ➢ Microsoft on the Web ➢ Product News. Either way, you'll end up in the same place:

```
http://www.microsoft.com/ie/default.asp
```

The Internet Explorer section of Microsoft's Web site offers several versions of the program, as well as several different download locations. To download an update, first choose the operating system you use, and then choose the nearest download site, and click on the link to start the download.

When the download is complete, you can install the update over your existing version of Internet Explorer. Your home page and your list of favorite places will be preserved, although you may have to reset some of the other options, such as link colors or character sets, if you've customized those settings.

Administrator Kit Fine-Tunes Internet Explorer

If your company wants to fine-tune Internet Explorer for internal use, you need the Internet Explorer Administrator Kit 3. With this kit, you can customize and distribute Internet Explorer version 3 for users of Windows 95 and Windows NT, and Internet Explorer version 2.1 for users of Windows 3.1 to meet the exact needs of your users.

The IEAK is available for three types of customers:

- Corporate administrators
- Internet content providers (ICP)
- Internet service providers (ISP)

All three can create specialized versions of Internet Explorer with preset links, preset home pages, and specific add-on applications; you can even display your own company logo instead of the Internet Explorer logo.

As the accompanying illustration shows, you can also format the browser for distribution via floppy disk or CD-ROM or in a self-extracting downloadable format.

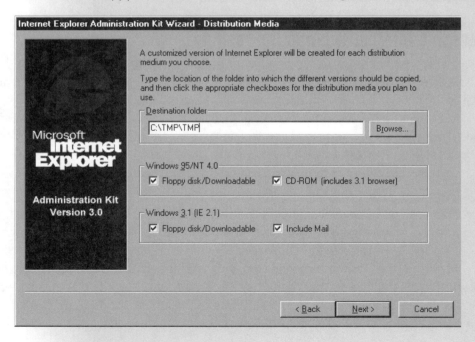

Corporate administrators have the most flexibility and can control the look and feel of the browser by presetting most browser options and then preventing users from changing them. You can specify which page your users access to get help when they choose Help ➤ Online Support. You can even specify the language version of Internet Explorer you want to include in your distribution package.

The kit is available free to companies that have signed the IEAK site license on Microsoft's Web site at

```
http://www.microsoft.com/ie/default.asp
```

Bear in mind that this kit requires a bunch of disk space to create those custom versions of Internet Explorer. Using nominal file sizes, calculate how much space you think you'll need, and then make sure you have at least *four* times that amount of free space for disk installations and an additional 80MB of free space if you opt for the CD-ROM distribution method. This disk space is used as temporary working storage when you're creating the custom versions of Internet Explorer; you'll get most of it back at the end of the process.

Configuring Helper Applications

When you link to a file that's not another HTML file on your intranet, such as a file that contains an audio or a video segment, you can have your browser automatically open an application to play or view the file; these programs are called *helper applications* or *plug-ins*. Both Internet Explorer and Netscape Navigator can manage many of the common audio and video file formats that you're likely to encounter.

Because of the close ties between Internet Explorer and the Windows Registry, Internet Explorer is already configured to launch any program you've installed on your system. You click on a link using the browser, and when the Confirm File Open dialog box opens, click on the Open button to launch the related helper application, which in turn opens and processes the file.

Things are not quite as straightforward in Netscape Navigator; you've got to go through a few extra steps to tell it which program is associated with which file type. Here's how to configure Lotus ScreenCam as a helper application with Navigator:

1. In Navigator, choose Options ➤ General Preferences, and select the Helpers tab.
2. Click on Create New Type to open the Create New MIME Type dialog box.

3.   Enter **application** into the MIME Type field, enter **x-screencam** into the MIME Subtype field, and click on OK to return to the Helpers tab.

4.   Enter **SCM** into the File Extensions field, and select the Launch the Application radio button.

5.   Finally, enter the complete path name of the ScreenCam application program into the directory field at the bottom of the tab. You can use the Browse button to help you find its exact location.

Figure 8.2 shows the Helpers tab with the ScreenCam information all filled in. The process is the same for any other helper or plug-in application, although the MIME type will certainly be different in each case.

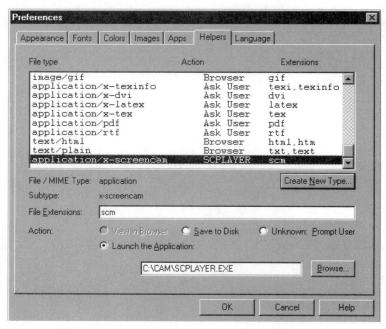

FIGURE 8.2: Setting up ScreenCam as a helper application in Netscape Navigator

You can perform many more operations with both of these browsers, and in the next section, we'll look at the ways you can collaborate with other intranet users by means of a browser.

Installing and Configuring Netscape's FastTrack Server

In this section, we'll look at how to install and then configure one of the most popular Web servers currently available, Netscape's FastTrack Server. The Netscape FastTrack CD contains several Netscape products, and as you'll see in a moment, the sequence in which you install them is important.

Before we start, let's look at the system requirements for running FastTrack:

32MB of memory   If you have less than this on your system, a dialog box opens during the first part of the installation process asking if you want to quit. To run additional copies of the server, you must have an additional 16MB of memory available; in other words, to run three copies, you must have at least 48MB of memory.

Windows NT 3.51 or 4   If you run NT 3.51, you must install the Windows NT Service Pack 4 or later. You can get this service pack from Microsoft's World Wide Web site.

Be sure that your DNS service is running before you start the installation. DNS allows you to use easy-to-remember server names, such as `server.megacorp.com` rather than the much more cryptic IP addresses, although you can certainly use IP addresses if you wish. For more on DNS, see Appendix B.

Once all these requirements are in place, installation is really just a question of following the on-screen prompts. Let's take a look.

FastTrack for Windows 95

By the time you read this, Netscape will have released a version of their popular FastTrack server that runs on Windows 95. FastTrack already runs on Windows NT and on several versions of the Unix operating system.

The Windows 95 version of FastTrack includes several of the features found in Netscape's high-end server product called Enterprise Server, including good browser-based administration features, excellent access-logging features, and support for Java and JavaScript as well as for secure transactions based on SSL 3.

The Windows 95 version of FastTrack also includes LiveWire for managing and developing applications and Netscape Navigator Gold for HTML for developing content.

There are several advanced Enterprise Server–level features that you won't find in this version of FastTrack, however, including database connections, revision control software, SNMP support, or the Verity search engine.

Installing FastTrack Server

The Netscape products on the CD-ROM must be installed in this sequence:

1. Navigator Gold
2. FastTrack Server
3. AppFoundry

Navigator Gold is the HTML editor and browser, and the tool you'll use to manage the server; FastTrack Server is the Web server software; and AppFoundry is a collection of reusable business applications, as well as other extensions. You can use the normal Netscape Navigator to manage your server, but if you also want to create HTML content pages for your intranet, you'll definitely need Navigator Gold.

The FastTrack CD-ROM contains the following directories:

FastTrak   Contains the FastTrack Server files for Windows NT and Windows 95 running on Intel hardware as well as NT running on Alpha hardware. *Note the spelling of this directory name.*

Gold   Contains the files for Netscape Navigator Gold for these same Windows platforms.

Navgator   Contains the files for Netscape Navigator for the same Windows platforms; again, *note the spelling of this directory name.*

AppFoundry   Contains AppFoundry files.

To install Navigator Gold, open the `NT_i386` directory inside the `Gold` directory, and double-click on `Setup.exe`. Follow the instructions on the screen, and choose No when asked if you would like to install CoolTalk (you won't need this to manage your FastTrack server).

Once Navigator Gold is installed, you're ready to install FastTrack Server. Here are the steps to follow:

1. With the CD in your CD-ROM drive, choose Start ➤ Run, and type the following into the Open field:

    `D:\FastTrak\NT_i386\SETUP.EXE`

2. When the Welcome screen appears, click on Next, and after you've read the terms and conditions displayed on the Software License screen, click the Yes button to signal your acceptance of those conditions.

3. Unless you have a specific reason to use a different name, accept the default installation directory, `C:\netscape\server`, in the Choose Destination Location dialog box. If you do specify a different directory, don't include any spaces in the name. Click the Next button to continue and to copy the server files onto your hard disk.

4. When the Configure Netscape FastTrack Server dialog box opens, type in the full name of your server and the user name and password for administrator access. The default user name is `Admin`, so be sure you use something different.

5. Enter the path indicating the location of your HTML document files. The default is `c:\netscape\server\docs`.

6. Click on the Finish button to end the installation.

And now that the installation is complete, we can move on to look at how to configure FastTrack Server with Server Manager. Since Server Manager works from the Navigator browser, you can in theory manage your server from any client. There are, however, several good reasons for performing certain management functions right on the server itself; see the accompanying sidebar for more information.

Managing from the Server or from the Client

You can perform the management functions for FastTrack Server from the server computer or from any browser running somewhere on the network that supports frames, tables, and JavaScript.

If you work directly on the server, all operations are essentially secure (unless someone is actually peering over your shoulder). But if you use a browser running on a client computer to perform management and administrative functions, be sure you understand the security implications. If you don't invoke Secure Sockets Layer (SSL), your server's security can be compromised.

Using the Server Selector

Accessing the management functions on FastTrack Server is similar to accessing HTML pages with a browser, except that rather than using the normal HTTP port number 80, a different port number is used, one that was assigned during the installation process.

You access the FastTrack administration functions using this URL:

```
http://name:port/admin-serv/bin/index
```

where *name* is the fully-qualified domain name for your server, something like `sales.megacorp.com`, and *port* is the port number assigned during the installation process. If DNS isn't available or is just not running on your system, you can use the server's IP address instead, in which case, the URL might look like this:

```
http://199.34.57.35:port/admin-serv/bin/index
```

> **TIP**
>
> **FastTrack Server runs as a Windows NT service, which means it's always running, even if no users are logged on to the system. And because no users are needed, services are more secure than normal applications.**

To start FastTrack Server administrative functions, choose Start ➤ Programs ➤ Netscape ➤ Administer Netscape Servers. Using one of the URLs just described, this option opens Netscape Navigator, accessing the Netscape Server Selector, as Figure 8.3 shows.

On the left side of the Server Selector screen, you'll see a list of the installed servers. If you've just completed your first installation, you'll see only one name in the list. In Figure 8.3, you can see that a server called Sales has been installed. Use the large On/Off switch to the left of this name to stop or start this server (the green light under this button indicates the server is running; a red light indicates that it isn't). By clicking on the server name, you can access the Netscape Server Manager, which we'll be looking at in a moment.

In the central part of the Server Selector screen, you'll see three buttons:

Install a New Netscape FastTrack Server   Click on this button to install another instance of the FastTrack server without repeating the whole installation procedure we described above.

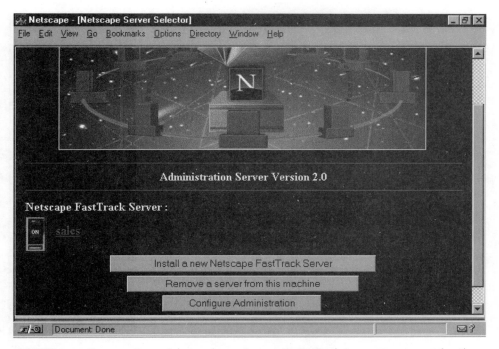

FIGURE 8.3: Netscape Server Selector gives you access to FastTrack Server management functions.

Remove a Server from This Machine	Click on this button to remove a server once you have used the On/Off switch to turn it off. If you have more than one server installed, don't remove the administration binaries, as they contain a set of configuration files, and any remaining servers won't be able to run properly.
Configure Administration	Click on this button to open the Administrative Configuration screen, which is the subject of our next section.

Configuring Administration Options

When you select the Configure Administration button in the Server Selector, you open the screen shown in Figure 8.4.

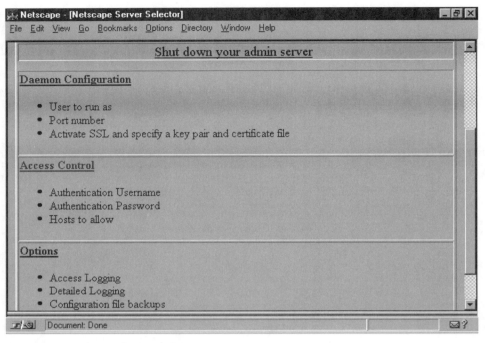

FIGURE 8.4: The Configure Administration screen

Before using the Server Manager, you can set certain specifications using this screen. Let's take a look.

Daemon Configuration This option lets you look at or change the Admin Server user account and password and the port number used to access these administrative functions. Remember that this port number was assigned by the installation program; you can change it to something more meaningful if you wish, but you can't change it to port number 80. Finally, you can turn on SSL security. As we've mentioned, if you plan on administering your server from a browser running on a client on the network, be sure to select this option. You'll have to obtain a digital certificate from a company such as VeriSign to implement SSL security.

Access Control This option lets you specify who is allowed to administer the server by user name and password, by hostname, or by IP address.

Options   These options all refer to logging administrative sessions and configuration changes. Assuming that there is only one genuine administrator, these logs may reveal any unauthorized attempts to change configurations.

You can also shut down the Admin Server from the Configure Administration screen if you select Shut Down Your Admin Server at the top of this screen. This action has the same effect as using the Services applet in the Control Panel to turn off this service. Once you've completed your administration choices, it's time to turn to the Netscape Server Manager.

Using Netscape Server Manager

When you click on a server name (we clicked on Sales) in the Server Selector screen, the Netscape Server Manager opens, as Figure 8.5 shows. All the settings and information shown in the Server Manager refer only to this specific server. You can return to the Server Selector screen if you click on the Choose button in the upper-left corner of the Server Manager screen.

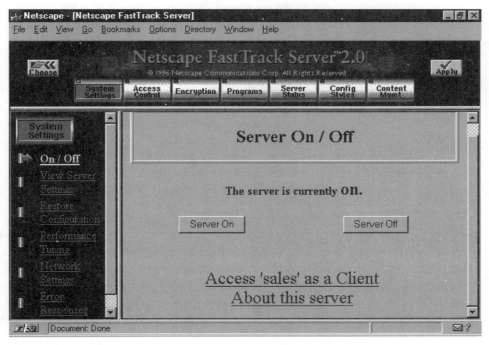

FIGURE 8.5: The Netscape Server Manager

> **NOTE**
>
> The Netscape Server Manager screen, shown in Figure 8.5, is actually a good example of how to use the HTML elements called *frames*. Each of the major elements in the screen is a separate frame; top horizontal box, left vertical box, and the main square window. You'll be hearing more about frames in Chapter 9, "Creating Intranet Pages with HTML."

The Netscape Server Manager screen, shown in Figure 8.5, has three individually sized windows, each of which is an HTML frame. As you make choices from the selections available across the top window, the information in the other windows changes dynamically.

The seven options available in the Netscape Server Manager are

System Settings   Gives access to basic server settings

Access Control   Allows you to specify the basic authentication and access restrictions

Encryption   Contains the main SSL security-configuration screens

Programs   Contains information on CGI, Java, and JavaScript directories and file types

Server Status   Gives you access to the server reporting and monitoring tools and the access and error logs

Config Styles   Lets you create and apply various styles

Content Mgmt   Allows you to specify hardware and software virtual servers, directory and file information, and URL forwarding

As you select a button, the items in the leftmost window change. Click on one of these items to open a page dedicated to that function in the main window; a small indicator appears next to the item you selected as a reminder of which page you're on.

Most of the functions also feature a Help button you can use to get more information on a specific topic. Once you're happy with your changes, click the Apply button to save your changes and put them into effect.

In the next few sections, we're going to take a closer look at the options available in the Netscape Server Manager.

System Settings

The System Settings screen, shown on the left in Figure 8.6, gives you access to several basic server settings:

On/Off   Lets you turn the server on or off and displays basic version number information.

View Server Settings   Displays the technical and content settings used by the server software; see Figure 8.6. This screen is a tremendously useful summary screen and should be one of the first places you visit when using the Server Manager. Much of this information is contained in the two configuration files `Magnus.conf`, which contains the technical settings, and `OBJ.conf`, which contains the content settings. All the value names in this screen are actually links you can use to go directly to the appropriate Server Manager configuration screen.

Restore Configuration   Lets you restore pervious server configuration information, effectively removing the effect of any recent changes; this can be a lifesaver. The number of configurations you can keep is unlimited, but we've found that about 10 is usually enough; click on the Configure Backups link to set the number of backups to keep.

Performance Tuning   Lets you turn DNS on and off and configure DNS caching.

Network Settings   Allows you to enter a new Server user name and password, server name, and port number.

Error Responses   Lets you enter a custom error response that is sent to a browser when the server generates an error. You can specify a file to send or an CGI script to run. You can customize the server's response to the following errors:

Unauthorized	Occurs when a user tries to access a file for which he or she does not have the appropriate permissions
Forbidden	Occurs when the server doesn't have the appropriate permissions to read a file
Not Found	Occurs when the server can't find a document or when the server has been told to deny the existence of such a document
Server Error	Occurs when the server generates a fatal error or when the system runs out of memory

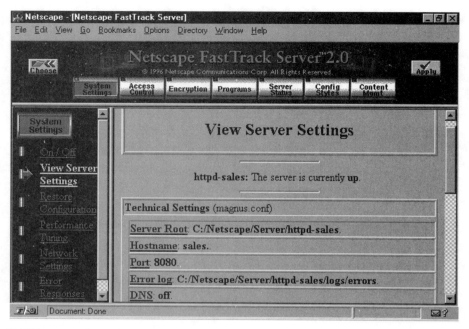

FIGURE 8.6: The System Settings screen with the View Server Settings option selected

> **TIP** You can also use the Access *server-name* as a client link on this screen to open a browser and see your server in the same way that your clients do. This is a useful troubleshooting aid you can use to make sure your server is actually operating in the way that you think it's operating.

Access Control

The Access Control screen, shown on the left in Figure 8.7, allows you to specify the basic authentication and access restrictions for your server.

You can have as many users in your user database as you wish, and you can group them; some users can belong to more than one group. You can even have multiple user databases, but it's much simpler if you just stick to one. The options on this screen include:

Create User Allows you to create a new user (see Figure 8.7).

Remove User Allows you to remove a user.

List Users Lets you list all the current users.

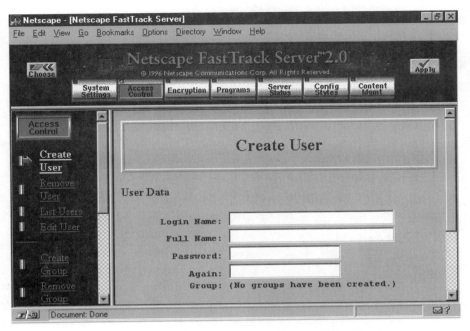

FIGURE 8.7: The Access Control screen with the Create User option selected

Edit User   Lets you edit information for a current user.

Create Group   Allows you to create a new group.

Remove Group   Allows you to remove a group.

List Groups   Lets you list all the current groups.

Edit Group   Lets you edit the information for a current group.

Restrict Access   Lets you restrict users' access to specified files on the server. If you have a set of confidential files on the server that you want only the people in the finance department to be able to access, you can specify that these files are off-limits to everyone by default, and you can then specify that the users in the finance group are an exception. You can also specify that the users in the finance group can not only read these files, but that they can also change (or write to) these files.

Manage User Databases   Allows you to create a new user database or delete an existing one.

Import Users   Allows you to import user information from an existing database contained in a text file.

Encryption

The Encryption screen contains the main SSL security-configuration entries, as Figure 8.8 shows:

On/Off   Turns encryption on and off.

Security Preferences   Lets you specify which SSL 2 and SSL 3 encryption options you want to use.

Generate Key   Lets you generate a key-pair file for the public and private keys for your server.

Change Key Password   Lets you change the key password.

Request Certificate   Walks you through the steps required to create the input data needed to apply for a digital certificate.

Install Certificate   Lets you install a digital certificate.

Manage Certificates   Lets you manage multiple digital certificates and contains details on several certificate-issuing organizations.

Stronger Cypress   Lets you choose between 40-bit and 128-bit encryption. Current U.S. law prohibits the export of 128-bit encryption, so be sure to make the appropriate selection if some of your users connect from overseas.

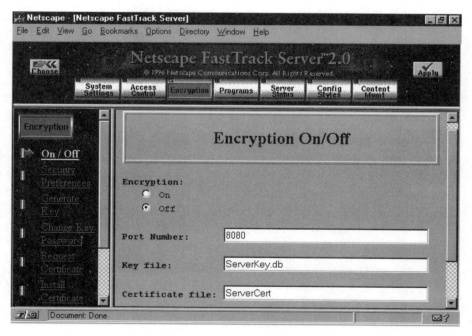

FIGURE 8.8: The Encryption screen with the On/Off option selected

> **NOTE** For more information on security, see Chapter 6, "Planning Your Intranet's Security," in particular the sidebar titled "Encryption Is the Key."

Programs

The Programs screen, shown on the left in Figure 8.9, contains information on CGI, Java, and JavaScript directories:

CGI Directory   Lets you specify a directory name for your CGI files (see Figure 8.9).

CGI File Type   Lets you specify a filename extension for your CGI files. You can use CGI, EXE, or BAT, and all files in the CGI directory with this filename extension will be treated as CGI scripts.

Java   Allows you to turn on the Java interpreter and specify a directory for your Java server-side applets. These applets must have a filename in the form `name.class`.

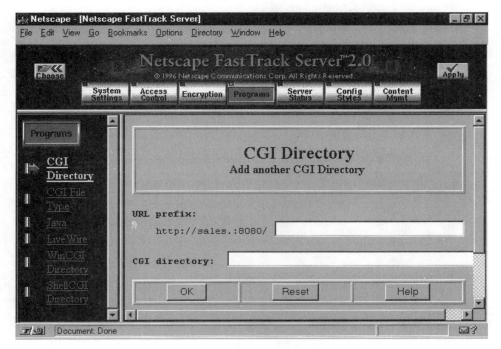

FIGURE 8.9: The Programs screen with the CGI Directory option selected

LiveWire   Lets you turn on the LiveWire application environment so you can run scripts written in JavaScript.

WinCGI Directory   Lets you specify a WinCGI-only directory.

ShellCGI Directory   Allows you to create a directory for your shell CGI files.

Server Status

The Server Status screen gives you access to the server reporting and monitoring tools and to the access and error logs.

These log files record all the activity on your server and can be helpful and instructive when it comes to troubleshooting your server. As shown in Figure 8.10, this screen includes

View Access Log   Lets you look at the access log that contains details of all the requests made of the server and at the server's response to those requests (see Figure 8.10). Use the Log Preferences option (described in a moment) to specify the information stored in the access log files

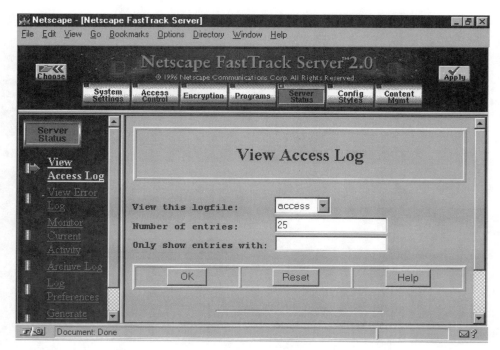

FIGURE 8.10:   The Server Status screen with the View Access Log option selected

View Error Log   Lets you look at the error log that contains information on the errors the server has encountered since it started running. It also contains informational messages indicating major events, such as the time and date that the server was started.

Monitor Current Activity   Opens a screen titled Server Monitor for Port *Number* where *number* is the port number used by your Web server. This monitor displays a selection of real-time information, including the amount of information transferred and the server status codes associated with the data.

Archive Log   Allows you to create an archive of your log files.

Log Preferences   Lets you specify the server variables to store in the access log file. This file can be created in the fixed Common Logfile Format or in a flexible format where you choose the variables to store.

Generate Report   Allows you to generate a report from a large set of server variables. You can create this report as an HTML document that you can look at using a browser or as a plain text file if you prefer. Three formats are available, containing totals, statistics, or lists.

Config Styles

A configuration style is an easy way to apply a preselected set of options to files on your server. A style can contain configuration information for any of the following:

CGI file type	The filename extension used for your CGI files
Character set	The character set in use
Document footer	The footer you want to attach to every Web page; for example, a signature
Error responses	The customized error responses for *4xx* and *5xx* series error codes
Log Preferences	Access log and error log preferences; discussed in an earlier section
Remote file manipulation	Allows one-button publishing from Navigator Gold
Require stronger security	Specifies 128-bit ciphers for SSL security; only available in the U.S.
Restrict access	Allows and restricts access to specific server files and directories
Server parsed HTML	Enables Server-Side Includes

The Configuration Styles screen, shown on the left in Figure 8.11, lets you create and apply styles:

New Style   Allows you to create a new style (see Figure 8.11)

Remove Style   Allows you to remove a style

Edit Style   Allows you to edit a style

Assign Style   Allows you to apply a configuration style to a file, a set of files, or to a directory

List Assignments   Lets you list the styles you have already assigned and the files and directories they apply to

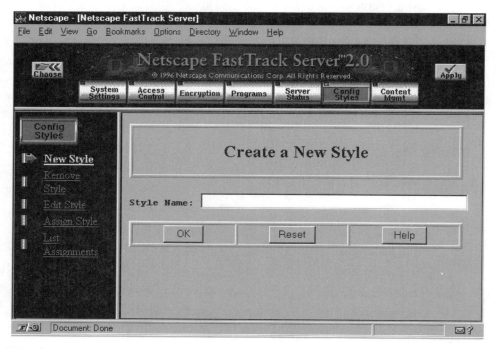

FIGURE 8.11:   The Config Styles screen with the New Style option selected

Content Management

The Content Management screen, shown on the left in Figure 8.12, allows you to specify hardware and software virtual servers, directory and file information, and URL forwarding information:

Primary Document Directory   Lets you specify the directory where you keep your HTML content files on the server (see Figure 8.12).

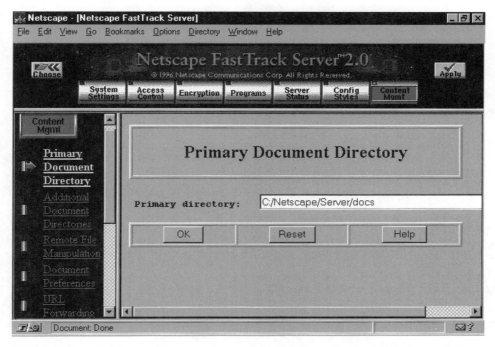

FIGURE 8.12: The Content Management Screen with the Primary Document Directory option selected

Additional Document Directories   Allows you to specify other document directories.

Remote File Manipulation   Allows clients to change documents on your server. Make sure all the appropriate permissions are in place so users can only write to specifically selected files.

Document Preferences   Lets you specify how directory indexing is performed if a file called Index.html or Home.html is not found, the location of the server home page, and the default MIME type for your HTML content files (usually text/plain).

URL Forwarding   Allows you to map a URL to another location. This can be useful if a URL changes or you want to send a user to another location.

Hardware Virtual Servers   Allows you to set up a hardware virtual server. FastTrack Server can manage up to 256 different IP addresses.

Software Virtual Servers   Lets you set up software virtual servers with different names but which all share the same IP address.

International Characters   Allows you to specify a different character set for a document or a set of documents.

Document Footer   Lets you specify a document footer that will be added to all HTML documents; for example, a signature.

Parse HTML   Allows you to specify that the server should search HTML documents for special commands before dispatching these documents to the client browser requesting them.

That brings us to the end of our coverage of Netscape's very popular and capable Web server, FastTrack Server. In the next section, we'll look at a more recent entry into the field of Web servers, Internet Information Server from Microsoft.

Installing and Configuring Microsoft's Internet Information Server

Microsoft's Internet Information Server (IIS) is bundled with Windows NT Server. It won't run on NT Workstation, but a similar product called Peer Web Services does run on NT Workstation, and another similar product called Personal Web Server runs on Windows 95.

Installing these products is easy and, in the case of IIS, is actually part of installing the operating system itself. Internet Information Server is closely integrated with the security systems in NT Server and provides separate Web, Gopher, and FTP services.

IIS is controlled and configured by the graphical Internet Service Manager application, and you can tailor IIS services to your needs using the property sheets. You can also configure IIS using Microsoft's Internet Explorer as long as you are logged into NT Server as an administrator.

The Elements of IIS Security

Internet Information Server uses all the security elements provided by the underlying Windows NT Server operating system and those built into the NT file system (NTFS). Internet Information Server also adds additional security by using IP address security and directory access settings. A simplified path through each part of the security system follows these steps:

1. Internet Information Server receives a request.
2. Is the IP address permitted?
3. If the IP address is permitted, is the user permitted?
4. If the user is permitted, do the IIS permissions allow the type of access requested?
5. If the IIS permissions allow the access requested, do the NTFS permissions allow this access?
6. If the NTFS permissions allow this access, access is granted.

If any one of these tests fail, access is denied. Let's look closer at some of these steps.

IP Address Security

The IP address of every data packet that IIS receives is checked against the settings in the Internet Service Manager property sheets, which we'll be looking at in a moment.

NOTE For more information about the TCP and IP protocols, see Appendix B, "The Intranet Protocol—TCP/IP."

You can configure these settings in two ways:

1. To allow access by all systems except those specifically excluded
2. To deny access to all users except those specifically included.

IP address security can exclude specific individuals or entire networks.

Username Authentication

All anonymous access requests use the IUSR_*computername* account created when IIS is installed. Username authentication is most useful if you want to deny a particular user or group access to your server.

IIS and NTFS Permissions

The Web server in IIS allows you to set three kinds of file and directory permissions:

Read Allows users to read the files in a directory.

Execute Allows users to change directories and to start applications or scripts stored in these directories. By default, all ISAPI and CGI scripts should be placed in the directory `\scripts`. For scripts and applications installed on IIS and NT Server, you must enable Execute Permission in both IIS and NT Server.

Secure SSL Channel   Allows users to send information to the Web server in encrypted form using Secure Sockets Layer encryption.

The FTP service supports read and write permissions only; the Gopher service supports only read permission.

Configuring IIS Using Its Property Sheets

You can choose to install IIS as part of your operating system when you install Windows NT Server, or you can add IIS at a later date. In either case, you'll configure your system using the IIS property sheets. Launch your IIS Manager and you can begin to configure your system.

The Service Property Sheet

The Service property sheet, shown in Figure 8.13, controls who can use your server and specifies the account used by anonymous users.

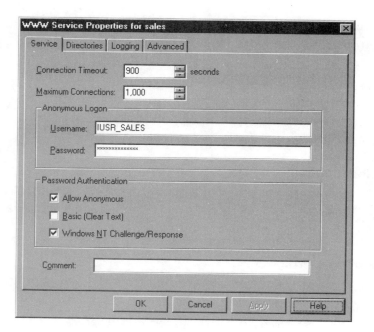

FIGURE 8.13:
The Service property sheet

This property sheet contains the following options:

Connection Timeout   Set the maximum length of the timeout for each connection before the server automatically disconnects an inactive visitor.

Maximum Connections   Specify the number of simultaneous connections you'll allow on your server at one time.

Anonymous Logon   If you want to use your current security settings to control access to your site, change the name in the Username field to an existing account on your server, and then enter the appropriate password.

Password Authentication   Select the level of password authentication you want to use on your IIS server. IIS supports three levels of authentication:

Allow Anonymous	When this box is checked, anonymous connections are processed, and the anonymous user name and password are used. If this box is left unchecked, all anonymous requests are rejected, and one of the two following authentication types must be selected.
Basic	When this box is checked, basic authentication is used. Remember, this level of authentication sends NT unencrypted user names and passwords over the network.
Windows NT Challenge/Response	When this box is checked, a proprietary system is used. Windows NT Challenge/Response authentication is currently available only with the Internet Explorer Web browser.

If you leave the Basic and Windows NT Challenge/Response check boxes unchecked and if you check the Allow Anonymous check box, all client requests are processed as anonymous requests. If a client does provide a user name and password, he or she will be ignored, and the anonymous account will be used instead, with all the security restrictions that may apply to this account.

If you're setting up an FTP service and the Allow Anonymous Connections check box is checked, all logons in which the user enters a user name of anonymous will be processed. If a user tries to log on with a user name of anything other than anonymous, he or she will be rejected. If you leave the box unchecked, your users must enter a valid NT Server user name and password to be able to use your FTP service.

The Directories Property Sheet

The Directories property sheet, shown in Figure 8.14, lists the directories available to IIS visitors in the Directory window. At the bottom of the Directories property sheet you will see these two check boxes:

Enable Default Document   Check this box to enable the file whose name appears in the Default Document field to be displayed to visitors who don't request a specific file when accessing your site. You can place a default document in each directory; if users don't make a specific request, they always see something.

Directory Browsing Allowed   When turned on, directory browsing lets visitors to your site look at a hypertext listing of the directories and files to help them navigate your system. A hypertext directory listing is sent to the browser if directory browsing is enabled and no default document is available.

WARNING   **Most administrators don't allow directory browsing because it exposes more of the underlying site structure than they want to show to a user.**

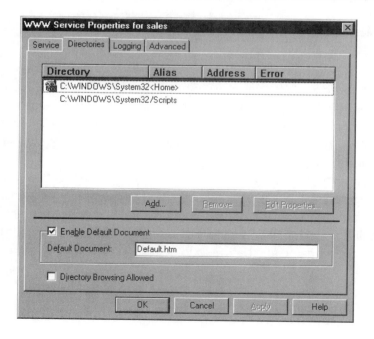

FIGURE 8.14:
The Directories property sheet

If you're using FrontPage, remember that it uses the default file name of `index.htm`, and IIS uses a default file name of `default.htm`.

Adding a directory to this property sheet allows the selected service (Web, FTP, or Gopher) to make information contained in the directory and in its subdirectories available to clients visiting your site. Directories not listed here aren't available to clients. Every service must have a home directory that is the root directory for that service.

IIS provides a default home directory for each of the three services—`\wwwroot`, `\gophroot`, and `\ftproot`—and you can also add other directories outside the home directory that appear to a Web browser as though they're a subdirectory of the home directory. Such directories are known as *virtual directories* and are most useful with the Web service. Because FTP is an older protocol, any virtual servers you create remain invisible. They're present, and any visitor who knows the alias can access them, but they won't appear in directory listings.

To configure a home or a virtual directory, follow these steps:

1. Select the appropriate service in the main Internet Service Manager window.
2. Open the Directories property sheet and click on the Add button.
3. When the Directory Properties dialog box opens, check either the Home Directory or the Virtual Directory check box, and then enter the name of the directory in the Alias text field.
4. Select the appropriate permissions.
5. Click on the OK button, and then click on Apply and OK.

Some FTP clients require that FTP information be presented in Unix format rather than in NT Server format. Set the Directory Listing Style to Unix rather than MS-DOS for the maximum level of compatibility.

The Logging Property Sheet

You use the Logging property sheet, shown in Figure 8.15, to specify when and how IIS service logging is performed.

After selecting the Enable Logging check box to turn on IIS logging, you have two choices:

> **Log to File**   Check this box to create a normal IIS log file, and then choose the interval to use when creating a new log file: daily, weekly, monthly, or when the file reaches a specific size. If you don't choose one of these options, the log file will continue to grow indefinitely.

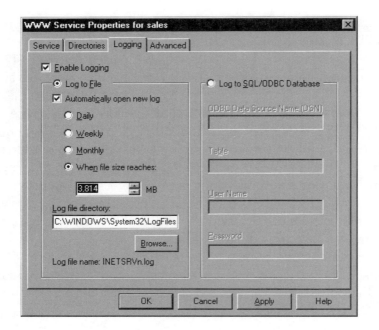

FIGURE 8.15:
The Logging property sheet

Log to SQL/ODBC Database   Check this box to send the IIS log information to a SQL or ODBC database. You must also specify the *data source name* (DSN), table, and a user name and password to the database. Using this option, you can direct logging of all IIS services to a single location and then use an ODBC-compliant application to look at your log data. This option is not available if you're using the NT Workstation Peer Web Services.

When logging to a file, the maximum total log line is 1200 bytes, and each field is limited to 150 bytes. When logging to a SQL or ODBC database, each field is limited to 200 bytes.

The Advanced Property Sheet

By using the Advanced property sheet, shown in Figure 8.16, you can control access to your server.

Two check boxes control overall default access:

Granted Access   Check this box to allow all computers access to your server except those specified by IP address in the box below.

Denied Access   Check this box to deny all computers access to your server except those specified by IP address in the box below.

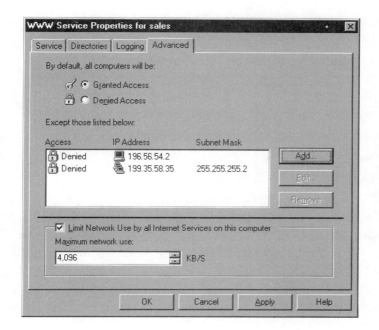

FIGURE 8.16:
The Advanced
property sheet

You can then use the list box to enter exceptions to the default access policy. You can block access to specific individuals or to whole networks based on their IP addresses.

You can also limit the amount of network bandwidth allowed for all services on your IIS server. Check the box marked Limit Network Use by all Internet Services on This Computer, and then select the maximum bandwidth you'll allow in the Maximum Network Use field. This value is in Kbps, or kilobits per second.

Limiting the network bandwidth is something of a two-edged sword—use it with care. You can certainly control the amount of network bandwidth your server makes available to visitors, but at the same time, by doing so, you may reduce the perceived response time of your server. Remember you can also specify the maximum number of simultaneous connections to your Web server on the Service Property Sheet. By carefully tuning the maximum number of connections and the maximum bandwidth, you can closely control access to your Web server.

The Messages Property Sheet

If you double-click on the FTP service in the main ISM window, you'll notice an additional tab labeled Messages. You can use the text boxes on this tab to specify various messages specifically for users of your FTP service, including

> **Welcome Message**   This long message is displayed to FTP clients when they connect to your FTP server, and you can use it to display the rules of your FTP site.

Exit Message   This short message is displayed as clients disconnect from your FTP server.

Maximum Connections Message   This text is displayed if a client attempts to connect to your FTP service when the maximum number of connections allowed are already in use; use it to display a message saying that your FTP server is at its maximum of *nnn* connections and that visitors should try again later.

These messages are not available to users of your Gopher or Web services.

Configuring IIS with Internet Explorer

Throughout this book, we've described how to use a browser as a front end so users can learn one common interface and then apply what they've learned to different tasks. To demonstrate just how effective a Web browser can be at performing user-interface tasks, Microsoft has provided the HTML Administrator in Windows NT 4, which you can use to configure IIS functions. All you need is a copy of the Internet Explorer browser. Here's how it works:

1. Install Internet Information Server on NT Server or install Peer Web Services on NT Workstation.
2. Log on as Administrator.
3. Use Internet Explorer to open `http://computername/iisadmin/`.
4. When Internet Explorer opens, as Figure 8.17 shows, simply follow the instructions on the screen.
5. Select a service from WWW, FTP, or Gopher. The HTML Administrator screens displayed using the Internet Explorer are similar to the ISM property sheets we looked at earlier in this chapter, although there are some minor differences in style and layout.

The one function that you can't perform from within the HTML Administrator is halting or restarting one of the three services; for that task, you must use the ISM or the Services applet in the Control Panel.

Several links provided in the HTML Administrator are actually shortcuts to Microsoft's own Web site on the Internet. If you're not connected to the Internet, when you click on one of these links, you'll see an Internet Explorer error message telling you the link could not be found. Connect to the Internet and try again, and your attempts will meet with success.

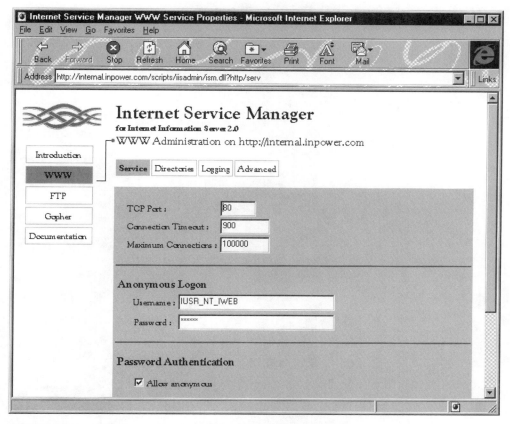

FIGURE 8.17:   Using the Internet Explorer to administer Internet Services

Next, we'll look at creating content for your intranet. As we get your content prepared, we'll cover HTML basics, finding existing materials to convert for use on your
intranet, and techniques to give your content some pizzazz.

Chapter 9

CREATING INTRANET PAGES WITH HTML

- **Understanding HTML**
- **Structuring your page**
- **Designing lists**
- **Using tables to arrange your data**
- **Using frames**
- **Formatting characters**
- **Dressing up your page with pictures**
- **Creating links**
- **Creating forms**
- **Looking at what's ahead for HTML**

Creating a successful Web page requires a good deal from both sides of your brain—the logical side that helps you write computer programs, and the artistic side that helps you compose a document that looks tasteful and inviting to a reader. That's why it's important to have several people test and critique your Web efforts; few of us can lay full claim to both sides of our brains!

This chapter will introduce you to creating Web documents, or *pages*. You'll see how to work with HTML, the page markup language, and, more important, you'll learn about the features in the language that you can include in your intranet pages.

As we continue discussing the creation of your intranet, we'll also get more detailed. This chapter is a little more technical and specific than some of the other chapters in this book. We're going to show you how to do some basic HTML *markup* or *tagging*. Markup and tagging are just different names for adding HTML formatting codes to your text. However, we can't cover everything about HTML, nor every trick in the book. For that kind of information, you'll want a book specific to HTML; you can also search the Internet for the latest HTML information. We'll include notes in this chapter on where to look for more information, including URLs where we can.

Introducing HTML

You create intranet pages with the *Hypertext Markup Language*, or HTML, the same language used to create Web pages on the Internet. In keeping with the original and ongoing theme of the Internet—openness and portability—the pages you create with HTML are just plain text. You can create, edit, or view the HTML code for a Web page in any text editor on any computer platform, such as Notepad under Windows 95 or NT, Simple Text on the Mac, or vi on a Unix machine.

> **TIP**
>
> **A good place to start learning about HTML is on the Web. Try**
> `http://www.yahoo.com/Computers_and_Internet/Software/`
> `Data_Formats/HTML/Guides_and_Tutorials/` **for the latest list of sites.**

Although it's easy to create a few simple intranet pages in a text editor, it can quickly turn into a grueling and mind-numbing task as your intranet grows. That's why many Web authoring tools let you create HTML intranet pages in the same way that you create documents in your word processor. You'll read about some of these tools and the advantages they offer in Chapter 11, "Using Intranet Authoring and Management Tools."

Browsing HTML Pages

When you open an intranet page in a Web browser, you don't see the HTML code that created the page. Instead, the browser interprets the HTML text and displays the page appropriately on the screen. If you're creating a Web page in a text editor, you use your browser to view the file you're working on to see the effects of your edits.

You will actually find that a page may not appear exactly the same when displayed in different browsers or on different computer platforms. This is because the *look* of a page is not always defined by the HTML language. Rather, the structure of the page and the function of the elements is described—the browser is responsible for coming up with a suitable representation.

> **TIP**
>
> Another good site for HTML information is the National Center for Supercomputing Applications (NCSA), *A Beginner's Guide to HTML* at `http://www.ncsa.uiuc.edu/General/Internet/WWW/HTMLPrimer.html`.

For example, later in this chapter you'll read about the six HTML codes you can use for creating six levels of headings on a page. You can specify that a paragraph of text be defined as one of the six heading levels, but the HTML heading code does *not* describe what that heading should look like. Let's say you define a primary heading using the HTML code `<H1>`. Your browser may display this heading in large, bold, serif type, or it may be in small, sans serif type. The key is that your browser knows it's a primary heading and displays it relative to the settings on your browser. It's up to the Web browser to differentiate each type of heading from the others.

One browser might display the first-level heading in a large font that is centered on the page, and another browser might display it as underlined boldfaced text that is left-aligned on the page.

The point is that a Web author can't prescribe exactly how a page should look, nor be sure how a page will be displayed by multiple browsers. Therefore, it's a good idea to see what your Web page looks like on several of the more popular browsers.

> **NOTE**
>
> The two biggest browser makers, Microsoft and Netscape, each have HTML and browser-specific information available. Microsoft's SiteBuilder is at `http://www.microsoft.com/workshop/author/` and Netscape's Creating Net Sites URL is `http://www.netscape.com/assist/net_sites/`.

The good news is that the browser market seems to be consolidating and standardizing. As time goes on, there should be fewer and fewer differences in the way browsers display the same page (except, perhaps, for the newest and not yet fully accepted, HTML features).

> **NOTE** While HTML describes the structure of a page and the browser interprets that information, page-layout programs, such as Quark or Frame, or page-description languages, such as PostScript, take a different approach. Page-layout software and PostScript define all the elements on a page using a set of complex commands to specify exact image and text placement, typefaces, and other attributes. The result is very controlled and static. HTML's simplicity makes it more flexible and quicker to display on-screen, but in a less static and controlled format that can drive graphic designers and your Marketing department crazy.

Now that we've covered some of the concepts, let's take a look at the actual elements and tags you'll use when creating your intranet's pages.

HTML Elements and Tags

A Web page is made up of *elements*, each of which is defined by an HTML code, or *tag*. A tag is always enclosed in angle brackets, and most tags come in pairs, with an opening and a closing tag. The closing tag is the same as the opening tag, but starts with a forward slash.

For example, to define text as a first-level heading in HTML, you use the <H1> tag, like this:

```
<H1>This is a Main Heading</H1>
```

A browser interprets these tags and displays the text within them appropriately, as shown here. The tags themselves, however, are not displayed within a browser, unless there is a problem

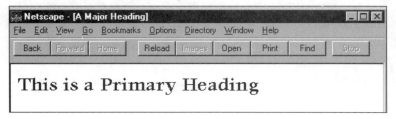

with a tag, such as one of the angle brackets being mistakenly left out (although most browsers will ignore any codes within angle brackets that they do not recognize).

NOTE

You can use either upper- or lowercase for a tag: because <H1> and <h1> are equivalent, the browser interprets them identically. Of course, your code looks nicer and is easier to read if you consistently use one or the other. In this book, we're using all uppercase.

Some tags have optional or required attributes. For example, the heading tag can take an optional alignment attribute:

```
<H1 ALIGN=CENTER>This is a main heading that is centered</H1>
```

TIP

Attributes are only used on the opening tag, never on the closing tag. Some tags can have a lot of attributes, and it may seem that the opening and closing tags don't match. If you get confused, check the part of the tag closest to the first angle bracket—that's usually the required part of the tag; it should match the closing tag.

You can also format HTML tags for readability. A browser ignores multiple spaces within a Web page and displays them as a single space. In addition, a browser ignores all hard returns within the HTML code—in other words, any blank lines you create in the code by pressing Enter a few times will not be displayed in the browser.

Say you're creating a table with the HTML code <TABLE>, you could make the code more readable (without affecting the actual table) by indenting the lines for the cells of the table, <TD>, beneath each row of the table <TR>, or by entering a blank line or two directly above and beneath the code for that table:

```
<P>A table is shown below.</P>

<TABLE>
  <TR>
    <TD>Cell A1</TD>   <TD>Cell B1</TD>
  </TR>
  <TR>
    <TD>Cell A2</TD>   <TD>Cell B2</TD>
  </TR>
```

```
<TR>
   <TD>Cell A3</TD>   <TD>Cell B3</TD>
</TR>
</TABLE>

<P>...and the page continues...</P>
```

Actually, there is one HTML element for which spaces and hard returns in the HTML code *do* count, and that is the *preformatted* tag, `<PRE>`. That tag instructs a browser to display the text in a monospaced font, which allows you to align text precisely, as you would when showing a program listing. The `<PRE>` tag is described later in this chapter in "Formatting Characters."

When Is a Standard Not a Standard?

Keep in mind that the HTML language is constantly evolving. Enthusiastic Web authors may happily include new and improved tags within their intranet pages to produce dazzling new effects. But, unfortunately, those effects will be lost on most users if their browser software has not been updated to the latest version that recognizes those new tags.

If you log on to your intranet one morning and find that you can't access certain features, it could be that you ignored an e-mail message from your Webmaster about upgrading your browser. Get in touch with your Webmaster pronto to find out what to do!

Officially, it's up to the World Wide Web Consortium (W3C) at the Massachusetts Institute of Technology (MIT) to define and establish a new version of HTML. Unofficially, leaders in the world of Webs and intranets, such as Netscape and Microsoft, come up with their own extensions to official HTML in the hopes of "improving" it. Eventually, many of these new codes are, indeed, included in the official HTML specification, but as the competition between the two companies increases, the two may use different enhancement tags for the same result. For more information, search the Web for information about HTML style sheets. Netscape and Microsoft both say they'll support them, but each has a different proposal. Based on the browser you choose, these differences can affect your intranet.

The Essentials of an Intranet Page

Every intranet page must include a few tags that define the page as a whole, so when a browser receives the page, it will recognize it as such. For example, the following HTML code produces a page that can be viewed in any browser; in Figure 9.1, it's shown in Microsoft's Internet Explorer browser:

```
<HTML>
<HEAD>
<TITLE>Greetings from the Intranet</TITLE>
</HEAD>
<BODY>
<P>Good morning! Welcome to our new intranet.</P>
</BODY>
</HTML>
```

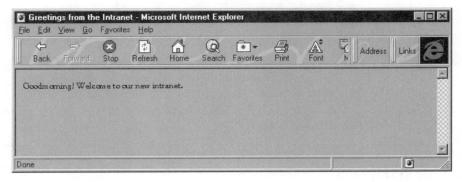

FIGURE 9.1:   The sample page displayed in a browser

Remember, this code is just a text file, plain and simple. Table 9.1 lists the tags that should be included in every page so any browser can view it.

You can incorporate dozens and dozens of other HTML tags into a Web page. The ones you use and how you use them depend only on your design and your imagination.

Table 9.1: Basic HTML Tags

Tag	What It Indicates
<HTML>	Declares that the text that follows defines an HTML Web page that can be viewed in a Web browser; the closing </HTML> tag ends the page.
<HEAD>	Defines the header area of a page, which is not displayed within the page itself in the browser.
<TITLE>	The text within this tag is the title of the Web page and is generally displayed in the Web browser's title bar, as in Figure 9.1. Be descriptive, as the title is frequently used by indexing programs as a name for your intranet page, and most browsers will offer a page's title as the default name when you save the page as a favorite or bookmarked location.
<BODY>	Delineates the actual content of the intranet page that will be displayed in the browser. In the example at the beginning of this section, only the words *Good morning! Welcome to our new intranet* will appear within the browser. Most of the other HTML features that we'll discuss in this chapter always appear within the <BODY> tag in a Web page. One of the optional attributes for this tag is BACKGROUND, which you can use to specify a graphical background image for the page.
<P>	Use the paragraph tag to mark the beginning of a new paragraph; the ending tag, </P>, is optional because the next <P> tag in the page marks the beginning of a new paragraph. You can include the ALIGN attribute to specify whether the paragraph should be centered or right-aligned on the page (left-aligned is the default).

Learning HTML

With the proliferation of sophisticated HTML editors (see Chapter 11, "Using Intranet Authoring and Management Tools"), it's unlikely that a text editor will be your first tool of choice for creating intranet pages. With any luck, you will never have to become an HTML expert, and you will forego the "pleasure" of wrangling your way through screenfuls of angle brackets, slashes, and other esoteric codes.

Even if you decide on an authoring tool that hides all the coding, understanding how HTML works and how it looks will prove invaluable to your Web-building experience. That's why this chapter and the next one give you a good introduction to what you can do with HTML—both basic and more advanced capabilities. But rest assured, we have absolutely no intention of molding you into a code cruncher.

There are many ways to learn about HTML without specifically studying it. Perhaps the most important method is already staring you in the face as you browse an intranet or the World Wide Web (WWW)—the pages themselves. All intranet pages are built from the same text-based HTML language, so when you're viewing a page in your browser that does something interesting, stop and take a look at the underlying code for that page. If you have an Internet connection, you can try it by starting your browser and opening the Sybex Web page at `http://www.Sybex.com`. Once you're there, you can look at the HTML that makes up the page. You can do that in one of two ways:

- Most browsers have a menu command, named something like View ➤ Source, that will display the current page's HTML code in a new window.
- Most browsers let you save the current HTML page to a disk. The resulting file, which you can open in your text editor or authoring tool, is the HTML code from which the page was built.

By viewing the HTML code for a page, you can get a feeling for how the page was created, even when you don't study every subtle nuance of that page's HTML code. Some other resources for learning about HTML include:

- *HTML: The Definitive Guide* by Chuck Musciano and Bill Kennedy, published by O'Reilly and Associates in 1996.
- The World Wide Web Consortium is a great place to look for information on HTML. The W3's URL is `http://www.w3.org/pub/WWW/` —remember `.org`, not `.com`! There is also a commercial company called W3 at `www.w3.com`.
- Web sites and intranet resources on the Internet are a great way to learn about HTML. We've already given you some, but you can find more by searching this Yahoo category: `Computers and Internet:Internet: World Wide Web:Information and Documentation`.

Now let's take the nuts and bolts you've learned here and use them to structure a page.

Adding Structure to a Page

Just about any HTML page you create for your intranet will benefit from imposing some sort of structure on it. For example, think about how you would put your company's procedures manual up on your intranet:

- If the manual is divided into chapters, you could make each one a separate intranet page.

- It's easy to mimic the manual's table of contents by using hypertext links in HTML.
- Each chapter in the manual might have several levels of headings, which you can also emulate with the heading tags in HTML.
- The body of the document would, of course, be divided into individual paragraphs.

You'll find that HTML offers several elements that let you create this type of structure in an intranet page. Let's look at them.

Using Paragraphs or Line Breaks

You create a paragraph by enclosing text within the paragraph codes <P> and </P>. Remember that any "paragraphs" you create by pressing Enter while editing HTML code will be completely ignored by a browser. You must specifically define a paragraph in the code by using the paragraph tag. Consider the text in the six lines of HTML code that follow:

```
<P>This is the first paragraph; its code
continues over several lines, but will be
displayed as a single paragraph in a
browser.</P><P>And this is a second paragraph
that will also be displayed as such in
a browser.</P>
```

This code would appear as two separate paragraphs in a browser, as shown in the upper portion of the browser in Figure 9.2. Note that their line lengths are determined by the width of the browser's window.

Most browsers insert some extra space between paragraphs, so in some instances, you will not want to use the <P> tag. For example, when you display your name and address in a page, you would not want a blank line between each line of the address.

In those cases, you should use the line break tag, <BR>. It tells the browser to wrap the text that follows onto a new line, without inserting any extra space between the lines. Here is an address within HTML code:

```
John and Joan Doe<BR>The Hanford Corp.<BR>123 S Proton
Dr<BR>Hanford, WA 98765
```

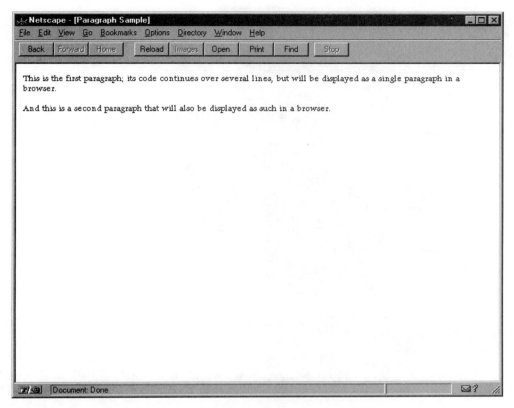

FIGURE 9.2: You use the `<P>` tag to define a paragraph.

Dividing Sections with a Horizontal Line

A simple and effective way to separate sections within a Web page is to insert a horizontal line, `<HR>`, also called a *horizontal rule.* By default, the line spans from one side of the page to the other.

For example, if your page has a banner across the top with your company name, you could insert a horizontal line beneath it. This would separate it from a table of contents of links to other pages, beneath which you could insert another line, followed by the main body of the page. At the bottom of the page, you could insert even another line, and beneath that line would be the important page identifiers, such as its URL, the date the page was last modified, a link back to a home page, and so on. (See Figure 9.3.)

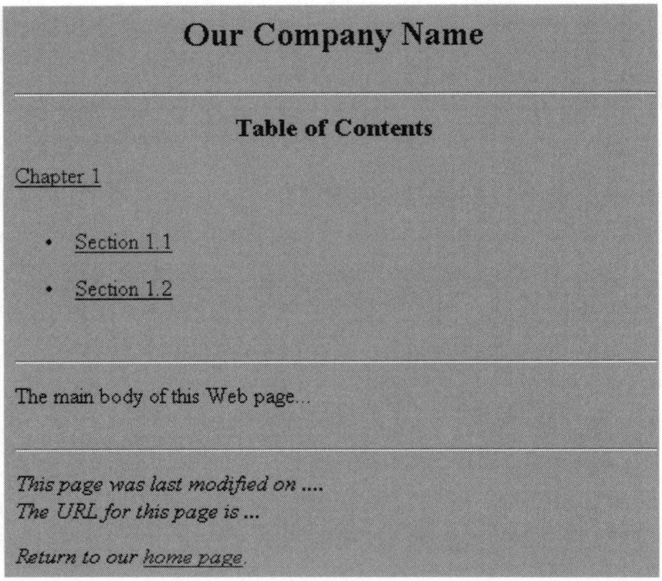

Our Company Name

Table of Contents

Chapter 1

- Section 1.1

- Section 1.2

The main body of this Web page...

This page was last modified on ....
The URL for this page is ...

Return to our home page.

FIGURE 9.3:
You can use the horizontal rule, <HR>, to divide a page into sections.

WARNING Horizontal rules can quickly clutter up a page. If your page has many distinct areas divided by several rules, try splitting the material into separate files.

The <HR> tag takes several optional attributes. You can specify the rule's thickness (the default is one or two pixels in most browsers) and how much of the browser's window it should span (as a percentage or in pixels); for example:

```
<HR SIZE=6 WIDTH=60%>
```

would display a line six pixels thick that spans 60 percent of the browser's window (centered in the window is the default).

Creating a Hierarchy with Headings

Another common way to add structure to a Web page is through the use of headings. This book, for example, uses headings to divide each chapter into logical chunks (or at least, that was our plan). Each chapter is divided into several main headings, each of which may contain several subheadings, and those subheadings may contain their own subheadings.

A Web page can have a maximum of six levels of headings, with HTML codes conveniently named `<H1>`, `<H2>`, `<H3>`, and so on:

```
<H1>This is a two-line<BR>first-level heading</H1>
```

As mentioned earlier, there is no inherent style to the headings—different Web browsers might interpret the look of a heading in slightly different ways. In general, a first-level heading will be in a larger, bolder font than a lower-level heading. Shown here is a sample of the six headings within Microsoft's Internet Explorer.

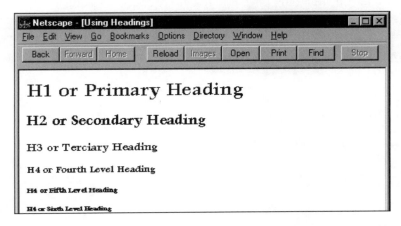

You're free to use the HTML headings in any order you like, but it makes good sense to use them as you would in an outline: the first-level heading, `<H1>`, being the highest level, and the sixth level, `<H6>`, the lowest or most subordinate.

Although the first heading you use should generally be the highest level that will occur on the page, this doesn't mean it must be the `<H1>` heading. You might start with `<H2>` because you know that most browsers display that heading in a smaller font than `<H1>`. In this case, then, the level-two heading would be the primary level, and you wouldn't use `<H1>` on that page.

Creating Lists

The bulleted or numbered list is a fast, easy way to apply some structure to a Web page, and you'll no doubt use it frequently. As always, the way a browser formats the list, such as the amount of indention and the style of the bullets, could vary from browser to browser. HTML offers several ways to arrange items in lists. The two most commonly used ones are bulleted lists and numbered lists:

- *Bulleted lists* (also called *unordered lists*) preface each item or paragraph in the list with a bullet; the <UL> tag begins the list.
- *Numbered lists* (also called *ordered list*) number each item in the list; the <OL> tag begins the list. The browser applies the appropriate number to each line when it opens the page. You can, therefore, add to or delete items from the list while you create the page and not worry about updating the numbering.

No matter which type of list you use, you define each item within it with the <LI> tag. The following unordered list

```
<P>Chapter I</P>
<UL>
<LI>Section 1</LI>
<LI>Section 2</LI>
<LI>Section 3</LI></UL>
```

looks like this in a browser:

Chapter I

- Section 1
- Section 2
- Section 3

You can also nest one list within another simply by beginning the new list with the appropriate list tag. This allows you to create outlines, for example, or tables of contents that have subheadings indented in their own list. Here's the list from the example above with a nested second list:

```
<<P>Chapter I</P>
<UL>
<LI>Section 1</LI>
<LI>Section 2</LI>
<UL>
<LI>Part A</LI>
<LI>Part B</LI>
<LI>Part C</LI>
</UL></LI>
<LI>Section 3</LI></UL>
```

In a browser, the secondary list is indented to set it off from the primary list. Again, the actual look depends on the browser that is viewing the page. Here is the indented list in Netscape Navigator:

Chapter I

- Section 1
- Section 2
     - Part A
     - Part B
     - Part C
- Section 3

Arranging Items within Tables

An even more powerful way to structure data within a Web page is the table. Like the tables you can create in your word processor or spreadsheet, an HTML table consists of rows, columns, and cells.

You can place just about anything you want within a cell in a table; there are few restrictions. Because of its flexibility, you'll find the table being used in countless ways in intranet pages.

Sometimes it will look like a table, with border lines dividing its rows, columns, and cells. In other applications, though, the structure of the table will be used but without displaying its borders. The table serves as a convenient way to organize elements of the page without making them appear to be within an actual table.

Like imagemaps (discussed in "Linking Pages"), tables are HTML elements that are best created in a dedicated HTML editor. You can build a small table "manually" in a text editor, but anything more complex and you'll be whining for the proper tools.

Table 9.2 lists the basic tags you use to define a table.

Table 9.2: Basic HTML Tags Used in Tables

Tag	What It Indicates
`<TABLE>`	Begins the table definition.
`<TR>`	Defines a new row in the table.
`<TD>`	Defines a single cell within the table.

Shown here is the code for a table that was used in the "HTML Elements and Tags" section at the beginning of this chapter:

```
<TABLE>
  <TR>
    <TD>Cell A1</TD>  <TD>Cell B1</TD>
  </TR>
  <TR>
    <TD>Cell A2</TD>  <TD>Cell B2</TD>
  </TR>
  <TR>
    <TD>Cell A3</TD>  <TD>Cell B3</TD>
  </TR>
</TABLE>
```

The result is a table with three rows and two columns; the text within the `<TD>` and `</TD>` tags is what appears in each cell. By default, as in this example, the table has no borders. You must specifically include them by specifying the width of their lines (in pixels). This tag

```
<TABLE BORDER=1>
```

would enclose all the cells in the table with a one-pixel wide border. On the left, here's the table without a border and on the right, the same table with a border.

Cell A1	Cell B1
Cell A2	Cell B2
Cell A3	Cell B3

To include a table caption, use the `<CAPTION>` tag once in a table. Any text between this tag and its closing tag is displayed as the table's caption, which by default is centered just above the table, much like the typeset tables in this book.

You use the table header tag, `<TH>`, instead of the `<TD>` tag, to create a header cell for the table. Most browsers display the text between the opening and closing table header tags bolded and centered within its cell. You will often use these table headers as titles in the first row or column of a table.

By default, a table will only be as wide as the longest entries in its cells; however, you can specify an exact width in the `<TABLE>` tag using the `WIDTH` attribute. The width can be expressed either in pixels or as a percentage of the browser's window. For example, this tag

```
<TABLE WIDTH=320>
```

creates a table that is exactly 320 pixels wide. If you want a table to be exactly half the width of the browser's window, no matter what width that might be, use the tag:

```
<TABLE WIDTH=50%>
```

If a table is less than the full width of a browser's window, it will be aligned with the left edge of the window. You can include the ALIGN attribute in the <TABLE> tag to specify whether the table should be left-aligned, centered, or right-aligned within the browser's window.

If you specify an exact width for the table, you might also want to set the width of each column using the WIDTH attribute within the <TD> tag for a cell. Just as you can specify the width of table, you can specify the width of a column either in pixels or as a percentage of the table (not of the browser's window).

You can also include many other tags and attributes in the table, such as the color of its borders and a background color or an image for the table or for any of its cells, and you can specify which borders should be displayed.

> **TIP** Remember, you'll get the best results with the least stress if you build your HTML tables within an HTML editor, such as those described throughout this book.

Splitting a Page into Frames

One of the newer HTML features is frames, which offers you a way to display multiple intranet pages within one browser window. In traditional Web and intranet browsing, if you click on a link in one page, a new page is opened and replaces the first page; when you click on a link in a page that serves as an index of other pages, the target page opens, but the index page is removed from the browser.

By splitting a page into two frames, the index page can be displayed in one frame, while the target of the selected link is displayed in the other frame in another part of the browser's screen. In this way, the index is always available, so you can easily make another selection.

The concept of frames is neat and simple:

- Create a single Web page as a *frameset* that contains no content other than the frameset definition.

- Specify how the frameset should be divided into frames.
- Assign a Web page to each frame.

You use the `<FRAMESET>` tag instead of the usual `<BODY>` tag to begin the frameset definition in the page. For example, this tag

```
<FRAMESET COLS="33%,67%">
```

creates a frameset page that consists of two frames arranged as columns. The first frame will be in a column on the left side of the browser's window; that frame will take up one-third of the browser's window. The second frame will be in a column to the right of the first one and will take up two-thirds of the browser's window.

To specify the source Web page that should be opened in each frame, use the `<FRAME>` tag:

```
<FRAME SRC="INDEX.HTM">
<FRAME SRC="INSTRUCT.HTM">
```

In this case, when the frameset is opened in a browser, the frame on the left will display the page `INDEX.HTM`, and the frame on the right will display `INSTRUCT.HTM`. You now have two intranet pages both sharing the same browser window. An example of a frame-based intranet page is shown in Figure 9.4.

To go back to the example from the beginning of this section, if the frame on the left contains an index of links, you can have each of those links display its target in the frame on the right. You do so by including the `TARGET` attribute in the anchor tag for the link and specifying the name of the frame (see "Targeting a Frame" later in this chapter).

In order to specify a target frame, you must first name the frame. You do so using the `NAME` attribute in the `<FRAME>` tag. In the previous example, you could name the tags in this way

```
<FRAME SRC="INDEX.HTM">
<FRAME SRC="INSTRUCT.HTM" NAME=RIGHT>
```

which gives the name `RIGHT` to the frame on the right. With that frame named, you can define each link in the index page so its target resource appears in the named frame, such as:

```
<A HREF="SOMEFILE.HTM" TARGET=RIGHT>
```

In this way, your index remains in the frame on the left, while the target of each link is displayed in the frame on the right.

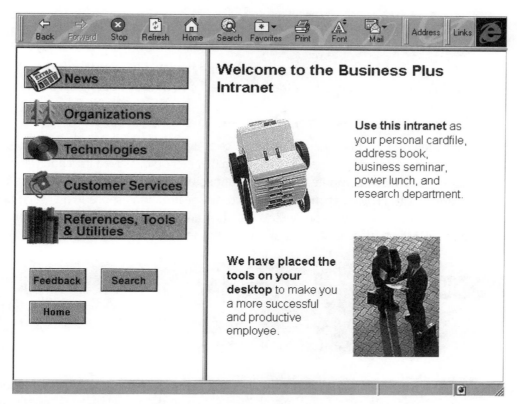

FIGURE 9.4: A frame-based intranet home page

Finally, even though Netscape and IE support frames, not all browsers do. For a browser that can't display frames, you can include the <NOFRAMES> tag within the frameset. Here's an example:

```
<NOFRAMES><BODY>
<P>Sorry, but this page uses frames, which your browser does
not support.</P>
</BODY></NOFRAMES>
```

As you can see, it includes the <BODY> tag, which is not used in defining a frameset but would be recognized by a frames-unaware browser. Anything within the <BODY> tags would then be displayed in the browser window.

Formatting Characters

One of the open-standard concepts behind the World Wide Web was that HTML should avoid literally describing the look of pages as much as possible. For example, a tag such as

```
<FONT FACE="TIMES ROMAN" SIZE=5 COLOR=#ff0000>
```

is frowned on by HTML purists because it goes against this theme. It means a browser has to have a specific, named font available that can be displayed in various sizes, and that the browser's computer has to be connected to a color monitor. Because these extensions to HTML assume that your browser functions more like a page-layout application than was previously required, they are one of the more debated changes to the HTML specifications. We'll explain all this in a moment.

> **TIP**
>
> As we discuss more complex tag options, you'll see multiword attributes within tags. When you can specify several options within a tag, you should include the options within quotation marks. The `<FONT>` tag shown above is a good example.

The days of trying to write standard HTML, or writing to the least common denominator, are waning quickly, and, in fact, the tag shown previously may soon be a part of the official HTML specification. It also illustrates two types of HTML tag attributes—*absolute* and *relative.* Generally, relative tags or attributes describe function and are truer to the spirit of the HTML specifications. Absolute tags or attributes describe formatting and are new to HTML. Here's what these attributes mean more specifically (refer to the example at the beginning of this section):

Absolute (literal)	The font type *Times Roman* is specified by name, and the color is specified by a hexadecimal RGB color value. There can be no doubt about how the author wanted this to look.
Relative (logical)	The font size five, however, does not refer to an actual point size. It's a size that is relative to the browser's default font size (which is size two) and gives the browser a little more flexibility in how it displays the font. The author wanted the font to be larger than the browser's default but was willing to let the browser assign the actual size.

Table 9.3 defines a few of the many HTML character-formatting tags. All require both an opening and a closing tag.

Table 9.3: Basic HTML Text-Formatting Tags

Tag	What It Does
`<ADDRESS>`	Most browsers display text that is surrounded by this tag in italics; use it to call out a Web page's author information, such as the page URL, author name, date of last revision, and so on (a relative tag).
`<EM>`	Most browsers display emphasized text in italics (a relative tag).
`<I>`	Italic text (an absolute tag).
`<PRE>`	The preformatted tag displays text in a monospaced (fixed-width) font, and multiple spaces, tabs, and hard returns within the HTML code are displayed as well; use this tag when the position of characters within each line is important, such as in program listings and columnar lists.
`<STRONG>`	Most browsers display strong text in boldface (another relative tag).
`<B>`	Bold text (an absolute tag).
`<S>`	Displays strikethrough text (an absolute tag); some browsers may use `<STRIKE>`.
`<U>`	Underlined text; you should generally avoid underlining text since that is how browsers usually indicate hypertext links in intranet pages (an absolute tag).

You can insert these tags where they are needed in a paragraph, and some tags can be combined. The page shown in Figure 9.5 is an example of HTML text formatting; this page was built using the following HTML code:

```
<HTML>
<HEAD><TITLE>HTML Formatting Tags</TITLE></HEAD>
<BODY><P>With HTML formatting tags, you can make text
<STRONG>bold</STRONG>, <EM>emphasized</EM>, or
<EM><STRONG>bold and emphasized</STRONG></EM>. You can also
<STRIKE>strike-out text</STRIKE> or make it <U>underlined</U>.
If you don't use the Preformatted tag, most browsers display
text in a proportional font, where different characters take
```

up different amounts of space. Here are 10 letter `<EM>i</EM>`s
and 10 letter `<EM>M</EM>`s; each line of the HTML code also had
five spaces entered between the fifth and sixth letters:`</P>`
`<P>iiiii     iiiii<BR>`
`MMMMM     MMMMM</P>`
`<P>`Here are those letters and spaces within the Preformatted
tags:`</P>`
`<PRE>iiiii     iiiii`
`MMMMM     MMMMM</PRE>`
`</BODY></HTML>`

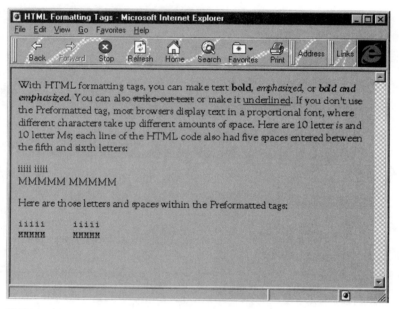

FIGURE 9.5: HTML formatting tags change the look of text in a intranet page.

Saying It with Pictures

While you can achieve a lot through the structure of your page and the formatting of individual characters, just about every intranet page can benefit from even one graphical image. Besides conveying 10,000 or so words, a picture can enliven an otherwise text-filled page, provide color, attract the eye, offer a little amusement, and help distinguish one page from another.

An image that you include in a Web page is called an *inline image*, as opposed to an image that is viewed separately in a browser, such as when the image file is the target of a link. In HTML, you reference the inline image in this way:

```
There's more <IMG SRC="images/arrow-rt.gif"> if you're
interested.
```

In this case, the image file ARROW-RT.GIF, located in the Images directory, is displayed within the text that surrounds it and might look like the one shown here.

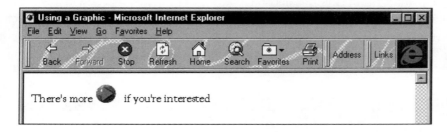

For more information on how to get the most out of using graphics on your intranet, see *Mastering Intranets,* also from Sybex.

Defining Image Attributes

The <IMG SRC> tag, used to reference images, can take quite a few attributes, all of which are optional. We'll look at a few of the more important ones here.

Specifying Alternate Text

When a browser cannot display graphic images, perhaps because the image file cannot be found or because the browser's image-loading capabilities have been turned off to save download time, you can include the ALT attribute in an image tag to display text in place of the image.

Many browsers will also display an image's alternative text while they are loading the image; if the text describes the image, the user will have some idea of what's being loaded, and it can actually enhance the image on the page.

Here's how you include the alternative text for an inline image:

```
<IMG SRC="picture.gif" ALT="The BusinessPlus logo">
```

TIP As with most multiword attributes within tags, you should include the text within quotation marks.

Sizing the Image

By default, a browser loads an image from the top down and displays the image in as large a box as needed. Until the complete image comes in, however, the browser cannot display the page in its final layout. If the image takes more than a few seconds to load, the reader is confronted with a page that may be in some disarray.

You can avoid this problem by including the image's dimensions within its HTML tag. Most image-editing or viewing programs will tell you the size of an image.

With that information, a browser can create a box of the correct size in the page and finish the other page formatting around it. It will then fill in the box with the picture, during which time you can be reading the text on the page. If there is alternative text defined for the image, the browser may display that in the box while the image is loading.

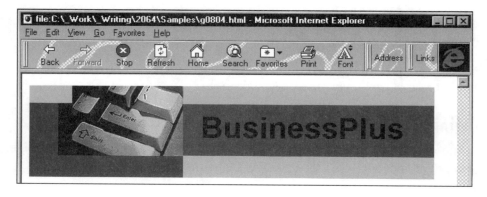

You can also use the WIDTH and HEIGHT attributes to specify the image size in pixels. If the graphic file PICTURE.GIF contains a picture that is 100 pixels wide by 150 pixels tall, this is how the HTML tag would look:

```
<IMG SRC="picture.gif" WIDTH=100 HEIGHT=150>
```

WARNING It's generally not a good idea to specify dimensions that are different from the picture's actual size. Most browsers will shrink or enlarge the picture to fit its defined box size and in the process will change the look of the picture in ways you may not anticipate. If you want the picture to be a certain size, crop or size it accordingly before you include it in your page.

Aligning the Image

When you display an image within a Web page, you can use the `ALIGN` attribute to position the image either flush-left, centered, or flush-right in the browser window. This tag

```
<IMG SRC="picture.gif" ALIGN=LEFT>
```

displays the image flush-left, which is the default, and any text wraps to the right of the image.

You can also use the `TOP`, `BOTTOM`, or `MIDDLE` attributes to align text with the top, bottom, or middle of the image. You would normally use these when there is only a single line of text next to the image, since anything with more than one line of text appears below the image. The default alignment is `BOTTOM`, which means the first line of text aligns with the bottom of the image.

To display an image so no text appears next to it, simply insert a paragraph tag before and after the image tag.

Using an Image as a Page Background

Earlier in this chapter, in the section "The Essentials of an Intranet Page," you read about the `<BODY>` tag. You also learned about one of its optional attributes, `BACK-GROUND`, with which you can create a background image for the page. This is how such a tag would look:

```
<BODY BACKGROUND="smallpic.gif">
```

A browser will fill the page's background with the specified image by tiling the image, as needed. This is one time when you can use a very small picture to great effect. It will fill the page while taking very little time to download.

> **TIP**
>
> **Many Internet sites offer images suitable for page backgrounds. You might start looking in the Yahoo search site under the category:** `Computers and Internet:Internet:World Wide Web:Page Design and Layout:Backgrounds`.

An image that is a pattern or texture can often be tiled into one seemingly seamless image. This can be effective if you're trying to give your intranet or even just one area or department a distinctive look. See Figure 9.6 for an example of a page with a background. For example, a woodworking company may want to give the wood descriptions page a background that looks like oak to convey a sense of the page's function.

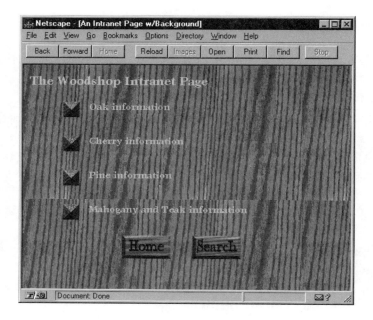

FIGURE 9.6:
An intranet page
with a background

WARNING If printing pages will be common from your intranet, remember that the background image doesn't print from any current browser. Don't make the background such an integral part of the page that the usefulness of the page is lost without the background. Chances are your intranet's pages will also be easier to read.

Remember that this is one feature of an intranet page you want to pay close attention to. Before you consider that page finished, be sure you can read all the text over the background image.

Linking Pages

At the heart of every Web page are the *hypertext links* (or just plain *links*) you create between text and graphic images or other pages on your intranet. When a reader clicks on a link, the browser jumps to a new resource and starts the processing needed to open and display it. That resource can be another HTML page, a graphic image, a sound or video file, and so on, and it might be located on your local hard disk or at another site anywhere on your intranet.

Creating a Link

You define a link with the anchor tag, <A>. Within its opening and closing tags, you specify the two components that every link must have:

- The target of the link, such as a URL or a filename
- The text or graphic image that you want to serve as the clickable link in a browser

After specifying the target within the opening anchor tag, follow that with the clickable text or image reference and end with the closing anchor tag:

```
<A HREF="target">Text for the link</A>
```

Most browsers display the link text underlined and in a different color from the default color for the Web page. For example, this HTML code

```
Here's <A HREF="help.htm">online help</A> when you need it.
```

would look like this when you're browsing its page:

```
Here's online help when you need it.
```

If you clicked on the underlined text, your browser would open the page named HELP.HTM. Note that when you point at a link in most browsers, the target of the link is displayed somewhere on the screen so you'll get some idea of what will happen if you click on the link.

The link example shown here is an example of using a *relative* address for the target. Because no path to the target file was specified, the target must reside in the same folder as the page that contains the link. Because it's not included in the address, it doesn't matter what the name of that folder is. Here's an example of another relative address:

```
Here's <A HREF="corp/dept/help.htm">online help</A> when you
need it.
```

This time the target file is in a directory (called a *folder* by some HTML authoring packages) named DEPT within a directory named CORP, which is within the same directory that contains the link's Web page.

You can also specify an *absolute* address that names the exact location of the target file, such as a complete URL. Here's the example with an absolute address (it's shown on two lines for clarity):

```
Here's <A HREF="http://www.domain.com/web/corp/
dept/help.htm">online help</A> when you need it.
```

When you create a link to a resource on your own intranet site, use a relative address instead of an absolute one whenever possible. That way, you can move your intranet to a new server or to a new directory on a server, and the links will still work correctly because they're relative.

Linking to a Named Location

When the target of a link is another intranet page, you'll see the very top portion of that page when it's opened in the browser. You can then scroll around within that page to see the other information it contains. But you can also link directly to a specific location within that page, which will then be displayed as soon as the page is opened. For this to work, that location must already be named.

You use the anchor tag to create what's often called a *named anchor* or a *bookmark* within a Web page. For example, this anchor tag

```
<A NAME="Sect1">Section 1.0</A>
```

gives the name Sect1 to the text Section 1.0. When viewed in a browser, the named text looks no different from the unnamed text. Therefore, it doesn't really matter if you name all the text in a line or just the first character, although it's generally best to name at least a few words in the line.

You'll often create named anchors for the main section headings in a page. In this way, you can jump directly to those sections from links in the same or from other intranet pages, or you can create a table of contents that gives you complete access to those named sections. Any links you create can have named anchors as their targets.

To specify a named anchor as the target for a link, you precede its name with a pound sign:

```
<A HREF="#Sect1">Section 1.0: Introduction</A>
```

In this case, because a URL wasn't included, the bookmark is assumed to be on the same page as the link. Clicking on this link (the text <u>Section 1.0: Introduction</u>) in a Web browser displays the line of text named Sect1 as the first line in the browser's window.

To link to a named location in another Web page, specify the target file as usual but append a pound sign and the name of the target named anchor. Here's an example, shown on two lines:

```
<A HREF="http://www.domain.com/somepage.htm#Sect1">Section 1.0:
Introduction</A>
```

This time, clicking on the link opens the file SOMEPAGE.HTM and displays the line of text that contains the named anchor Sect1 at the top of the browser window.

Targeting a Frame

Earlier in this chapter, you read about the frameset, which is an intranet page that you divide into multiple frames, each of which can open and display a separate page.

When a link resides in one frame of a frameset, you can display the target for that link in any of the frames in that frameset. You do so by including the TARGET attribute in the link's anchor tag, along with the name of the frame that should receive the target of the link.

For example, here's the linking example shown earlier, but this time the target will be displayed in the frame named RIGHT:

```
Here's <A HREF="help.htm" TARGET=RIGHT>online help</A> when
you need it.
```

When a user clicks on this link, the target file HELP.HTM will be opened in the frame named RIGHT in the current frameset.

By default, if you don't specify a target frame for a link in a frameset, its target resource will be opened in the same frame, replacing the Web page that contained the link.

Linking to Other File Types

The target of a link is often another Web page, but it can also be any other type of file. In most cases, a file's type is determined by its filename extension, such as TXT for text files and HTM or HTML for intranet pages.

> **TIP** The HTM extension indicates a file that was probably created in the DOS/Windows 3.x world. The HTML extension indicates a file that was created in the Unix, Win95, Windows NT, or Macintosh world.

Most browsers can open intranet pages, text files, and GIF or JPEG graphic-image files. For other file types, however, a browser must fall back to the operating system to open or otherwise handle that file. The operating system, in turn, will pass the file along to the appropriate program.

For example, sound files (WAV or AU) and movie files (AVI, MOV, MPG, or MPEG) would be played by the appropriate sound and movie player. However, if the target of a link is of an unknown file type (unknown to the browser and its operating system, that is), the link may fail, but most browsers notify you of the problem and offer to save the file to disk instead of opening it. If you know that you're using a specific file type on your intranet, you can preconfigure your browser to open that file type. See your browser's documentation for information on how to set up this feature.

Chapter 10, "Adding Other Content to Your Intranet," discusses a variety of files you can include in your intranet site, all of which can serve as targets for links.

Linking to an E-mail Address

The target for a link can also be an e-mail address. When a user clicks on the link, the user's e-mail program should open with a new message displayed and already addressed to the address in the link. The user can then create the body of the message and send it to the target address in the usual way.

You use the keyword *mailto* to indicate that the link is to an e-mail address:

```
<A HREF="mailto:ballard@domain.com">Send your comments to
Ballard</A>
```

When a user clicks on the link <u>Send your comments to Ballard</u>, the user's e-mail program will open with a new message addressed to `ballard@domain.com`.

Using Clickable Images and Imagemaps

Earlier in the chapter, you read about the ways you can incorporate graphic images in your intranet pages. An image in a page can also serve as the source for a link—clicking on the image activates the link. You can go even further, though, and create more than one link within an image. The result is called an *imagemap*.

You can utilize clickable images in countless ways in your intranet pages; here are a few of the possibilities:

- A small image next to descriptive text can serve as a button; this is similar to real-world buttons, such as the doorbells by an apartment building's front door, which have the name of an occupant above each doorbell.

- A small picture of a product listed in a catalog can link to the page for that product. In this case, little or no descriptive text may be needed if the picture is self-evident. When in doubt, even a little descriptive text goes a long way in dispelling confusion about the purpose of a graphical image link.

- A row of images can serve as a menu, such as at the top of a page. Again, including a little text next to or within each image is usually the best way to go so your users can tell what clicking the icon does.

- A larger image can serve as an imagemap, such as a site map of your corporate offices—you can click on a part of a building to open the relevant page for that department.

- A catalog of office furniture might contain an imagemap of a furnished conference room. The chairs, the table, the coffee pot, and so on, could each link to information about that item.
- An image that displays a time line could include links at different points along the line. The chronology could be in a geologic scale, with images of a dinosaur, a woolly mammoth, a prehistoric man, and so on; or your time line could illustrate something with a shorter time span, such as a construction project, on which the links would be images of a surveying instrument, a dump truck, a cement truck, a framed building, and so on.

Defining an image as a link is almost the same as defining text as a link. Instead of entering the link text, you specify the image file's URL. Here's how you could revise the link example shown earlier in "Creating a Link." The image file HELP.GIF is used as the source of the link. Clicking on that image would open the target of the link, which is still the Web page HELP.HTM:

```
<A HREF="help.htm"><IMG SRC="images/help.gif"></A>Here's
online help when you need it.
```

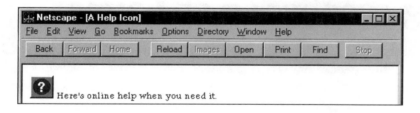

Creating an imagemap is not so simple, however, because you must define the coordinates of each clickable region, or *hotspot*, within the image and the target for each region. You also have to define how the imagemap will be controlled.

Traditionally, imagemaps were handled by the server. When you clicked on a hotspot in an imagemap, the browser sent the coordinates of your click to the Web server, which looked up those coordinates in a map of the image to determine which link region had been clicked. It then processed the request for the target of that link.

Many of today's browsers can also support client-side imagemaps, in which the coordinates of the hotspots defined for the image are included in the HTML file, along with the target names. When you click on the image, your browser determines which link was clicked and opens the target of that link.

WARNING One large imagemap can take much longer to load than several small images used to create the same effect. Unless your intranet is running fast clients on a quick network, smaller images are more usable for the average intranet user.

Creating either type of imagemap is best accomplished within a full-fledged HTML editor. In that case, you simply drag out an outline of the shape that you want to serve as a hotspot within the image, and then you specify the target for that link. You can usually define regions that are rectangles, circles, and polygons.

How you group the hotspots within the image is up to you. Most HTML editors also let you define a default target for the image as a whole. If you should click in an area that happens to be outside any of the defined regions, the default target is opened rather than one of the specific targets.

Getting Feedback with Forms

So far in this chapter, all the HTML elements we've discussed have been display-oriented, in that they affect the way a page appears within a browser. Now we'll look at the HTML form, an element that not only affects the display but also allows the user to send information back to *you*.

Those two issues, *display* and *send*, are the primary functions of a Web-based form:

- The form controls that you create on a Web page are displayed in a browser, and the user can enter data in them, select check boxes or radio buttons, select items from a list, and so on.
- Once the user has entered data into the form, there must be a mechanism to send the data back to your server. Once the data has been received on the server, there needs to be another mechanism to store or manipulate that data for further use.

Designing a Form

Designing a form for a Web page isn't especially difficult if, as with tables, you do the job in an HTML editor. The forms you create for the Web look and behave a lot like any other computer-generated forms you may have come across. For example, an

HTML form can have a one-line data-entry field (sometimes called an *edit field*), in which the reader can type an e-mail address.

Enter Your Email Address

Email [   ]

[Send]

To begin the form definition, use the <FORM> tag. As part of that definition, you specify where the data should be returned (a URL) by using the ACTION attribute. The destination might be the server for the form's Web page or some other server that will accept the data. You also specify *how* the data should be returned, using the METHOD attribute.

There are two different ways to send information to your server: POST or GET. Using METHOD=POST, you send all the information from the form separately from the form's URL, while METHOD=GET creates a single string that begins with the form's URL and ends with the form's data. Sometimes this can create a string that is long enough to exceed the maximum allowed URL length, causing an error that results in lost data. The POST method is the most common way to handle the job.

Within the opening and closing <FORM> tags, you lay out the controls of the form. You can include any other HTML elements, as well; these elements will appear in the page along with the form controls. Some of the more common form control tags are shown in Table 9.4 and a resulting form in Figure 9.7.

Table 9.4: Common HTML Form Control Tags

Tag	Form Control	Description
<INPUT TYPE=TEXT>	Data-entry field	Displays a one-line data-entry field.
<INPUT TYPE=PASSWORD>	Password field	Displays characters as asterisks in a one-line data-entry field.
<TEXTAREA>	Multiple-line data-entry field	Enter a paragraph or more of text.
<INPUT TYPE=CHECKBOX>	Check box	Select an item by clicking on its check box.

Table 9.4: Common HTML Form Control Tags (continued)

Tag	Form Control	Description
`<INPUT TYPE=RADIO>`	Radio button	Select one of a group of radio buttons.
`<SELECT>`	List	Select one or more items from a list.
`<INPUT TYPE=SUBMIT>`	Button	When clicked on, sends the form's data to the server.
`<INPUT TYPE=RESET>`	Button	When clicked on, resets all form controls to their defaults.

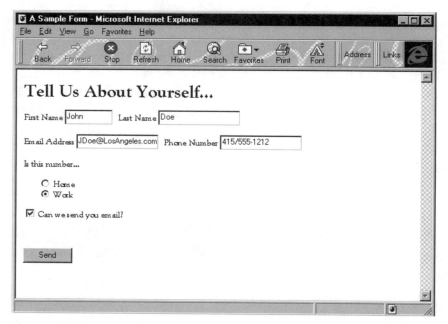

FIGURE 9.7: A user can enter information or select items in an HTML form.

The definition for each control (other than the Submit and Reset buttons) must include its name, which is sent to and used by the server to identify the data that control returned. Each control may also have several other attributes that define how it behaves. For example, the single-line data-entry field has the following attributes:

Size   The displayed width of the field in the form.

Maxlength   The maximum number of characters that can be entered into the field.

Value   The characters that appear within the field when its page is first opened or the Reset button is clicked; you might use *(none)* as this default value, so when the data's returned to the server, this entry would indicate that the reader hadn't entered any data into this field.

Here is an example of the code for a data-entry field:

```
<INPUT TYPE=TEXT NAME=COMPANY SIZE=25 MAXLENGTH=100 VALUE=(none)>
```

When the user has entered all the necessary information into a form, that data is still on the user's local computer—it hasn't reached the server yet.

Getting the Data Back to the Server

In a form, such as the one shown in Figure 9.7, the user clicks on the Submit button (labeled *Send* in the figure) to send the data back to the server. The browser collects at least two pieces of information about each control in the form: the name of the control and its current value.

For example, if a user entered **John Glanton's Arizona Tours** into the data-entry Name field, the browser would send back the following information:

```
COMPANY="John Glanton's Arizona Tours"
```

By naming each individual piece of data, the server can identify each piece of information it receives. Note that radio buttons are organized into named groups, so only one button in a group can be selected. The value of the selected button is returned for the named group.

The possibilities for what you do with that data once it comes back are wide open. Web servers usually have built-in form-handling tools that let you choose how incoming data should be manipulated; you could, for example:

- Format the data into a standard HTML page, and display it to the user to confirm what the reader has entered.
- Write the data to a database file in any of several file formats.
- Send the data to an e-mail address.
- Let the data trigger the display of another Web page, such as the home page of a company catalog that the user selected in the form.

Beyond using a server's built-in tools to handle the incoming data, programming work will be needed to create the necessary script or program to manipulate the data. For details, see Chapter 11, "Using Intranet Authoring and Management Tools," and for information on CGI scripts and other ways to transfer data to and from the server, see Chapter 10, "Adding Other Content to Your Intranet."

Looking at HTML and the Future

The amazing thing about the hypertext markup language, HTML, is that it seems to grow and change almost faster than people can incorporate it into their Web sites. Some other features you should investigate include the following:

- Scrolling marquees that display a band of scrolling text within a window in the browser. As of this writing, only the Microsoft browser, Internet Explorer, can display scrolling marquees. A similar effect can be created using a Java applet or JavaScript.
- Page background sounds that play when you access the page.
- Style sheets and cascading style sheets that give the layout of your intranet pages the same flexibility and consistency that styles give to your word-processing documents.
- Watermark background images that don't scroll with the page (at this time, only the Microsoft browser has this feature).
- Inline programs, such as Java or ActiveX, that allow intranet pages to "run" rather than just being viewed as a document. We'll be looking at both Java and ActiveX in Chapter 10, "Adding Other Content to Your Intranet."

Although the pressure to add new features to HTML is tremendous, the Web-related industry is also working hard to try to maintain standards in the midst of the ongoing revolution.

You now have some HTML basics (maybe more than you wanted!), and you're ready to move on to more advanced intranet content. Our next chapter will continue to help you create your intranet's content and increase its functionality.

Chapter 10

ADDING OTHER CONTENT TO YOUR INTRANET

FEATURING

- **Collaborating with a browser**
- **Using multimedia**
- **Using Acrobat on your intranet**
- **Extending HTML**
- **Programming for your intranet**

You want your intranet to be more than a static set of HTML pages—you want some zip and excitement that, at the same time, adds value to the content. In the last chapter, we took you on a quick tour of HTML and showed you how you can use HTML tags to prepare the content for your intranet. We covered both text and graphics and looked at linking to other HTML pages and at how to use imagemaps. In this chapter, we'll look at livening up your intranet pages by adding sound, video, and Adobe Acrobat files.

The HTML pages we looked at in the last chapter are essentially static in the sense that they pass information from the server to the browser. In this chapter, we'll look at several ways you can pass information in the other direction, from the browser (or in other words, from the user) back to the server, and we'll take a brief look at the programming techniques you can use to access that data once it gets to the server, including Common Gateway Interface programming as well as the two major APIs—NSAPI from Netscape and ISAPI from Microsoft.

One of the most interesting technical debates that will continue into the foreseeable future is the debate between Sun Microsystems and Microsoft over Sun's Java Programming Language and Microsoft's ActiveX technologies. The former is an open approach to the problem, while the latter, so far at least (although there are signs that things are changing here) is a more proprietary and closed approach. We'll take a look at all the components in this debate later in this chapter.

> **TIP**
>
> Be careful to evaluate all this technology in the same way you would any other new business strategy. The arguments that "because it's cool" and "because we can" are not sufficient reasons to chase after every single advance. Ask the same questions you always ask: What's the payoff? What's the return on this investment? What benefit will my users see and at what cost? And be prepared to leave out some of the "cool stuff" if you don't perceive a quantifiable benefit for your company.

Some of the most cost-effective advances will be in those areas that facilitate communications between the Web server and the corporate database. The large database developers have a long, long lead over Web server developers and aren't likely to be caught. Look for advances from companies such as Oracle, Sybase, and the like, in the areas of SQL (Structured Query Language), communications, and OLTP (online transaction processing). Much of the technology we take for granted is still in its infancy, and changes that seem imminent may in fact be several years in the future. But no matter what you call it, change is coming.

Collaborating with a Browser

Are you fed up with running around trying to organize people to attend face-to-face meetings? Or trying to get the production manager to go over the schedule with the sales rep in San Francisco? It's not easy to get everyone in the same place at the same time. With some of the collaboration tools available for use on your intranet using standard browsers, people can stay at their desks and participate; they don't have to all be in the same place at the same time.

To this end, several collaborative technologies for intranet users are emerging—including text-based conferencing, video conferencing, and whiteboard (or chalkboard) applications—in which several participants can work on the same project at the same time, and everyone can immediately see the effects of changes made by one member of the group. Most of the packages support basic drawing tools, including pen, underline, and annotation tools, and some allow you to show other participants the output from another application running on your system. One program even lets you pass control of an application running on your machine to another conference participant. On many of these applications, a status line at the bottom of the screen displays the names of the participants.

Administrative utilities accessible from within a Web browser allow system administrators to create conferences, establish access controls and security options, and add or remove users from the conferencing system.

Let's take a look at two popular conferencing applications: NetMeeting and CoolTalk.

NetMeeting versus CoolTalk

The recently released NetMeeting conferencing application from Microsoft is a business-oriented collaboration application that allows several people working in different locations to collaborate simultaneously on the same project, using any Microsoft-compatible program to edit documents. NetMeeting can also support audio conferencing over the Internet.

Microsoft NetMeeting supports the rapidly emerging International Telecommunications Union (ITU) T.120 multiuser–data-conferencing standard, which is also supported by collaboration products from at least 20 other companies. Participation in all the CoolTalk modules is, however, limited to two people.

Netscape's CoolTalk is a consumer-level Internet phone application, supported by several other smaller collaboration applications, including a clever answering machine. This answering machine will be of limited appeal to Internet users because the connection must be open for the answering machine to work, but intranet users may find it useful. CoolTalk supports Netscape's own Internet Interactive Collaboration Environment (IICE).

Both applications offer different compression techniques for use with communication links capable of different speeds. They also provide whiteboard and chat functions, but only NetMeeting allows application sharing and provides a file-transfer function. You and your coworkers can now collaborate on a sales document in Word, work together on your expense report spreadsheet in Excel, or prepare a presentation in PowerPoint. Here's how it works.

As the host of the session, you click on the Share icon, and select which application you want to share. This sends a copy of the application's screen image to all participants in the conference, and all the other remote users have access to the application's tools and any documents that you have open.

Initially, the NetMeeting session defaults to a work-alone mode that allows remote users to look at but not control the application or change the document. Once the host of the session changes into collaboration mode, anyone can take control of the application by clicking on the program's image. This means a remote user can use any of the program's functions, including Delete, Save As, and Exit. NetMeeting shows you who is in charge by placing that person's initials next to the mouse cursor.

Whiteboard functions in both programs are similar to basic image-editing applications, with additional features so you can transmit drawings, images, and annotations to the other party or parties in your group in real time. In CoolTalk, you have to use a single page of 640-by-480, whereas NetMeeting lets you use multiple, much larger pages. NetMeeting also lets you edit your comments by maintaining the images separately from the added annotations; in CoolTalk you can erase but not edit your comments. Figure 10.1 shows a CoolTalk whiteboard session in progress.

FIGURE 10.1: A CoolTalk whiteboard session

Advances in Multimedia

As we said in the introduction to this chapter, the HTML pages we looked at in the last chapter are somewhat static, and by incorporating sound, animation, and video into your intranet content, you can do a lot in terms of adding interest and a certain amount of value to your pages. Just imagine the applications—a video of the company president's speech to shareholders at the annual meeting, a demonstration of a new product either for a customer presentation or as a training tool, or an animated sequence that explains how to assemble a product in the manufacturing department.

You'll be hearing a lot about using multimedia on your intranet site as more and more audio, animation, and video technologies converge to constitute a toolkit of genuinely useful products. One of the continuing problems is that of available network *bandwidth;* multimedia applications can generate large files that simply gobble up bandwidth. Here are two common approaches to this problem:

- *Encapsulated multimedia* consists of the appropriate data segments in a file that is transferred as a single large entity and "played" after the download is complete. This approach is becoming less and less popular.
- *Live multimedia* consists of the data streams sent over the network that can be "played" in real time so the person using the browser can interact with the data stream. Most current products use this approach.

Live multimedia components are often called *streaming* or *continuous-delivery* audio and video to differentiate them from encapsulated multimedia. We'll look at these two technologies in a moment, and we'll look at some experimental aspects of this kind of data transmission. But we'll begin with a quick look at how you can assess the case for using multimedia on your intranet site in the first place.

Using Multimedia on Your Web Site

As with any new technology, you want to carefully evaluate the return on your intranet site investment. Therefore, before describing these multimedia technologies in detail, ask yourself a few questions about what you hope to achieve by using audio or video on your intranet site:

- Why are you providing a multimedia service? What are you trying to accomplish? Is there some specific part of the message you want to get across that can only be presented using audio or video, or could you use some other, less intensive method?

- What is the value to your company of a multimedia presentation, and how will you quantify the returns on this investment?
- What is the value to your customers of a multimedia presentation? Can they access your site using a communications link that is fast enough to get the benefits, or will they just find it enormously frustrating as they wait, and wait, and wait?
- Can you condense the message you want to get across to one simple but direct statement and use multimedia to enhance that message while leaving the rest of your intranet as a more traditional combination of text and graphics?
- How soon do you need to add this element to your Web site?
- What will the consequences be for the current server hardware and software? Do you need to upgrade the client computers out there on the network, or do they all have sufficient processing horsepower, and do they all have sound cards and the appropriate video monitors? If you do have to upgrade, what is the anticipated cost, and how do you weigh that cost against the benefit you perceive?

Remember that other essential services must always continue to receive support and bandwidth.

Evaluating Transmission Mechanisms: TCP, UDP, and IP Multicasting

The TCP/IP family of protocols was originally designed to deliver files over the network reliably, but with some measure of allowable delay and so are generally unsuitable for applications that require continuous real-time data. For streaming audio or streaming video to work, compromises have to be made in the transmission mechanism. Currently, three mechanisms are in use: TCP, UDP, and IP multicasting.

NOTE   Most corporate firewalls will pass TCP-transported information, but some will not pass information transported by UDP. This is not a security issue, but it may have an impact on your ability to receive information from beyond the firewall.

TCP

TCP (*Transmission Control Protocol*) is probably the most common protocol in use. It's used to transmit large packets of information and to guarantee delivery of those packets. TCP also includes flow-control mechanisms that ensure it doesn't saturate the communications link.

A drawback from the audio-video point of view is that TCP retransmits a packet that is lost. This introduces a gap in the data, which is quite noticeable and which usually interrupts playback until the errant packet is retransmitted and received successfully. Even with these concerns, TCP is a good all-purpose solution to transmitting audio-video data over an intranet. (For much more on TCP, see Appendix B, "Intranet Protocols—TCP/IP.")

UDP

UDP (*User Datagram Protocol*) is a maintenance protocol that can transmit a large number of small packets very quickly at a high priority but that cannot guarantee packet delivery. The receiving application must manage this potential for dropped packets in some way. Using UDP in this way can also saturate communication links; therefore, don't use it without some flow-control mechanism to manage the link. User Datagram Protocol is well suited to transitory applications, such as Internet phones.

IP Multicasting

In IP (*Internet Protocol*) multicasting, a host group is created, and all members of the groups receive every IP datagram. Membership is dynamic. You join that group when you start receiving audio-video data, and you leave the group when you stop. IP multicasting is a good solution when you need to send the same audio-video information simultaneously to a group of people.

Creating the Files

The steps you take to prepare audio, animation, or video for transmission are essentially the same. We'll just discuss the steps in general terms; refer to your specific multimedia application for details:

1. Digitize or convert the audio or video source to an electronic file using a sound card, a video frame grabber, or both. Given that much of the processing still to be done to these raw data files will result in a loss of quality, do as much as you can to capture the cleanest signal possible.

2. Encode and compress the raw data. Each type of technology uses a different lossy compression algorithm, and the more you squeeze the data down into smaller and smaller files, the more distortion appears as the quality degrades.

3. Code the appropriate HTML tags into your intranet page so browsers can find the encoded files on your server.

4. Load the multimedia files onto your server. The server registers the filename extension as a MIME type.

TIP   You must download and install the appropriate plug-in application or browser before trying to play a file. All the encoding technologies are slightly different, so be sure you get the right one. We'll look at some of the multimedia plug-ins in a moment; for extensive detail on all sorts of plug-ins, see `http://www.microsoft.com` and `http://www.netscape.com` for the latest plug-ins available.

Now when you select a media link, your browser sends a message to the server; the server returns a token file that tells your browser which add-in application (player or viewer) to open. Once this application is running, it sends a request to the server, which transmits the file to the player; after a few seconds wait as the file is buffered, playback begins.

Streaming Audio

The main bottleneck in receiving audio information is the capacity of the communications link between the browser and the server. This is less of a concern if you have a direct network connection, but if you usually dial in using a modem and telephone line, the connection type assumes a larger significance. This is where streaming audio comes in.

Streaming audio not only allows a browser or add-in application to play the file as it arrives, but with it, you (the user) can manipulate the data by fast forwarding, rewinding, or pausing the data stream. You can also search for a specific packet of data. Prerecorded data can be compressed before it's sent, something that's all but impossible to do with live audio. Audio data can be stored in a variety of different file formats, including AU, RA, or WAV files.

Table 10.1 lists some common connection types and indicates the quality of audio you might expect.

Table 10.1: Connection Types and Sound Quality

Connection Type	Speed	Audio Quality
Dial-up modem	9.6 to 14.4Kbps	8kHz (mono or AM radio)
Dial-up modem	28.8Kbps	16 or 22kHz (mono)
Frame Relay/ISDN	56 to 64Kbps	16 or 22kHz (stereo) or 44kHz (mono)
ISDN	128Kbps	44kHz (stereo)
T1	1.544Mbps	VHS quality stereo

Streaming audio products for your intranet are available from a variety of sources, as Table 10.2 shows, and in many cases, you'll find that the player application or browser plug-in is free and that there is a charge just for the application used to create or edit the audio files themselves.

Table 10.2: Some Streaming Audio Products

Product	Company	URL
Crescendo	LiveUpdate	`http://www.liveupdate.com/`
Internet Wave	VocalTec	`http://www.vocaltec.com/`
RealAudio	Progressive Networks	`http://www.realaudio.com/`
StreamWorks	Xing Technology	`http://www.xingtech.com/`
ToolVox for the Web	VoxWare	`http://www.voxware.com/`
TrueSpeech	The DSP Group	`http://www.dspg.com/`

TrueSpeech and Windows 95

The DSP Group's TrueSpeech product is an excellent choice for small sites for several reasons—the most obvious being if you have Windows 95, you already have their encoder; it's a licensed component of the Windows 95 Sound Recorder.

TrueSpeech is a data compression technology used in a wide range of products, including digital answering machines, telephones, and dual simultaneous voice/data modems.

In 1994, the DSP Group licensed their TrueSpeech 8.5 algorithm to Microsoft for inclusion in Windows 95. This version provides a compression ratio of up to 15:1. Or, in other words, it can reduce a MHz 16-bit audio stream to approximately 8.5 kilobits per second—just right for real-time playback on a 486 or Pentium system.

Streaming Video

Streaming video places demands on the server that are more stringent than those of any other Web content. Consequently, its development is a little behind that of streaming audio. There are currently two slightly different approaches to streaming video:

- *Stand-alone video players* let you preview the video clips as they arrive on your system, and then let you replay them at your convenience. They're typically packaged as Netscape plug-ins or as ActiveX controls (we'll be looking at ActiveX controls later in this chapter) that you install on your browser. Stand-alone video players work with a wide variety of standard digital video file formats, including AVI, MOV, and MPEG.

- *Client-server video players* use special software on the server to transmit highly compressed digital video, and they require that you install a special player on the client for viewing. These systems provide broadcast streaming video for viewing in real time. Because these server products assume that a significant portion of the data will be lost in transit, you can't save the file for later.

Products are available from several sources, some of them are shown in Table 10.3.

Table 10.3: Streaming Video Products

Product	Company	URL
CineWeb	Digigami	`http://www.digigami.com/`
ClearVideo	Iterated Systems	`http://www.iterated.com/`
InterVU MPEG Player	InterVU	`http://intervu.com/`
Streaming Videogram	Alaris	`http://www.alaris.com/`
StreamWorks	Xing Technologies	`http://www.xingtech.com/`
VDO Live Video Player	VDOnet	`http://vdo.net`
VivoActive Player	Vivo Software	`http://vivo.com/`
Vosaic Browser	Vosaic	`http://www.vosaic.com/`

StreamWorks from Xing Technology Inc., and VDOLive from VDOnet Corporation are the current leaders in this emerging technology; Vosaic is not far behind.

MBONE Explained

MBONE, the abbreviation for *multicast backbone,* is an experimental technology used to transmit digital video over the Internet. Even at relatively modest data-sampling rates, a video broadcast can easily saturate an ISDN circuit or a fractional T1 link, so imagine the likely effects on the owner of a 14.4Kbps modem.

MBONE requires the creation of another Internet backbone service using special hardware and software to accommodate the high data-rate transmissions needed for digital video. For some time, MBONE has been used to transmit concerts and conferences to a limited number of people.

The Internet protocol committees are currently working to add support for broadcast modes to the next version of IP (known as IPng). Support for multimedia and multicasting is seen as a key requirement for this new protocol.

Two other World Wide Web sites of interest are MPEG Plaza, an easy-to-navigate collection of MPEG products, services, and technical information. Check out

`http://www.visiblelight.com/mpeg/`

TB's Video Site also contains a great collection of links to all the best video-related World Wide Web Sites at

`http://www.plantaganet.com/tbvideo`

Streaming Animation

It seems that there are even fewer choices in the world of animation. Narrative Communications, a company founded by former Lotus Development Corporation technologist John Landry, has created a system for those interested in publishing a large quantity of CD-quality multimedia material. The Enliven package includes a free plug-in viewer (which works as a Netscape Navigator plug-in or as a Microsoft Internet Explorer ActiveX control), the Enliven Producer authoring tool, and the Enliven server software. Find out more at

`http://www.narrative.com`

Using the FutureSplash Player plug-in, you can view animations created by the FutureSplash Animator from FutureWave Software, Inc. One of the Animator's most notable features is that you can create interactive elements without doing any pro-gramming at all. Visit their Web site at

`http://www.futurewave.com/`

And finally, Sizzler, from Totally Hip Software, a plug-in player for Navigator and Internet Explorer lets you play real-time interactive multimedia and animation. A con-version tool allows you to convert existing animation files into the Sizzler format. Check them out at

`http://www.totallyhip.com/`

Putting It All Together with Shockwave

Shockwave for Director from Macromedia is a plug-in that plays Macromedia Director files downloaded from the network. But it's also much more. It's a multimedia development environment for the creative professional who doesn't want to spend time leaning how to program, but who just wants to make stuff happen. And stuff will happen, too; your intranet pages will come alive with sound, animation, video, and perhaps most important of all, you can interact with your users.

There are three steps to the process:

1. Create a Macromedia Director file using one of the authoring tools; you'll hear more about them in a moment.

2. Compress, or "shock," the Director files using the postprocessor Afterburner. Shockwave doesn't use a lossy compression method to shrink the files, so the file you see in your browser is exactly the same as the file originally created by the authoring tool. On one hand, there is none of the loss in quality associated with such compression methods, but on the other, Shockwave files tend to be on the large side.

3. Use the Shockwave plug-in to retrieve the file, decompress the contents on the fly, and view the result. Playback is seamless, so Shockwave elements appear as an integral part of your HTML page.

This plug-in is available free from

`http://www.macromedia.com/shockwave/`

Macromedia offers three Shockwave-enabled authoring tools:

Director   An application used to create movies you can deliver over an intranet. Director employs a film-making metaphor; you assemble your cast of multimedia elements on the stage (or screen) using a powerful scripting language called *Lingo*. A multichannel score manages sounds, color palettes, text, video, scripts, animation, and sprites.

Authorware   An application aimed at intranet developers and used to create interactive multimedia. It features large file-streaming on demand, asynchronous preloading of data before it's needed, icon-driven scripting control, and data-measurement functions you can use to send data back to the server for storage and analysis. When you create an Authorware segment using Afterburner, the segment is compressed and divided into pieces. As the segment is played in the browser, the separate pieces are downloaded to the client computer only as they're needed.

Freehand   A high-end–vector-graphics drawing program that you can use to embed graphics into your HTML pages. Freehand includes several impressive tools to create a link out of anything on an HTML page by drawing an irregularly shaped hotspot.

Shockwave is not currently a true streaming technology, which means the whole file is normally downloaded before viewing can begin.

Using Acrobat on Your Intranet

Adobe's Acrobat can add a different kind of information to your intranet. Acrobat allows you to store and display your documents with the same formatting and page-layout control that you'd expect from a desktop publishing package like FrameMaker or QuarkXPress. Like HTML pages, Acrobat documents can contain hypertext links to other parts of a page, other pages in the same file or another completely separate file, including URLs. Also, like HTML pages, Acrobat files are readable on most computing systems, including Macintosh, HP-UX, Windows 3.*x*, Windows 95, Windows NT, OS/2, SunOS, AIX, Linux, and Sun Solaris. A free Acrobat Reader is available for all listed platforms that will allow you to view the files after you've downloaded them. If you're using IE or Netscape, you can also view the files directly in your browser using either a Netscape plug-in or an IE ActiveX control.

TIP

Find out more about the system requirements and availability of Acrobat or download a copy of the free Acrobat Reader from Adobe's Web site at `http://www.adobe.com/Acrobat/`. Two other good Acrobat-information sites are *Acropolis: The Magazine of Acrobat Publishing* at `http://plaza.interport.net/acropolis/` and Emerge, a resource for Acrobat information at `http://www.emrg.com/`. For an interesting example of Acrobat on the Web, see Project Cool: The Acrobat Developer Zone at `http://www.projectcool.com/developer/acrobat/`. Both `http://www.dev-null.com/dn-pdf.html` and `http://www.best.com:80/~dglazer/adobe/` have some great examples of dynamic Acrobat forms.

On your intranet, you can use Acrobat documents to replace paper versions of human resource forms, marketing brochures, and software manuals. You can also use

Acrobat to create interactive online forms, much like HTML forms. Like sound or video, Acrobat files can be streamed from your server to a browser to speed the download of the file. Files may also be downloaded and opened later or kept for reference.

Acrobat or HTML?

Acrobat is an extra tool in your intranet's toolbox. It isn't a replacement for HTML, but it does function in some similar ways, making it tricky to decide when to use Acrobat and when to use HTML. In general, if a precise layout or "look" of a document is an integral part of its function, then choose Acrobat. If the information or content is the prime reason for the document existing on your intranet and the presentation is secondary, choose HTML. Even with streaming technology, sending a plain-text HTML file is faster than sending a binary Acrobat file over your intranet.

Acrobat files use the *Portable Document Format* (PDF). PDF is based on PostScript, Adobe's page-description language. The PDF format includes compression, allowing complex, graphic-intensive files to remain relatively small. For example, an 800+ page manual we printed to a PostScript file was about 55MB. After we converted it to PDF, the file was about 11MB. Of course, most documents on your intranet will probably be smaller.

So how to you use Acrobat documents? The simplest way is to just add a link to them using the HTML <ANCHOR> tag:

```
<A HREF="/PDFs/MyDocument.pdf">My Acrobat Document</A>
```

Acrobat files may also be incorporated directly into an HTML page by using the <EMBED> tag. Think of the <EMBED> tag as a generic version of the <IMG> tags that allow you to embed images into HTML. If you've embedded an Acrobat file into an HTML page, your browser can display the Acrobat file as an integrated part of the page. Figure 10.2 shows you an example of how that looks.

If you were to click on a link within the displayed Acrobat document, you'd move through it using your browser, just as if you had opened it using the Acrobat Reader. Currently Netscape also allows you to open the file directly in the browser by double-clicking on the embedded file.

Creating Acrobat Documents

You can create Acrobat documents in three ways:
- Printing to PDF
- Capturing in PDF format
- Distilling PostScript files

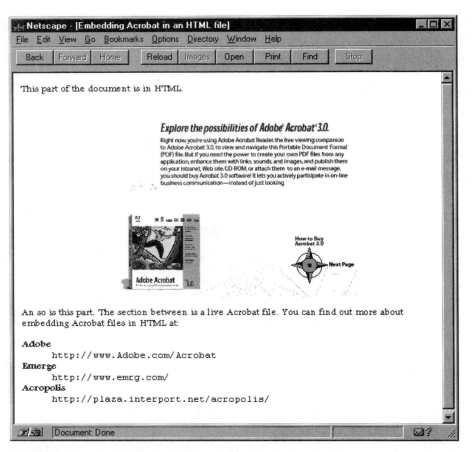

This part of the document is in HTML.

Explore the possibilities of Adobe® Acrobat® 3.0.

Right now, you're using Adobe Acrobat Reader, the free viewing companion to Adobe Acrobat 3.0, to view and navigate this Portable Document Format (PDF) file. But if you need the power to create your own PDF files from any application, enhance them with links, sounds, and images, and publish them on your intranet, Web site, CD-ROM, or attach them to an e-mail message, you should buy Acrobat 3.0 software! It lets you actively participate in on-line business communication—instead of just looking.

Adobe Acrobat 3.0

How to Buy Acrobat 3.0

Next Page

An so is this part. The section between is a live Acrobat file. You can find out more about embedding Acrobat files in HTML at:

Adobe
        http://www.Adobe.com/Acrobat
Emerge
        http://www.emrg.com/
Acropolis
        http://plaza.interport.net/acropolis/

FIGURE 10.2: An HTML page with an embedded Acrobat document

To create files, you'll need to purchase a copy of Acrobat 3—the free Reader only allows you to view, navigate, and print PDF files. Once Acrobat is installed, you'll have a new print option to print to a PDF file. This allows you to create PDF files quickly, although the quality can be lower than using the other methods. Use the PDF writer if you're converting fairly simple pages that you want in PDF, so they'll match the rest of the sites' files. For example, your marketing area may have high-concept brochures in PDF format and may want their less-complex product fact sheets in PDF, so users get every document from them in the same format.

> **WARNING**
>
> The Acrobat family includes several applications with similar names: Acrobat Reader, Acrobat (also called Exchange), Distiller, and Capture. Acrobat utilities include the PDF Writer, Scan, Capture plug-in, and Touch-up. This may lead to some confusion as you decide what you need for your intranet. Only the Reader is free. To create files, you'll need at least Acrobat or Capture. See Adobe's Web site at `http://www.adobe.com/Acrobat/main.html` for a complete description of each Acrobat package.

If your documents contain EPS images or are fairly complex, use Acrobat's Distiller program to create your PDF files. To do this, simply print to a PostScript file from your authoring tool. Start Distiller and open the file. Distiller then converts that PostScript file to PDF format. Distiller can also be configured to watch directories on your network and automatically distill PostScript files that you put there.

If your site contains documents that come from paper-only sources, you'll use Acrobat Capture to move the information from paper to PDF using a scanner. A Capture plug-in ships with Acrobat, but you can also purchase a full-featured, stand-alone Capture program that gives you more control over your PDF scans. The Capture plug-in is to Capture as the PDF Writer is to Distiller. For basic operations it works beautifully.

Acrobat is a great way to extend the capabilities of your intranet to deliver graphically rich documents that complement your other intranet functionality, such as video and sound. However, HTML itself is "extending" to add new functionality. Unfortunately these extensions are often part of "the browser wars" that Netscape and Microsoft wage. Let's look at some of those issues next.

Extensions to HTML

Extensions to HTML are being proposed all the time to add the new features that Web page designers think they need. As this process continues, it's becoming more and more evident that HTML is moving away from describing the structure of a document, which was the original intention behind its design, and is moving toward being a page-description language.

And despite all the talk of standards, there are still subtle differences in the way that certain HTML tags are displayed in the two front-running browsers, Netscape Navigator and Microsoft's Internet Explorer. We'll explore those differences in this next section and then go on to look at Microsoft's implementation of Cascading Style Sheets (CSS).

What's So Standard about That?

There's no doubt about it—both Netscape Navigator and Internet Explorer do a good job of displaying a basic HTML page, but the Internet Explorer seems to have an edge when it comes to displaying some of the newer and more advanced HTML features.

Both browsers support frames, which let multiple panes of information appear in a single browser screen, but in subtly different ways. Navigator recognizes attributes that define the thickness and color of the frame border, while Internet Explorer supports the advanced concept of floating frames that can appear anywhere on the HTML page.

Both browsers support tables, including multiple columns and rows, borders, nested tables, and cell background colors, but Microsoft is closer to supporting the World Wide Web Consortium (W3C) RFC 1942, the proposal likely to be accepted as the formal definition of tables. Internet Explorer can draw different types of borders between cells in a table and can place background images in table cells. Some of these features may seem a little esoteric, but they're bound to have an impact on any data displayed in tables, such as financial spreadsheets and general ledger entries.

Navigator's < MULTICOL> tag flows text into multiple columns automatically, with adjustable column width and column spacing. In the past HTML designers have simulated columns using tables, which has always been an uneasy compromise. Their <SPACER> tag allows you to insert either horizontal or vertical white space of a specified number of pixels.

On the graphics front, both browsers can manage the basic graphic formats, including JPEG, GIF, and so on, but Navigator supports the LOWSRC attribute to the <IMG> tag, which lets you specify a low-resolution preview version of an image that loads before the complete image. On the other hand, Internet Explorer supports the DYNSRC attribute that loads an AVI animation rather than a simple static graphic. Internet Explorer also allows for built-in MPEG playback, while Navigator does not.

Both Navigator and Internet Explorer allow background graphics, but only Internet Explorer supports watermarks or nonscrolling backgrounds, a built-in marquee that can generate scrolling text, and horizontal rules of different colors. And, of course, Internet Explorer supports Cascading Style Sheets too.

Internet Explorer and Cascading Style Sheets

As we've mentioned previously, HTML defines the structure of a document and not the details of its presentation; the details are left to the browser. Then along came a draft proposal from the World Wide Web Consortium (W3C) for Cascading Style Sheets (CSS) to give HTML designers an unprecedented level of control over typography and the appearance of their pages. Microsoft implemented a version of CSS Level 1 in the Internet Explorer.

CSS Level 1 brings a complete set of typographical controls to HTML. You can specify paragraph margins (top, bottom, left, and right), indention, line spacing, text highlighting, even different fonts. All this means the designer can now create precise margins, use different font styles, and specify amounts of white space around graphical elements and text, along with other desktop-publishing-like controls.

CSS uses rules to define the presentation of an HTML page; a rule can be as simple as

```
H1 {color : green}
```

where `H1` is any HTML element acting as a selector, and `{color : green}` is the declaration. The declaration has two parts, a property (`color`) and a value (`green`). There are about 35 properties, including font properties, color and background properties, text properties, box properties, and classification properties, and they can be specified in a variety of ways. In addition to this new level of control, CSS gives designers two important new features:

- The ability to create display elements in HTML that previously required a bulky GIF file.
- The ability to separate style information from the HTML document, making updates easier and the site much easier to maintain. Multiple HTML pages or even a complete site can use a single style sheet, so changes in that style sheet will ripple across every page on your intranet.

If you're careful, you can design HTML pages with style sheets in such a way that they are transparent to browsers that don't yet support them, so you don't need two sets of HTML pages, one with and one without style sheets.

How to Invoke a Cascading Style Sheet

You can invoke CSS from within an HTML document in different ways, depending on the needs of your intranet. Let's take a quick look at the HTML used to invoke CSS:

```
<HTML>
<HEAD>
<TITLE>Title</TITLE>
<LINK REL=STYLESHEET TYPE="text/css"
      HREF="URL" TITLE="Fab">
<STYLE TYPE="text/css">
@import url;
H1 {color : blue}
</STYLE>
</HEAD>
<BODY>
<P STYLE="color:green">
</BODY>
</HTML>
```

Here we have four ways of invoking style sheets:
1. A `<LINK>` element to link to an external file containing a style sheet
2. A `<STYLE>` element inside the `<HEAD>` tag
3. An imported style sheet using the CSS `@import` notation
4. A `<STYLE>` attribute on an element inside the `<BODY>` tags

To review the official W3C working draft for Cascading Style Sheets, go to
`http://www.w3.org`
and for other resources try
`http://www.w3.org/pub/WWW/Style/`

To review a recent article from *Websmith*, along with an easy-to-read description of CSS and some examples, see
`http://www.smithing.com/issues/i3/ws51.html`

And finally, you might visit these two sites for Microsoft's version of the CSS story:

`http://www.microsoft.com/truetype/css/intro.htm`

`http://www.microsoft.com/workshop/author/howto/css-f.htm`

A Brief Introduction to Intranet Programming

So far we've looked at how to publish mostly static information on a Web site, but how do you create truly interactive applications for your intranet? Fortunately, there are several answers to that question. You can write *scripts*, or external programs, using almost any 32-bit programming language, such as Perl, the C or C++ programming languages, or Windows CGI, Pascal, REXX, or Visual Basic. You can also use NT batch files, although we don't recommend it. You just have to make sure that you use one of the standard server interfaces:

- CGI (*Common Gateway Interface*) is the traditional definition of how server and browser interact. Despite what you might hear, CGI is not a programming language, but a definition of how servers and browsers communicate. A CGI script is simply a script that conforms to this CGI standard.
- NSAPI (Netscape Server API) from Netscape and ISAPI (Internet Server API) from Microsoft are two programming interfaces available as an alternative to using CGI.

While an extensive discussion of intranet programming is beyond the scope of this book, let's take a quick look at these two interfaces.

> **NOTE**   For more on programming and using CGI and APIs, see *Mastering Intranets* by Pat Coleman and Peter Dyson, available from Sybex.

CGI Programming

The term *script* originates in the Unix world, where it describes programs written in and interpreted by one of the Unix shells. Scripts are external programs that the Web server runs in response to a request from the browser. When a visitor requests a URL that points to a script, the server executes it, and any output that the script creates is sent back to the browser for display. Figure 10.3 shows the basic information flow.

FIGURE 10.3: Information flow through the CGI or API interfaces

You can use a script for tasks as varied as creating an interface to a relational database system, to your own search engine, to anything in between—there are really very few limits. CGI also allows the server to create new documents on the fly—that is, at the moment the browser requests them.

The truly major benefit of using CGI is that any CGI-compliant script will run on any CGI-compliant Web server (and most of them are), and that simple fact can save you a whole lot of time. There is a good chance that someone somewhere has already solved a problem similar to yours and created a CGI script to do it. He or she may well have posted the solution on one of the many Web sites that carry lots of CGI scripts. Start your search at one of these sites:

```
http://hoohoo.ncsa.uiuc.edu/cgi/
http://www.boutell.com/cgic/
```

Bear in mind that much of the early work with CGI scripts was done in a Unix environment. If you've decided on a Unix server for your intranet, you shouldn't have any problems. Some of the scripts might work on Windows NT, others almost certainly won't. Always check first before you run anything on your own system. A disadvantage of using CGI is that scripts can be inefficient and can slow server performance in some cases.

A Few Words of Warning

You can use many sources to find CGI scripts that have already been written and debugged. But if you do download a CGI script from one of these sources, don't assume the script is harmless and ready for use. Writing CGI scripts is not particularly easy, and writing secure scripts is a job for the experts.

All sorts of things can happen; some programmers add back doors in the scripts to ease the problems of debugging the script and then forget to take them out when the script is finished. This is particularly important if your intranet maintains outside connections to the Internet. You may think that you have just installed a nifty utility that will save you hours of work, when, in reality, you have just installed an open door to your system. You should always test shareware or freeware thoroughly on an offline system *before* installing it on one of your online intranet servers.

The problem is not really in CGI itself, but in the power that it gives to script writers, who may be system administrators or users. There are really two main areas at risk:

- The accidental disclosure of confidential information, such as passwords or registry files
- The potential for fooling or spoofing the CGI script into doing something you had not anticipated, such as executing system commands

Fortunately, there are several things you can do on your intranet to minimize any risk from CGI:

- Locate all your CGI scripts in the same directory on the server, and be sure the Webmaster is the only person with write permission for that directory.
- Never, ever, trust input data from a user. If your script manages information that a user has entered into a form, don't make assumptions about any data you receive. Even though you have asked someone to enter his or her zip code in the form, don't assume that the field will actually contain numbers—you can never predict what a user will enter. Always scan for nonalphanumeric characters and throw them away before you process the input. This can go a long way toward keeping your system safe.
- Consider using a compiled executable program with NSAPI or ISAPI to do the job instead of using CGI. Besides security, another benefit to this solution is that programs written to these APIs are compiled and execute faster than the same function written as a CGI script.

If your users ask that they be allowed to write their own CGI scripts, carefully consider the management problems of tracking a changing list of CGI scripts. And besides that, do you really want users writing programs to run on the server? Probably not. If you feel that using CGI scripts poses a security problem on your server, revisit Chapter 6, "Planning Your Intranet's Security," for more ideas on how you can manage potential security threats.

Programming with the Netscape and Microsoft APIs

Aside from the security and other risks we looked at in the last section, there are other drawbacks to using CGI scripts; they offer poor scalabililty and low efficiency. Each instance of a CGI script runs in its own address and process space, not in the Web server space. This means that a new copy of the script is run each time it's called, with a new address space and a new process. In some cases, when the script actually does very little, system overhead becomes a significant portion of the total script running time.

The newer generation of Web servers promise to increase the flexibility and add new functions to the server side by using proprietary APIs, such as NSAPI (Netscape Server API) from Netscape and ISAPI (Internet Server API). Using this sort of approach over the conventional CGI approach has several advantages, including:

- APIs can be more efficient in their use of memory because initialization occurs only once.
- APIs let a server application stay connected to the Web browser without losing important information. In CGI scripting, the browser disconnects from the server after each request and has no memory of any previous transactions between browser and server.
- APIs let you plug in custom applications, such as user authentication routines or database logging applications.

The major disadvantage to using an API is that it's bound to a specific server or group of servers; whereas CGI scripts are, in theory at least, portable to any environment. The APIs are definitely aimed squarely at professional programmers and usually require a detailed knowledge of the C programming language.

Netscape's NSAPI

Netscape's NSAPI is not easy to summarize; it's a large, complex, proprietary API, closely tied to the server setup. Each NSAPI function has to be configured in the Netsite Object Configuration database. A detailed description of how to use NSAPI is beyond the scope of this book, but if you're interested, you'll find lots more information on NSAPI at

```
http://www.netscape.com/newsref/std/server_api.html
```

Microsoft's ISAPI

Microsoft's ISAPI is a new API released with the Internet Information Server that was jointly developed by Process Software, creators of the Purveyor IntraServer and other intranet and Internet software products. ISAPI is also proprietary and is only available on Microsoft and Process Software products. For details of how to use this API, see Microsoft's World Wide Web site, contact the Microsoft Developer's Network (MSDN), or see the BackOffice Software Development Kit (SDK) and look for details on how to access the BackOffice series of products from this interface. Check out

```
http://www.microsoft.com/intdev/
```

NOTE To help convince software developers that ISAPI is the way to go, Microsoft plans to provide a simple wrapper for ISAPI applications that will make them CGI-compliant. That way, software developers can have their cake and eat it too.

Undoubtedly, the increasing use of these APIs will lead to the addition of new functions to the current stock of server software as third-party software developers create new applications to improve performance and add security and logging functions currently not available.

In the next section, we'll look at another comparative newcomer on the scene, the Java programming language developed by researchers at Sun Microsystems, and we'll show you how it has a completely different focus from these inward-looking APIs.

The Sun Shines on Java

Java is a serious programming language originally developed by Sun Microsystems (and not just a source of bad coffee-related jokes). With Java, you can create absolutely any kind of software imaginable that will work across the Internet. What this means to most users is that instead of browsing from site to site, you can now think of the Web as a giant hard disk that contains all the applications you could ever want. Java has the power to add dynamic, interactive content to your Web pages, sending static HTML pages the way of the dinosaurs.

Microsoft's Internet strategy, like that of many companies, has always been to try to impose its own standards on the rest of the industry, and this has usually been done by locking the customer into the set of Microsoft products. Sun, on the other hand, comes from the Unix world, where standards are traditionally much more open. Sun is trying to build Java into a broad, acceptable alternative to several Microsoft initiatives.

Microsoft may bundle products, and sometimes give products away as free promotions, but it would never have distributed Java in the way that Sun has done.

Almost all the popular Web browsers now support Java, and a small group of Java developers have created animated and interactive Web sites. Sun maintains that if you can write an application in C++ (and you can write almost any application in C++), you can write that same application in Java and distribute it across the Web.

Why Java Is So Important

But what is all the fuss about? Why, exactly, is Java so important? To answer this question, we need to take a step back and look at how the elements of the client-server relationship between Web browser and Web server have changed. In the beginning, a Web browser was able to access all kinds of information coded in HTML, but it was a one-way street; there wasn't any interaction between the user and the server. Users couldn't change anything on the HTML page or interact with the server.

Then along came the Common Gateway Interface (CGI), which allows for somewhat limited interaction, but is too clumsy for complex, real-time application programming.

The Java Programming Language (to use its full name) represents the third stage. Java allows complex and secure remote interaction in real time over mixed networks. It also runs on all major platforms. And that makes Java's potential in distributed computing simply enormous.

Using Java Applets

Java requires a multithreaded operating system, which means that Windows 95 and NT are in and that Windows 3.1 is definitely out. A Java applet (an *applet* is a small application running under the control of another application, usually the Java-enabled Web browser) is downloaded from the server and executes under the control of the Java interpreter in the computer running the browser. Many early Java demos concentrated on sizzle rather than steak, but one of the major long-term benefits of Java is the ability to manage new data types as soon as they are developed and to create distributed interactive applications.

Right now, you can't "play" a new type of data file until you find the appropriate helper or add-in application that knows how to manage and decode the data. With Java, an applet can contain the viewing mechanism along with the data, or alternatively, the Java applet can instruct the browser to collect the viewer from another Web site.

Another potentially large impact is in the area of interactive applications, created and managed until now by CGI or Perl scripts. Java will almost certainly displace CGI programming simply because it's both more efficient and more powerful. CGI scripts are host based and place overhead on the server for every script that runs; Java runs on the local processor in the computer running the Web browser.

Some of the early Java demos won't run until the whole Java program has been received from the server; the effect is rather like waiting for a large graphic to load. Until it arrives, the Web page you're viewing has a hole in it. Other demos require a large number of GIF files to present an animated image; in this case, the image files take longer to download than the animation itself takes to run. Most of these effects are because Java is still very young; once programmers start to optimize their code and invent the tips and tricks that are common in other languages, you'll see some astonishing things done using Java.

Java and HTML

Java applets are opened by using an HTML link and the <APPLET> tag, so providing a Java effect on a Web page can be as simple as copying a Java file to your server and adding the HTML link. The HTML to do that might look like this:

```
<HTML>
<HEAD>
<TITLE>A Java applet </TITLE>
</HEAD>
<BODY>
<APPLET CODE="MYAPPLET">
</APPLET>
</BODY>
</HTML>
```

Note that no filename extension is used in the applet name. You can also use other modifiers with the <APPLET> tag to align the applet on your Web page, retrieve the applet from another URL, and so on, as Table 10.4 shows. If your browser doesn't understand the <APPLET> tag, it just ignores it and displays any alternative text you specified instead.

Because Java is considered an interpreted language, there is a performance penalty when it's compared with a C++ compiled program. The Java program runs somewhere between ten and twenty times slower than the equivalent compiled C++ program, but it's still much faster than most scripting languages, such as Perl or Tcl.

Table 10.4: Attributes Used with the <APPLET> Tag

Modifier	Description
CODEBASE	This optional attribute specifies the absolute or relative-base URL (directory) of the applet to be displayed.
CODE	This required attribute specifies the actual file that contains the applet; not a URL.
WIDTH	This required attribute specifies the initial width, in pixels, that the applet needs in the browser window.
HEIGHT	This required attribute specifies the initial height, in pixels, that the applet needs in the browser window.
ALT	This optional attribute specifies text that a browser that understands the <APPLET> tag but doesn't support Java should display instead of the applet.
NAME	This optional attribute gives a name to the applet instance; this allows applets to find each other by name and communicate.
ALIGN	This optional attribute specifies the applet's alignment on the page and works just like the <IMG> tag.
VSPACE	This optional attribute specifies the amount of space above and below the applet that the browser should leave and works just like the VSPACE attribute of the <IMG> tag.
HSPACE	This optional attribute specifies the amount of space on either side of the applet that the browser should leave and works just like the HSPACE attribute of the <IMG> tag.
PARAM	This modifier, along with its NAME and VALUE attributes, specify a named parameter and a string that are passed to the Java applet.

Java compromises by creating a byte-code so the final Java interpreter has considerably less work to do than a normal stand-alone interpreter. When this byte-code file arrives in your computer, it provides 70 to 80 percent of the data needed to run the applet; the other 20 to 30 percent is provided by the Java runtime environment and tells the applet how to perform on that specific platform.

How Does It All Work?

So how does a Java applet get from the server to a Java-enabled Web browser? Here are the steps:

1. The Web browser requests an HTML page from the Web server.
2. The Web browser receives and displays the Web page.

3. The Web browser interprets the `<APPLET>` tag and sends a request to the server for the file specified in the tag.
4. The Web browser receives the specified file, verifies the byte code, and starts executing the Java applet on your system.

Any Web server can send out the Java file; no special requirements are placed on the server, and no modifications are required. And because execution takes place on the client computer, Java applets are largely unaffected by restrictions in bandwidth or by limitations in HTML.

Security in Java

Inherent in the Java system are several important security aspects. Java downloads include a byte-code verification process; if the packet's size changes along the way, the transfer is aborted. The Java loader assumes that the data stream may have been tampered with and so it checks very carefully to make sure it hasn't changed en route to protect against viruses or Trojan Horses.

Once the Java applet is running on your system, the operations it can perform are strictly limited by your Web browser. In general, Java applets don't do the following:

- Read or write files on the local system
- Delete or rename files on the local system
- Create a directory on the local system
- List a directory, check for the existence of a specific file, or obtain the size, type, or modification information for a file
- Manipulate network connections (other than the connection to your Web site)
- Run other applications on your system
- Load any DLLs on your system
- Make native function calls to the underlying operating system
- Access memory directly
- Obtain the user's name or the home directory name
- Define any system properties
- Manipulate any thread that isn't part of the same threadgroup as the applet
- Terminate the Java interpreter

In some cases, a Java applet may be allowed to read files named on a read-access control list.

In Java version 1.1, you'll find RSA's public-key encryption scheme to provide security for commercial and credit card transactions. Java will also be compatible with Netscape's Secure Sockets Layer (SSL) and with the Microsoft and Visa Private Communications Technology (PCT).

Java on Your Intranet

Software developers are not just interested in Java because it's new and interesting and can bring sparkle to their Web pages; they're interested in Java because it's hardware and operating system independent. Many developers will use Java because the applications they create will run on any platform, provided the user has a Java-enabled browser.

This single aspect of Java has many programmers—who face a company full of different kinds of hardware running several variations of different operating systems—smiling all the way back to their cube. They can now write a Java applet to solve that nagging integration problem. If you're looking for a low-cost way to distribute applications across your enterprise, take a look at Java; it might just be the answer to your prayers.

JavaScript

Sun and Netscape jointly developed *JavaScript,* a Java scripting language designed to make it easier for nonprogrammers to create Java applets, and released it into the public domain. JavaScript used to be called *LiveScript,* but the name was changed in late 1995.

Use the `<SCRIPT></SCRIPT>` tags in your HTML page to define a JavaScript script. However, some browsers ignore these tags, and any text that appears in the HTML page between them will be rather ugly in those browsers.

You'll find lots of information on JavaScript on the World Wide Web; take a look at some of these sites. The Unofficial JavaScript Resource Center at

```
http://www.ce.net/users/ryan/java
```

includes lots of links to other sites, tips, and tutorials. Another good site is the JavaScript Tip of the Week at

```
http://webreference.com/javascript
```

with tips and information on programming with Netscape Navigator. And for a coherent discussion of how and why you might use JavaScript, see *Mastering Netscape FastTrack Server* by Robert P. Lipschutz and John Garris, available from Sybex; or *The ABCs of JavaScript,* by Lee Purcell and Mary Jane Mara, also available from Sybex.

Should You Use Java?

Is Java the answer on your intranet? As always, the right answer is that it all depends. If your site's content is simple and can be presented in text and simple graphics, the answer is probably no, you don't need Java. You should also look at the programming skills you can draw on in support of your site. If programming in C++ gives you the mother of all headaches, again, the answer is probably no, you don't need Java.

Also, keep in mind the type of communications link that the majority of your users can access. If you run a fast corporate intranet, bandwidth may be less an issue, and you may find that you can use Java to add a little spice to your HTML pages. If some people connect to your intranet using 14.4Kbps modems, however, they'll be spending a lot of time waiting as more and more stuff is downloaded from your site.

Java may well be the best thing since sliced bread, but it's also a topic that attracts a great deal of overstatement and inflated claims when discussion turns to what will happen in the future. Don't use it just because it's there; use it because it fills a well-defined need on your intranet.

The Future According to Microsoft

Microsoft came to the Web late, but has not lagged behind in recent developments; huge amounts of money and resources have been allocated to develop Microsoft's presence in this exploding market. Much of the current storm between Netscape and Microsoft is in terms of their two browsers and each company's version of several so-called standards.

Developments on many fronts form Microsoft's plan of attack, including Windows NT, the Internet Information Server, the Internet Explorer, proposed emerging standards, such as ActiveX and ISAPI, additions to Windows 95, and the creation of HTML development tools and editors.

We looked at all sorts of browsers, including the Internet Explorer in Chapter 7, "Choosing Intranet Hardware and Software," and we looked at servers in Chapter 8, "Installing Intranet Software." Here we'll look at the other major components in Microsoft's strategy, ActiveX and the Common Internet File System.

Microsoft's ActiveX

Microsoft's answer to Sun Microsystems's Java programming language is the ActiveX specification, which consists of three main elements:

- *ActiveX controls*, which function just like conventional OLE controls (OLXs). They can be located on your browser or can be downloaded from the server and used for something as simple as a button all the way to something as complex as a whole report. ActiveX controls can also interact with one another.
- *ActiveX documents*, which allow you to view active documents as well as HTML pages, thus presenting you with a common interface for several tasks.
- *ActiveX scripting*, which allows you to coordinate ActiveX controls on your Web site using the two available scripting languages, JavaScript and the Visual Basic–based VBScript. Eventually, we may even see ActiveX scripting implementations of Sun's JavaScript and Perl. At this point, VBScript has a smaller runtime module, at 50K compared with the 1.2MB needed for Java.

ActiveX is a careful repackaging of Microsoft's COM (*Common Object Model*), the foundation that supported OLE. By adding network capabilities (and so creating DCOM or Distributed COM) and by reducing the scope of OLE to create ActiveX, Microsoft has created a comprehensive suite of component-based Internet- and intranet-oriented applications. ActiveX controls are not completely incompatible with Java, and Microsoft has not only licensed Java from Sun, but also agreed to provide a wrapper to make Java applets behave just like ActiveX objects.

But there are other, absolutely fundamental differences, between Java and ActiveX, including portability and security. Java has security designed in right from the beginning, and ActiveX can make no such claim. Java applications are secured from both accidental and intentional attacks on system integrity. ActiveX can only offer the alternative of cryptographic certificates, whose protection is aimed at a completely different target.

> **TIP**   You can find out more about ActiveX and even download some sample ActiveX controls from `http://www.microsoft.com/activex/gallery/`.

Microsoft has also announced a set of drop-in ActiveX controls for nonbrowser applications, including the following:

- FTP ActiveX Control, which lets applications use FTP

- HTML ActiveX Control, which lets applications launch their own simple Web browser
- HTTP ActiveX Control, which lets applications behave like simple Web servers
- NNTP ActiveX Control, which gives applications access to Usenet newsgroups and other NNTP news
- SMTP/POP3 ActiveX Control, which lets applications use e-mail without the need to start a separate program
- WinSock ActiveX Control, which provides an interface to the TCP/IP suite of protocols in Windows 95 and Windows NT

These controls are all contained in Microsoft's Internet Control Pack (ICP) and were jointly developed by NetManage, Inc. and Microsoft.

How Does ActiveX Work?

An ActiveX Control is a reusable software component that has been developed by Microsoft or by a third-party software vendor. As Table 10.5 shows, an ActiveX Control can be as small as a single button and as large as a Web Browser Control, and this is, of course, only a partial list. You can use these controls in your intranet pages, in desktop applications, or in development tools.

Table 10.5: ActiveX Controls

Control	Description
Web Browser control	Displays HTML pages, ActiveX controls, and ActiveX Documents and is based on Internet Explorer 3
Marquee control	Scrolls an HTML page in any direction, at a specified rate
ActiveMovie control	Displays streaming and nonstreaming video and audio
Label	Creates a text label
Textbox	Creates a multiline text-entry and text-display box
Listbox	Creates a drop-down list box
Option	Lets users choose among several options
Toggle button	Creates a button with two states, such as On and Off
Scrollbar	Creates horizontal and vertical scrollbars
Chart	Creates different kinds of charts
Menu	Creates a menu on a Web page

According to Microsoft, there are currently more than 1,000 commercially available ActiveX controls that you can access using Microsoft's C, C++, Visual Basic, or Visual J++ programming languages. You don't have to be a programmer to use many of the ActiveX controls, although you may find that you need a certain amount of script support to use some of them. Many controls you can use simply as prefabricated components that you can incorporate directly into your intranet pages.

> **TIP**　Netscape Navigator supports ActiveX controls through the ActiveX plug-in available from Ncompass Labs at `http://www.ncompasslabs.com/`.

When Internet Explorer comes across a Web page containing an ActiveX control, it first checks the System Registry to see if that component is available on that machine. If it is, the Web page is displayed and the control is activated. If not, Internet Explorer finds the control in a location specified by the creator of the HTML page and installs it automatically. When a component has to be downloaded, you'll see a message to this effect, so you can choose to cancel or continue with the download. If the control has been digitally signed, you'll see a message that verifies the name of the software developer and that the control has not been tampered with. By default, all downloaded controls are placed in the directory `\WINDOWS\OCCACHE`.

Nearly all the ActiveX technical papers, downloadable software, tips and tricks can be found on Microsoft's Web site at

`http://www.microsoft.com/intdev/controls/controls-f.htm`

but you should also visit the ActiveX Component Gallery at

`http://www.microsoft.com/activex/gallery/`

The ActiveX Gallery includes a library of ActiveX applications, as well as instructions for downloading the software development kit (SDK) from

`http://www.microsoft.com/intdev/sdk/`

ActiveX and Open Standards

As you saw earlier in this chapter, Sun's Java programming language is independent of both the underlying operating system and the basic hardware (computer, video card, and monitor) that it runs on. Sun has been an active member of the Unix community for years, and this open approach to Java reflects a similar fundamental philosophy. Java applets can run on *any* system for which there is a Java interpreter.

ActiveX, on the other hand, is available only on the Windows/Intel, or *Wintel*, platform used in PCs, and for many companies actively engaged in software development, that severely limits any appeal that ActiveX might have for them; they are still faced with solving the problem of how to program for the Wintel platform as well as for all the other platforms that their software has to run on.

To counter the charges that ActiveX is an inward-looking proprietary system, Microsoft recently took several important steps to open up ActiveX.

In late 1996, after spending $100 million over seven years, Microsoft agreed to cede control of a subset of ActiveX technology to the Open Group, an industry group that will now control the software's future design standards.

Microsoft has released the following components:

- COM/DCOM object model
- Remote procedure call implementation
- NTLM security interface
- Structured Storage format for files
- System Registry for storing object information
- Moniker object naming scheme
- Remote authorization for running remote objects

Microsoft has not released these elements of its systems:

- Source code for ActiveX controls on the desktop
- Win32 API set

Find out more about the Open Group at

```
http://www.opengroup.org/
```

Common Internet File System

Several companies have joined with Microsoft in support of the proposed *Common Internet File System* (CIFS), a file-sharing technology based on the SMB (*Server Message Block*) protocol. SMB is an open protocol available in the Unix world that allows users read and write access to files on remote systems without needing to download the files first, as with FTP and other similar protocols.

CIFS adds several enhancements over the existing SMB protocol to allow support for DNS name resolution as well as support for slow-speed dial-up lines and remote printer sharing. In addition, CIFS also supports authentication, file locking, data sharing and file-system security, all of which will become increasingly important as companies establish their own corporate intranets.

The Intranet Database

Connecting your intranet to an existing corporate database is one of the most powerful ways to take existing data and present it in new, useful ways. You can put your product catalog online for sales reps to look at during sales calls; you can use an intranet to access your personnel records and enroll in a benefits plan. The major database players—Oracle, Informix, and Sybase—are developing sophisticated database Web tools that you can use on your intranet. Third-party vendors are also developing database-connectivity tools for those databases as well as using ODBC (Open DataBase Connectivity) to connect to other databases such as Microsoft Access. ODBC uses database drivers to translate database-specific information into a standard format allowing your intranet to read data from any ODBC-compliant database.

> **TIP**
>
> Ah, more information! *Mastering Intranets, Mastering Internet Information Server,* and *Mastering Netscape FastTrack Server,* all from Sybex, should get you started. Also check out Oracle at `http://www.oracle.com`, Sybase at `http://www.sybase.com`, Informix at `http://www.informix.com`, and for the latest connectivity information, see Yahoo's current listings at `http://www.yahoo.com/Computers_and_Internet/Internet/World_Wide_Web/Databases_and_Searching/`.

If you're interested in connecting a database to your intranet, seek out the database administrator in your organization and begin discussing the options. You'll also need to do some research because database connectivity is well beyond the scope of this book. If you already have a specific DBMS (DataBase Management System) selected or in use, you can contact that vendor for specific solutions or see some of the references we've given you in this chapter.

In this chapter, we've given you a pretty detailed overview of some ways to enhance your intranet's content with video, sound, and Acrobat. We also briefly discussed connecting a database behind your intranet front-end. You now have some ideas on how to extend your intranet beyond basic HTML and some leads on where you can get more information on the specific products you'll need. Our next chapter will show you examples of some specific intranet sites and give you information on where to learn more.

Chapter 11

USING INTRANET AUTHORING AND MANAGEMENT TOOLS

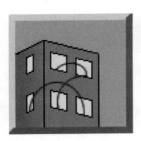

FEATURING

- **Using Microsoft's Internet Assistants**
- **Converting documents for use on your intranet**
- **Creating pages with HTML authoring tools**
- **Managing your intranet now that it's online**

The days when you had to be an HTML guru living in a cave to create exciting HTML pages are long gone; now you can stay in your office and use one of the large set of popular and capable HTML authoring tools instead. Many of them are so easy to use that you can leave HTML-content preparation to the people that know all about the content, rather than having them pass the content to people who know all about HTML. This means you can spend more time setting overall intranet guidelines and attending to site administration and other important tasks.

We're going to start this chapter by looking at Microsoft's Internet Assistants, one of the easiest ways to create intranet pages. We'll also look at some programs you can use to convert your existing files into HTML before delving into HTML authoring tools such as FrontPage.

Which brings us neatly to the focus of the second part of this chapter, in which we'll be looking at some tools you can use to manage and administer your intranet site. We'll cover the day-to-day operations you're likely to encounter and describe how to get the best out of some of the popular site-management tools. Let's start by looking at how you can create HTML pages at a simple level using a text editor or your word processor.

Quick Intranet-Page Editing

In the "old days," you used a standard text editor or basic word processor, such as WordPad, to create HTML files, essentially coding everything by hand and then saving the resultant HTML pages as text files. You had to remember all the HTML tags and take care of HTML syntax yourself. If you want, you can still do that, but many better and more convenient ways are now available.

An alternative to creating your HTML files from scratch is to use a word processor or other desktop application to do the job for you and then convert the file into an HTML version of the file. Microsoft has made a set of Internet Assistants available for its popular Office applications—Word, Excel, and PowerPoint. We'll look at the Internet Assistants for Word and Excel here.

> **TIP**
>
> Another PowerPoint file converter, called PowerPlus Maker, is available from Net-Scene. This program converts PowerPoint presentations into a compact file format that you can view using Net-Scene's PointPlus plug-in with your browser. Find out more at http://www.net-scene.com/.

Microsoft Word Internet Assistant

The Microsoft Internet Assistants all use your existing Microsoft Office applications to create HTML content quickly and easily. The original Word Internet Assistant was released for Word 6 and has been updated for Word for Windows 95 and integrated into Office 97. All you have to do is save your documents, and the Internet Assistant converts them for you. Here are the steps to follow to save an existing Word document as an HTML page:

1. Prepare your Word document, or open a document you have previously prepared.
2. Choose File ➤ Save As to open the Save As dialog box.
3. Select HTML Document (*.HTM) from the Save As Type box. The file name is automatically changed to this new filename extension.
4. Click on the Save button to save your file.

NOTE Remember that HTM is the HTML extension in the Microsoft world. Its Unix, Mac, Windows 95, and Windows NT counterpart, which you often encounter on the Internet, is HTML.

Basically, the Word Internet Assistant is a set of Microsoft Word templates that add HTML functions to Word's command structure. When you open or save an HTML file, the menu choices available for the file change.

Word Internet Assistant changes any of the styles it knows about to HTML tags, but you can manually create HTML equivalents of your own. Although the conversion may not be perfect, it's good enough for many purposes and a good place to start.

NOTE Word Internet Assistant 1 for Word 6 doesn't support tables. Any tables in your Word document will be converted to preformatted text, which you may or may not find satisfactory, depending on your specific application. You'll need Word 7 or higher and Internet Assistant 2 to convert tables properly.

One nice feature in Word Internet Assistant is that it converts any graphics in your original Word file into GIF form. The converted files are stored in the same directory as the current file, with working links to the current file. All you have to do is to remember to copy all the files—HTML content and GIF graphics files—onto the server when the time comes to start using your intranet.

As well as performing simple conversions, Word Internet Assistant is also an almost-WYSIWYG (*What You See Is What You Get*) HTML editor. When you are working on an HTML document, a new toolbar appears in Word containing most of the commands for the Internet Assistant.

> **TIP**
>
> If your carefully constructed HTML page looks strange when you view it in your browser, you may have accidentally saved it as a Word DOC file. Word DOC files are not simple text files, but binary files, and although you may recognize some of the text you see on the browser screen as coming from your content file, much of it will be rendered as gibberish and funny little squiggles. Go back to Word and be sure to save the file as HTML (*.HTM) if you are working with the Internet Assistant or as a text file (*.TXT) if you are using Word without Internet Assistant as your editor.

Unfortunately, Internet Assistant for Word doesn't do much in the way of HTML syntax checking, although it's easy enough to switch into HTML source mode by clicking the HTML button once you've found an error.

Microsoft Excel Internet Assistant

Just as Word Internet Assistant makes creating HTML documents a snap, Microsoft Excel Internet Assistant, installed as an XLA add-in file, makes creating HTML tables quick and easy and is designed to convert your Excel spreadsheets into intranet pages fast.

Excel Internet Assistant doesn't let you create links to other pages, so its main use is in preparing tabular materials for publication. Once the spreadsheet has been converted into HTML, you can then use another HTML editor to add links and other text. Excel Internet Assistant also supports background colors and formatted text.

To convert all or part of an Excel spreadsheet into HTML, follow these steps:

1. Open Excel, and load or create your spreadsheet.
2. Choose Tools ➤ HTML Wizard.
3. Follow the instructions on the screen to select the cells for conversion and the name of the file in which to save the HTML content.

> **TIP**
>
> Just to make sure everything is as you think it should be, once the conversion is complete, review the new HTML file in your browser *before* you load it onto the server.

These Internet Assistants do a good job converting Word or Excel documents into HTML, but as you might expect, they're somewhat limited. In a moment, we'll take a look at some of the most popular HTML authoring tools, but first, let's see if one of the HTML translation tools will meet your needs.

Finding and Using Converters

If you already have a large collection of legacy documents that you want to convert into HTML automatically, you have several options. If you primarily work with Microsoft products, you can, of course, use the Internet Assistants we looked at in the last section, but what do you do if you work with different kinds of data files created by a mixed set of products? In this section, we'll look at some applications that can help take the grunt work out of just this sort of conversion.

CorelWeb.Data

CorelWeb.Data from Corel Corporation is a tool for converting database files into HTML. You can select the records and fields that you want to export, and the program sorts the data and sets field layout. CorelWeb.Data can access files created by Access, dBASE, FoxPro, Lotus 1-2-3, Oracle, and Paradox applications, as well as programs that use these same data formats. For more information, check out

    http://www.corel.com/

Web Publisher

Web Publisher from SkiSoft, available in the Standard and the Pro versions, converts Rich Text Format documents into HTML. Web Publisher can also convert files from Microsoft's Excel and PowerPoint applications.

Because you can define a template to use when converting a document, you can impose a standard look and feel to the resulting HTML pages. Web Publisher can also process files in batches, create buttons that jump between pages, build links from existing indexes, and convert graphics images into GIF format. Find out more at

    http://www.skisoft.com/

KEYview

KEYview from FTP Software is a combination converter and viewer that you can use to translate files in a variety of formats into HTML. You can also view files from a variety of word processors, including spreadsheet files and vector and raster graphics files.

KEYview comes bundled with Conversion Tool, a stand-alone utility that actually performs the conversions and works with the Windows Explorer. You can, therefore, convert files using drag-and-drop. Check out this Web site for more details:

    http://www.ftp.com/

WordPerfect Internet Publisher

WordPerfect integrates HTML functionality directly into its application. This program lets you edit documents in a WordPerfect window that contains a special HTML toolbar. You can then work on your text in this window, adding text using WordPerfect's character and paragraph styles, and then export the file in HTML form. The program uses WordPerfect's bookmark feature to add links, but it can't convert graphics into GIF format. Find out more at

    http://www.corel.com/products/wordperfect/cwps7/

Using HTML Authoring Tools

As more people work to create intranet pages, the software companies are offering better tools to help in this process. To create an HTML page in times past, as we saw earlier in this chapter, you wrote the content, added the HTML tags by hand using a text editor, and then used your favorite browser to look at the results. This was not only tedious and time consuming, but also it was easy to make a mistake in HTML that prevented the document from displaying in the browser.

HTML editors make the creation of intranet pages much simpler; however—although you can get add-on products for most word processors, as we saw in the last section—they lack essential features and are somewhat under-powered. Many HTML errors are subtle and occur when two tags overlap in a way that makes no sense or because you forgot to terminate a tag. The result is a page that doesn't look like you expected it to—or doesn't display at all. This is where HTML authoring tools can be enormously helpful.

Not all HTML authoring tools are created equal. Some will have features you like and use; others will be less attractive. The basic feature set is still evolving because this software category didn't even exist a few years ago. Also, software vendors are faced with the interesting task of keeping their browsers up-to-date with their HTML authoring tools, as well as keeping an eye on the competition's products. All in all, it may be somewhat confusing, but in the end, it benefits you—the consumer.

As these high-level HTML authoring tools gain a foothold in the software market, knowing HTML will actually become less important, and intranet content creators will be free to concentrate on the other important aspects of their work, such as design and layout.

In the sections that follow, we'll deal with Microsoft FrontPage in some detail, and then we'll a take a quick look at Netscape Navigator Gold.

Redux: The Web by Any Other Name...

As we tour through these products, bear in mind that they do not all use the same terminology. Microsoft FrontPage, for example, defines a *Web* as any group of HTML pages, from a single page to an entire intranet.

Most of the other HTML authoring packages refer to the World Wide Web as the *Web* and refer to a collection of HTML pages as an *intranet*, as a *site*, or even in one case as a *MiniWeb*. FrontPage uses the term *hyperlink*, which is of course correct, but most of the other products refer simply to *links*.

Microsoft FrontPage

Because of the popularity of Microsoft FrontPage, we're going to spend a large part of this chapter looking at it in detail. We'll look at how you can use it to create intranet content and later, in the "Managing Your Intranet" section, we'll look at how you can use it for management and administration tasks.

FrontPage consists of four components that together make a comprehensive Web publishing package:

1. The Personal Web Server, which is the scaled-down Windows 95 version of Microsoft's Internet Information Server
2. The Explorer
3. The Editor
4. The To Do List

NOTE The FrontPage 97 Bonus Pack also includes both the Microsoft Image Composer and the WebPublishing Wizard for using FrontPage with server software that does not support the Front-Page extensions.

With these components, you can create and maintain a Web site, build and edit new intranet pages, and manage the links in your pages. The latest version of FrontPage also includes Microsoft Image Composer, an application you can use to manipulate graphical files and perform conversions.

NOTE Windows NT Server 4 includes a free version of FrontPage, but it's version 1; most of the discussion in this chapter centers on later versions of FrontPage.

This section will concentrate on the component you'll probably use the most—the FrontPage Editor.

Editing Documents in the FrontPage Editor

You can create a new Web page in the Editor simply by clicking on the New button on the toolbar to access a new blank page. But when you use the Editor's File ➤ New command, you can create a new page based on a FrontPage *template* or a *Wizard*.

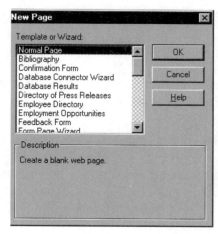

A template is simply a ready-made page that you can use as a starting point. A Wizard helps you create a new page by asking you a series of questions about the content or layout of the page. It then builds the page based on your responses, and you can get to work on the result.

When you have a intranet site open in the FrontPage Explorer, you can use the Editor's Edit ➤ Open from Web command to open a page from that Web site and make your changes. The intranet pages are listed both by their URL and their page title, which greatly simplifies the process. Figure 11.1 shows an example Web site displayed in the FrontPage Explorer.

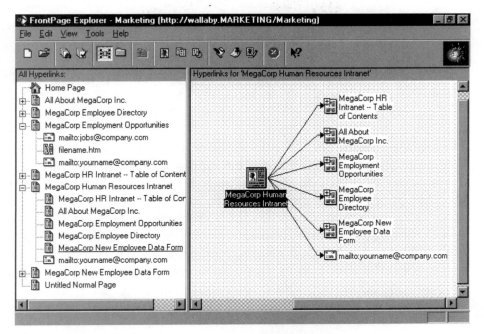

FIGURE 11.1: Example Web site displayed in the FrontPage Explorer

You can also use the File ➤ Open command, which lets you open files outside the current intranet site. You can open HTML files, Rich Text Format (RTF) files, or plain text files. Finally, if you use the File ➤ Open Location command, you can open a file by specifying its URL.

Just Pretend You're Using a Word Processor

When you're working in a page in the Editor, you can pretty much go about your job as though you were creating a document in a Windows word processor:

- You simply type text, pressing Enter only at the end of a paragraph (the HTML code is <P>) or using the Insert ➤ Break command (or press Shift+↵) to break a line without creating a new paragraph (the code for this is <BR>).
- You can select text or graphic images with the mouse or keyboard.

- You can invoke a command to act on the selected data (either from the menu bar or by right-clicking on the items in question), such as to make text bold (<STRONG>) or emphasized (<EM>) or to turn selected paragraphs into a bulleted list (<UL>).
- You can move, copy, and delete data in the usual ways.
- You can insert data from another file using the Insert ➤ File command.

One big difference between the FrontPage Editor and a word processor—and it's an important one—is that the options the Editor offers you on its menus and toolbars are all HTML-related. Let's take a quick look at some of the editing tools you'll find for creating intranet pages:

- Use the Insert ➤ Symbol command to create characters that don't reside on standard keyboards, such as ½ or the copyright symbol, ©. FrontPage will automatically assign the correct HTML code for any nonstandard characters, such as &#189 for ½ and &#169 for ©.
- Use the Tools ➤ Spelling command to check the spelling in your Web page.
- Use the Find or Replace commands on the Edit menu to find text within the current page or replace that text with other text. If you want to find or replace specific HTML tags within a page, for example the <STRONG> tag, you can use a text editor such as Windows Notepad. Remember, the HTML file you create in the Editor is just plain text, like any other HTML file.

Adding Structure to Pages

Perhaps the simplest way to affect the structure of a Web page is by inserting a horizontal line (<HR>, often referred to as a horizontal rule) that spans from one side of the page to the other. It's a simple but effective way to delineate one section from another.

To modify the look of a horizontal line, right-click on the line and choose Horizontal Line Properties to open the Horizontal Line Properties dialog box. Here you can set the width and height options, the alignment, and the color to use for the line.

Before we go on, let's take a quick look at a couple of other tools you can use to structure your intranet pages.

Creating a Hierarchy

A common and effective way to add structure to a Web page is through the use of headings. A Web page can have a maximum of six heading levels, whose HTML codes are conveniently named <H1>, <H2>, <H3>, and so on. As with all HTML codes, there is no inherent style to the headings—different Web browsers might interpret the look of a heading in a different way. In general, however, a level one heading will be in a larger, bolder font than a lower-level heading. The way headings appear in the FrontPage Editor just happens to be the same way they look in Microsoft Internet Explorer. What a nice coincidence!

Structuring Your Pages with Lists

Another common structural tool is the list. Examples of bulleted lists and numbered lists can be found throughout this book, and both those styles are available in HTML pages in the Editor. As you'll recall from Chapter 9, the numbered list is often called an ordered list (`<OL>`) and a bulleted list is called an unordered list (`<UL>`) in the world of HTML.

To begin a list, you can click on either the Numbered List or the Bulleted List button on the toolbar. For a numbered list, the Editor will insert a number at the left of the current line; for a bulleted list, it will insert a bullet.

Then you simply type the text for this item in the list. The text is indented from the bullet or number and wraps to a new, indented line as needed. Press Enter to start a new item in the list. When you want to end the list, you can press Ctrl+↵ once, press Enter twice, or click elsewhere on the page. To add even more structure to your intranet pages, you can also place a list within a list; the subordinate list is indented farther to the right.

Now let's turn our attention away from the page as a whole and focus in on how you can affect the formatting of individual characters on a page.

Formatting Characters

You can change the appearance of text on a page with the Format ➤ Font command. The Font dialog box will then offer several groups of enhancements, as Figure 11.2 shows, on two tabs:

Font   This tab lets you choose a font by name, a font style (regular, italic, bold, or bold italic), and size. You can also choose a color and an effect (underline, strikethrough, or typewriter).

Special Styles   This tab lets you apply special character styles to the selected text; just be sure to use the blinking text tag with discretion. Choose Vertical Position to create a subscript or superscript (Normal is the default), and specify the level to which you want to raise or lower the text. A higher number increases the distance above or below the baseline.

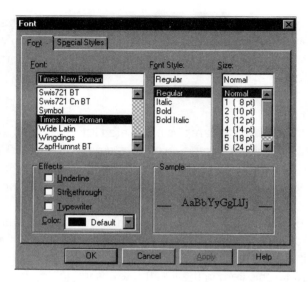

FIGURE 11.2:
The Font dialog box contains the Font and the Special Styles tabs.

> **TIP** You should generally avoid using underlined text in your pages; by convention, most browsers interpret underlines as hypertext links. It can be confusing for a user to have to look twice at a page to see if the underlined text is actually a link.

You can change a variety of properties for the Web page you're editing by choosing File ➤ Page Properties. The options in this dialog box offer several ways to enhance the look of a Web page, including background colors and background images. Be careful how you use these options, however—there's nothing like black letters on a dark purple background to make a user decide it's time to jump to a new page. You can change the colors of hypertext links on the page with three options: Hyperlink, Visited Hyperlink, and Active Hyperlink. Now let's take a look at how you actually create those links.

Linking Pages to the World

To create a hypertext link, first you select the text or image that will serve as the link in the Web page, and then you specify the target of the link, which can be another location on the page or another Web resource that will be accessed when the link is clicked on or activated.

You can create a link in the Editor in several ways, but the method you'll probably use most often is simply this:

1. Select the text or image that will serve as the link.
2. Click on the Create or Edit Hyperlink button on the toolbar to open the Create Hyperlink dialog box. It contains four tabs where you specify the target for the link.

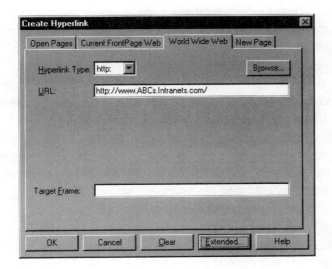

Open Pages   Choose one of the pages currently open in the Editor. You can also choose a bookmark in the selected page to serve as the target (bookmarks are discussed in the next section) as well as a frame.

Current FrontPage Web   On this tab, choose a target from the current Web site (the Web site that is open in the Explorer).

Word Wide Web   Specify a target by its URL on the World Wide Web and the protocol required to access it. For example, you can choose HTTP for standard intranet pages or MAILTO to allow a reader to send mail to the target address you specify.

New Page   Enter a page title and a URL to create a new Web page in the Editor that will serve as the target for the link.

3. When you've specified the target for the link, click the OK button.

The text you selected in the Web page is now underlined and in the color blue (or the color you specified for links in the Page Properties dialog box). As you pass the mouse pointer over a link, the name of its target appears on the status bar. If a link points to a target in the current intranet site, you can hold down the Ctrl key and click on the link to have the Editor open the target page for editing.

Creating Links to Bookmarks

Before you can create a link to a *bookmark,* you have to define the bookmark. A bookmark is simply a named location within a page to which you can create a link. For example, you can create a table of contents at the top of a page that contains links to various locations (bookmarks) within the page. When a user clicks one of those links, the target bookmark location is displayed immediately in the Web browser.

To define a bookmark, select the text or an image, choose Edit ➤ Bookmark, enter a name for the bookmark, and click on the OK button. Now you can create a link to that bookmark as described in the previous section.

To change the target of a link, click on the text or image that forms the link, and then click on the Link button on the toolbar. FrontPage displays the Edit Hyperlink dialog box, in which you can modify the target of the link. To change the underlined text that serves as the link, simply edit the text in the usual way.

Letting FrontPage Track Your Links

One of *the* most frustrating aspects of building an intranet site is trying to track all the links your pages contain. Your intranet site might have many internal links that refer to resources within the current intranet site, and it might have many external links that refer to resources outside the current site. You can use the Explorer's Verify Hyperlinks command on the Tools menu to check each link to see if it's still valid.

If an internal link is broken (the target can't be found), you can choose to edit the link and let the Explorer update all links to the new target URL you specify. You can also choose to have the Explorer verify all the external links in the intranet site, although this could take a long time if there are lots of them.

Displaying Images in Pages

To place a graphical image in one of your intranet pages in the Editor, first position the insertion point at the location where you want the image to appear. Then choose Insert ➤ Image. In the Image dialog box, you can select an image in the following ways:

- Select an image from the list of images that already reside in the current FrontPage Web.

- Use the Other Location tab, and then click on the From File button to choose an image from outside of your intranet site, or click on the From Location button and specify the URL of an image.
- Select the Clip Art tab and choose a category, and then choose an option from the Contents box.

FrontPage can import a wide variety of graphic file formats, including GIF, JPEG, BMP, TIFF, WMF, PCX, and EPS.

TIP   When you save the page that contains the image, FrontPage will ask if you want to save the image to the current intranet page, which you'll generally want to do. When the image is saved, FrontPage converts it to either the GIF or the JPEG format, the two most widely supported formats among Web browsers. When you save a JPEG image, you can choose the level of compression for the file.

You can modify the properties of an image in the Editor by either right-clicking on the image and choosing Image Properties or by selecting the image and choosing Edit ➤ Image Properties. Either way, the Image Properties dialog box with these three tabs opens:

General   On this tab, you can specify the source of the image, the type of image, and any alternative text you want to associate with the image.

Video   On this tab, you can specify the source of the video clip, control the repeat parameters, and specify how you want the video to be triggered.

Appearance   On this tab, you can specify the exact screen location for the image or video clip, along with its border thickness and its width and height.

You can also choose to make one color in a GIF image transparent so the underlying Web page will show through any part of the image that contains that color. To do this, click on the image to select it, click on the Make Transparent button on the Image toolbar, and then click on the color in the image that you want to make transparent. The Image toolbar appears whenever you click on an image in the Editor to select it.

Creating Hotspots in an Imagemap

By using the tools on the Image toolbar, you can create *hotspots,* or clickable areas of an image, in an *imagemap.* An imagemap is just an image with areas that contain hypertext links. The Image toolbar has three buttons you can use to define hotspots of different shapes: a rectangle, a circle, and a polygon.

To create a hotspot, follow these steps:

1. Select the image by clicking on it.
2. Click on one of the three buttons on the toolbar.
3. Drag within the image to define the perimeter of the hotspot.
4. Release the mouse button, and the hotspot is outlined in the image. FrontPage will then display the Create Hyperlink dialog box.
5. Define the link and deselect the image.

After completing this last step, the hotspot outline disappears. But if you pass the mouse pointer over the hotspot, you'll see the name of the link's target in the status bar.

If you find it difficult to see the outline of a hotspot in a selected image, click on the Highlight Hotspots button on the Image toolbar. Doing so hides the image beneath a single color so the hotspots stand out.

You can choose between two methods of processing hotspots in your imagemaps:

Server-side The Web server interprets the mouse click on the imagemap and sends the appropriate target back to the browser.

Client-side The imagemap in the Web page contains all the necessary hotspot and link information so the browser can interpret the mouse click on the imagemap and request the appropriate target resource.

The second method frees the server from doing any extra work—it all happens within the browser. The only caveat is that earlier versions of browsers don't support these client-side imagemaps, although by now almost all the current versions of most browsers should.

You choose the method of imagemap handling for your entire intranet via the Advanced tab in the dialog box that appears when you select FrontPage Explorer's Tools ➤ Web Settings command.

Using Microsoft Image Composer

Microsoft Image Composer, a top-level–image-editing application, is included as part of the FrontPage 97 Bonus Pack. You can use it to create department or corporate logos, to modify existing graphical elements, or to create stunning new effects. Figure 11.3 shows an image loaded into the Image Composer main editing window.

The native file format of Image Composer is MIC, but this program also supports a variety of other graphical file formats, including Adobe Photoshop 3 PSD, GIF, JPEG, Windows BMP, PCD, Targa TGA, and TIF.

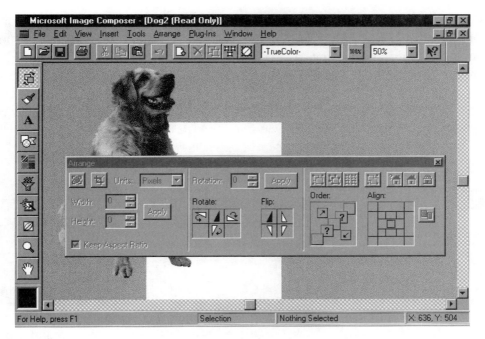

FIGURE 11.3: Image loaded into the Image Composer

If you double-click on an image in the FrontPage Editor, the Microsoft Image Composer opens over the image, so you can edit it using the options on the various tool palettes. Once you've finished editing the image, you can send it back to FrontPage. Here are the steps to follow:

1. Open the page in the FrontPage Editor that contains the image you want to edit.
2. Double-click on the image to open the Image Composer.
3. Use the toolbox to display the tool palette that you want to use with the image. (We'll look at some of the effects you can use in Image Composer in just a moment.)
4. Choose File ➤ Save to send the image back to the FrontPage Editor. If you think you might want to work on the same image at some point in the future, consider saving it in the native Image Composer file format before you exit Image Composer.
5. Choose File ➤ Exit to leave the Image Composer and finish your work in the FrontPage Editor.

You can use the Art Effects tool palette in Image Composer to change an ordinary image into something quite startling. Art Effects are grouped according to the graphical media they resemble—Paint, Sketch, and Graphic. You can also use Exotic and Utility to transform an image into gleaming chrome or rippled glass. Art Effects works best on high-quality scanned images that have areas of light and dark and a large range of colors. With Image Composer, you can work on one image, or you can work on several images at the same time. And if you make a mistake, you can always use the Undo command to remove the most recent application of an effect.

> **NOTE**
>
> To find out more about FrontPage, see *Mastering Intranets*. This book contains information on creating tables, forms, and frames, and on using FrontPage WebBots, a user-friendly automation tool. Or if you really want to delve into FrontPage, see *The ABCs of FrontPage 97* by Gene Weisskopf. (Both books are available from Sybex.)

We've spent a lot of time on FrontPage because it's an easy-to-use and capable HTML-authoring package that will continue to be popular with many people. Next we'll look at some other popular authoring tools.

Netscape Navigator Gold

Netscape Communications' Navigator Gold is a special version of the immensely popular Navigator browser with a built-in WYSIWYG HTML-authoring tool. This editor is capable and easy to use if you want to create a modest number of intranet pages, but you might not use it to create a large corporate intranet; other products are better suited to that particular task.

The editing window looks just like a normal Navigator window, except that there are three toolbars at the top: one for character formatting, links, and graphics; one for file functions, and a third for paragraph formatting. Each toolbar button's function is displayed when the mouse pointer passes over it. You can open as many editing windows as you like.

To create a page, just start typing. You can add formatting from the common tags on the toolbar or from the more complete list in the menus, while you use another toolbar button to clear all the tags from an area of selected text.

You can add a graphic using drag-and-drop, and you can change many of its attributes—such as its size, location, and border—by double-clicking on it; a dialog box opens containing thumbnail illustrations of the possible options. And you can create links by dragging a Link icon from the browser window or by dragging a file from the Windows Explorer.

Navigator Gold can create tables, but not forms or frames, and you won't find any assistants or Wizards in the package either. Figure 11.4 shows an HTML template in Navigator Gold. We selected the table in this template and then right-clicked to open the properties menu you can see in the figure.

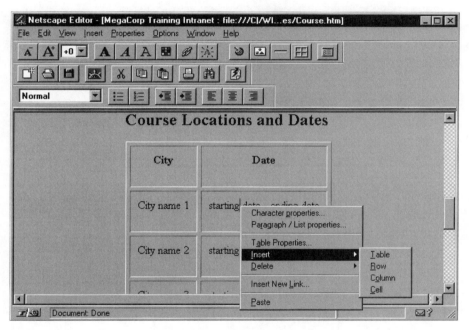

FIGURE 11.4: Navigator Gold open on an HTML template

When you've created your HTML pages, you can use the built-in FTP to transfer them to your server. For more information, consult the Web site at

    http://www.netscape.com/

Adobe PageMill

Adobe's PageMill for Macintosh, and soon for Windows, has been enhanced for version 2. Now you can create tables and frames as well as edit them in a WYSIWYG environment. PageMill supports importing text from word processors and Excel spreadsheets and allows you to incorporate Java applets and to use Netscape plugins. You can find out more about PageMill from Adobe at

```
http://www.adobe.com/
```

HTML Editors on the World Wide Web

You don't have to look far to find a lot of freeware or shareware HTML–authoring tools on the World Wide Web. And as you might expect, they range in capability from thinly disguised text editors to large, complex applications worthy of commercial products.

You might start your search by selecting an operating system and then searching on **"HTML"** and **"editor"** at

```
http://www.shareware.com/
```

or at the Yahoo site:

```
http://www.yahoo.com/Computers_and_Internet/Software/
Internet/World_Wide_Web/HTML_Editors/
```

Two other good sites are

```
http://www.tucows.com
http://pilot.msu.edu/user/heinric6/soft.htm
```

Managing Your Intranet

Your site may be small enough that one person can perform all the duties needed to keep it in top condition, but if you run a large corporate intranet, you may find that you need a department of people to keep everything running smoothly. No matter how many people it takes to do the job, the range of duties is essentially the same and includes some or all of the following:

- Preparing and adding new HTML content
- Inspecting system logs
- Testing active links and locating new links

- Testing CGI scripts
- Responding to feedback from users
- Keeping up with the latest developments in Web technology
- Backing up the server
- Installing software upgrades and system patches
- Troubleshooting server problems
- Upgrading system hardware

In the sections that follow, we'll look at how several of the most popular products can help you perform some of these tasks, beginning with FrontPage.

Managing Your Intranet with FrontPage Explorer

We looked at how to use the HTML-authoring aspects of Microsoft's popular FrontPage package earlier in this chapter; here we'll be concentrating on how to use it for managing and administering your intranet. When you create a new intranet site in the FrontPage Explorer, the Explorer creates a new folder for the intranet site off the root Web (within the folder `FrontPage Webs\Content` by default) and installs the files it needs for managing your intranet.

> **TIP**
>
> **Just as it's easy to confuse the Windows Explorer with Internet Explorer, remember that FrontPage Explorer is a third—and still different—Explorer.**

In the Explorer, choose File ➤ New Web, or click on the New Web button on the toolbar to display the New Web dialog box. You can create the new Web with either a template or a Wizard, just as you can when creating a new page in the FrontPage Editor. If you want to start a new, empty Web, choose either the Normal Web or the Empty Web option. The first contains a single blank Web page; the latter doesn't contain any pages.

When you create a new intranet site, you must choose the server on which it will reside (if you have multiple servers) and give the intranet site a name, which will also name the site's folder or directory on disk. When you have a Web site open in the Explorer, the dialog box for the File ➤ New Web command lets you add the new site to the current intranet. All the pages associated with the new site will be imported into the current intranet. For example, if you've finished a human resources site, you can now add it to your intranet.

Unlike the pages you work on in the FrontPage Editor, there are no data that you must save in the Explorer because all changes are saved automatically. Note, however, that you should always exit the Explorer *after* you exit the FrontPage Editor. When you do so, the Explorer is aware of any changes you make to intranet pages in the Editor.

To open an existing intranet site in the Explorer, choose File ➤ Open Web, or click on the Open Web button on the toolbar. You choose a server from the Open Web dialog box and then choose a FrontPage intranet site from that server.

> **WARNING**   You can't work with multiple intranet sites in the Explorer; opening a new site closes any other open site.

Changing Explorer's View of the Intranet

The main FrontPage Explorer window is divided into two parts: an outline pane on the left that shows all the pages in your intranet and a Hyperlink View pane on the right that shows all the links. You can change from Hyperlink View to Folder View to see page-related details on every file on the intranet, such as the date and time each was last modified. Use either the relevant commands on the View menu or their buttons on the toolbar to change views.

In the Folder view pane, you can sort the list of items in the usual way: Click on a column title to sort by that column; click on it again to sort by that column in reverse order. Change the size of the panes by dragging the center divider to the left or right.

When the Hyperlink View is displayed, you can choose to expand the view using one of three commands on the View menu (or their corresponding buttons on the toolbar):

Hyperlinks to Images   Displays links to any image files; you can turn this off to reduce the number of icons in the Hyperlink View pane.

Repeated Hyperlinks   If a page links to a target multiple times, this option displays every link to that target; turn this off to reduce the number of icons in the Hyperlink View pane.

Hyperlinks inside Page   Displays a link to the same page that contains the link, such as a link that refers to a bookmark on the same page. Again, you can turn this off if the Hyperlink View pane is too crowded.

Importing Intranet Pages and Resources

You can import individual pages or other resources into the FrontPage Explorer, where they'll be incorporated into the current intranet site. To do so, follow these steps:

1. Choose File ➤ Import.
2. Click on the Add File button in the Import File to FrontPage Web dialog box, and go to the folder that contains the file or files you want to import.
3. Select the files you want to import; you can use the Shift+Click and Ctrl+Click methods for making multiple selections.
4. Click on the Open button to add the files to the list of files to import. To select files from another location, click the Add File button again.

In the Import File to FrontPage Web dialog box, you can change the URL of any of the files you've selected before you import them, or you can remove files from the list. You can even close the dialog box for now and return to it later. You can select only those files you're ready to import and then click on the OK button. As the files are brought in, those that contain links to existing files in the current Web will show the appropriate arrows to those files in the Link View pane. Any graphical image files are placed in a default folder named *Images* within the Web site, so you may have to change the URL for graphic images in the incoming pages.

Managing Links in an Intranet Site

There is one routine but time-consuming task that the Explorer turns into a quick and easy task—tracking links within intranet pages. To verify hyperlinks, simply select Tools ➤ Verify Links, and then click on the Verify button in the Verify Hyperlinks dialog box that appears. If you move a file to another folder, the Explorer will automatically update all links to that file, so they point to the new location. If you rename a file, the Explorer will display the Rename dialog box, asking if you want to update all the hyperlinks to this file. Choose Yes, and the links will be updated.

You can also take advantage of the Explorer while you're working in the Editor. To create a link in a page, drag the target's icon from the Explorer's Hyperlink or Folder View into the Web page in the Editor. The resulting link's text will be the target page's title (or URL for other resources), but you can edit the text as needed.

Managing Your Intranet with Netscape Server Manager

If you're using the Netscape FastTrack server, you can use the Netscape browser as your main administrative tool. Choose Programs ➤ Netscape ➤ Administer Netscape Servers. Enter the user name and password you used during installation, and the browser will open on the Netscape Server Selector screen. Click on a server name here, and the Server Manager will open; the Server Manager interface uses HTML pages containing frames, tables, and JavaScript elements.

> **TIP** For more detailed information on Netscape's FastTrack Server, see *Mastering Netscape FastTrack Server* by Robert P. Lipschutz and John Garris, available from Sybex.

The Server Manager contains seven selections, each accessible from a button on the Management page:

System Settings   Contains basic information on the server.

Access Control   Contains authentication and access restrictions.

Encryption   Contains the screens for controlling Secure Sockets Layer (SSL) security.

Programs   Contains information on Java, JavaScript, CGI and WinCGI directories and file types.

Server Status   Contains server monitoring and access tools, as well as the access and error logs.

Config Styles   Contains an area where you can create and apply styles to server resources. Styles can contain configuration information for several different areas of server configuration, including the character set in use, CGI filename extensions, and access and error log preferences.

Content Mgmt   Contains management and configuration information for hardware and software virtual servers, URL forwarding, and file and directory information.

Managing Your Intranet with Adobe SiteMill

Adobe SiteMill is currently available for the Macintosh. SiteMill provides a graphical environment to view your site's structure, links, page titles, and other functionality.

SiteMill uses *views* to define the ways you look at your site. Following are some of the views.

Site view   Lets you can create links by dragging page icons from and to *Page view.* In Site view, you can also see all your resources including your page titles and locations.

External Reference view   Lets you see all links you've made to outside destinations. You can edit those links using drag and drop.

Error view   Shows all broken links and allows you to make fixes quickly.

You can find out more about SiteMill from Adobe at:

```
http://www.adobe.com/
```

This chapter gave you some ideas on what authoring and management tools are out there and an overview on how to use some of them. Between the writing and the publishing of this book, many new versions of existing tools or even entirely new intranet authoring applications will become available, but with the information you've learned in this chapter, you should be able to decide which features you need to create and administer your site, as well as if a new version's features make an upgrade worthwhile. Now that you've learned about the tools, it's time to put them to use. Our next chapter will give you examples of setting up specific intranet sites, such as a technical support or sales and marketing intranet.

Chapter 12

SETTING UP SPECIFIC INTRANET SITES

- **Setting up a technical support site**
- **Creating a training site**
- **Creating an effective sales and marketing site**

Up to now we've been pretty general in our discussion of the specific kinds of activities and functionality you might provide on your intranet. This chapter will take some of those big-picture ideas and show you how you can put them to practical use. Even though we'll be getting more specific, don't expect every little detail—after all, these are only examples. Some of these scenarios are covered in more depth in *Mastering Intranets*, where you'll even find HTML templates for your intranet to get you started. Other ideas will come from your employee's needs or off the net.

> **TIP**
>
> We'll give you some examples of the kinds of things you should think about as you plan a specific site for your intranet. For some in-depth case studies, see Microsoft or Netscape's intranet information on their respective Web sites or see *Mastering Intranets* from Sybex.

Here is a list of some Web sites that have excellent, practical intranet ideas:

Netscape Intranet Solutions `http://www.netscape.com/comprod/at_work/`

Microsoft Intranet Solution Center `http://www.microsoft.com/intranet/`

Intranet Design Magazine `http://www.innergy.com/`

The Intranet Journal `http://www.intranetjournal.com/`

WebMaster Magazine's Intranet Resource Center `http://www.cio.com/WebMaster/wm_irc.html`

You can find even more intranet information by using the major Internet search engines. These include

Excite `http://www.excite.com`

Yahoo `http://www.yahoo.com`

OpenText `http://www.opentext.com`

Lycos `http://www.lycos.com`

WebCrawler `http://www.webcrawler.com`

Creating an Intranet Technical Support Site

No matter how large your organization, you can manage many important technical and customer support functions on your intranet. In this section, we'll look at some of the technical support areas in which an intranet can add value to your organization.

Technical support, perhaps along with research and development (R & D), will most likely be one of the first departments to apply intranet technology extensively in your organization. Part of the reason is that people in technical support will use whatever tools are available to help them do their jobs faster or more easily. Being out there on the front line and dealing with angry customers can concentrate the mind wonderfully.

Even though this part of the chapter specifically concerns technical support, you can take the ideas you'll find here and apply them in a range of settings, including customer service, research and development, and engineering. Figure 12.1 shows you a sample site with many technical support features such as online help, a tech support form used to report problems, and a feedback page.

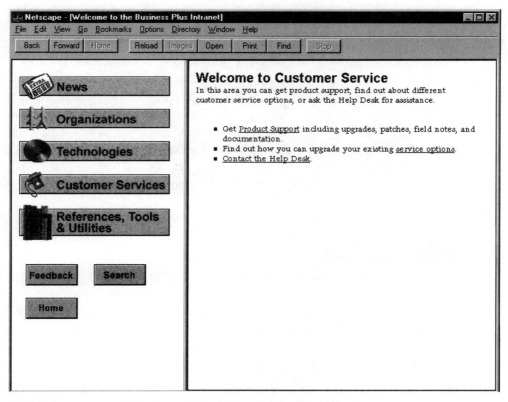

FIGURE 12.1:   A sample site featuring some customer support areas

How Bechtel Does It

Bechtel, an engineering procurement company based in San Francisco, California, uses its own internal intranet to document its external World Wide Web site, including information on how to configure the Internet connection and how and where to place new or updated HTML content files on the server, as well as information on new Web technology and future plans for Bechtel's Web site.

Bechtel's intranet, known as BecWeb, has evolved into one of two important components of Bechtel's Global Knowledge Network (GKN), developed so the company's 20,000 employees scattered all over the world can get information for their project quickly. The other component of GKN is Documentum's InfoWorks, a document management system currently used for human resource information.

A small committee, who comprise the Web Advisory Board and who encourage and coordinate the spread of intranet technology, oversee BecWeb. However, individual departments are encouraged to take responsibility for their own pages on the intranet.

More and more employees are gaining access to BecWeb, and the aim is to give all employees access by 1997 when the current migration to Windows 95 and NT will be complete.

Deciding on Content

Technical support can cover a wide range of activities, from an internal help desk designed to answer questions from people within the company, to a major hardware or software technical-support organization designed to resolve issues brought up by angry customers who may have paid thousands of dollars for a product. Any actual implementation will depend on the needs of your company. Figure 12.2 shows you a sample feedback form used to troubleshoot problems.

With this broad view in mind, let's take a look at the areas in which an intranet can benefit your organization:

- Help desk assistance
- Problem tracking and resolution
- Troubleshooting procedures for common problems

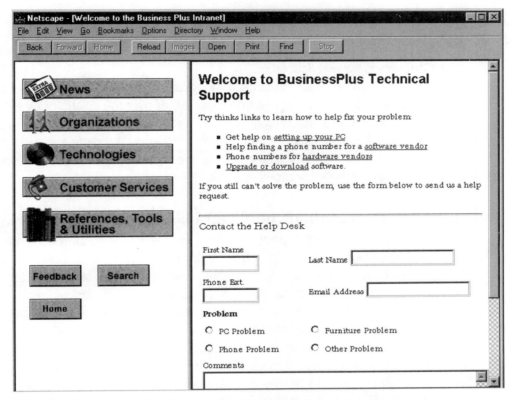

FIGURE 12.2:   A form like this one can be used to gather information about customer support issues.

- Documentation and technical library
- Distribution of software bug fixes, upgrades, and patches
- Software release notes
- Status of software releases
- Engineering change orders
- Product test results and benchmarks
- Links to other related intranet sites within the company
- Glossary of technical or product terms
- Product technical specifications
- Blueprints and engineering drawings
- Technical FAQ (Frequently Asked Questions)
- Technical policies and procedures

- Forms and surveys
- Collecting statistical information
- Helping other departments research and implement their own intranets
- Conferencing and collaboration

Your technical support staff can consult the topics in this list for information they need to pass on to the customer in some form, either over the phone or by e-mail. Other information will be available directly to the user. It makes little difference in theoretical terms whether that user is a company employee, a third party, such as a contractor or supplier, or a real paying customer. In the sections that follow, we'll look at some of these suggested applications in detail.

Placing Technical Documentation on Your Site

One of the most important aspects of making your technical documentation available is that you can keep it up-to-date. This can be especially important in companies that produce a large volume of technical information that needs to be updated frequently, whether that information is a technical library, product testing results and specifications, or troubleshooting procedures for your service engineers in the field.

You can also maintain a list of current company documentation—including title, part number, revision level and revision date, and stock on hand—so employees can locate physical copies of documentation to send to customers quickly and easily.

Also, you can create links between sales and marketing information and more detailed technical information. When a customer asks a sales representative for more detailed information, the rep can find technical specifications, test results, and product manuals on the intranet. Figure 12.3 shows you a sample page with links to technical documentation, help files, and other information.

Here are some more ideas that relate specifically to technical documentation on your intranet:

- Product specifications can contain links to other related technical information, and the complex technical terms in those documents can be defined in a linked glossary. We'll look at how to do this in "Creating a Glossary of Technical Terms" later in this chapter.
- Keeping configuration information for networked systems, workstations, printers, and other technical information on the intranet can save people time previously spent hunting down the appropriate support staff member.
- Engineering change orders can be communicated to the Engineering, manufacturing, and purchasing departments in a timely fashion.

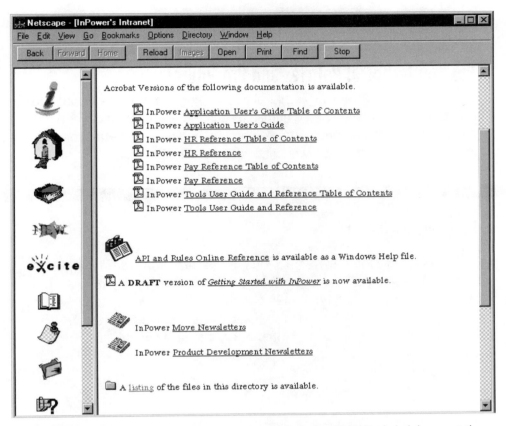

FIGURE 12.3: This sample site has links to Acrobat versions of published technical documentation, online Help files, and newsletters.

- Software release notices and technical documentation on an intranet can cut printing and distribution costs. In some cases, you may even be able to use the intranet to distribute released software to interested parties and to customers.
- You can publish product testing and performance benchmarks for your products or if you work in the medical field, reports on clinical trials and newly developed protocols.
- If the work you do falls under the domain of one of the national or international standards-setting organizations, you can publish the latest revision of those standards on the intranet, helping staff keep up-to-date.

In the next section, we'll take a closer look at one aspect of technical documentation that lends itself particularly well to an intranet—technical policies and procedures.

Posting Technical Policies and Procedures

By posting copies of your technical policies and procedures on your intranet, you can realize the benefits that the human resources department receives when it places copies of policies and procedures on an intranet, namely, better communications, improved productivity, and lower printing and distribution costs.

How Motorola Does It

A division of Motorola Semiconductor Products in Austin, Texas, uses an intranet to share policy and procedure information with interested parties. Before implementing the intranet, the company used several different *and* incompatible e-mail systems, which made document interchange a frustrating and difficult process. Now, the intranet has made it possible to share documents easily, obtain fast technical feedback, conduct discussions, and exchange new product ideas.

Here are some technical policies and procedure documents you might consider making available on your intranet:

- Network security policy
- Hard-disk backup policy
- PC virus-detection policy
- Software duplication and software piracy policy
- Network access procedures for remote users
- Policy on Internet access by company employees
- Password usage policy

If your company specializes in a specific industry segment, look for other examples of policies and procedures that you could place on your intranet. For example, if your company handles toxic chemicals, you can put OSHA regulations for those chemicals and procedures for treatment of accidental spills on your intranet.

Creating a Glossary of Technical Terms

In most corporations, one of the first elements to be implemented is a glossary of technical and product-related terms.

A glossary could include an alphabetic listing of unfamiliar technical or product terms, abbreviations and acronyms, even industry slang and jargon, and, in some cases, graphical images. You can set up your glossary in many formats, from a simple, *direct look-up link* to something more complex, for example, linking other documents on your intranet, such as press realeases or product specification pages, to the glossary. In this case, a direct look-up link is a self-contained glossary file, where the letters of the alphabet are at the top of the HTML file, and the glossary entries are arranged, in order, below but in the same file, and there are no links to any other file. It's that simple.

The row of letters at the top of the screen is a quick navigational aid; click on one of the letters to jump directly to the first glossary entry referenced by that letter. Even if you don't have entries for every letter, leave them all in place; you might need them later, and as we have said before, an alphabet consisting of only a few letters is very disorienting to most people. Figure 12.4 shows a sample glossary.

Here's a piece of the HTML used to create the glossary shown in Figure 12.4:

```
<HTML>
<HEAD>
<TITLE>Intranet Glossary</TITLE>
</HEAD>
<BODY>

<IMG SRC="graphics/bannerKeys.gif" HEIGHT="129"
WIDTH="548"><BR><BR>
<FONT SIZE="+2" FACE="arial, helvetica"><B>Intranet
Glossary</B></FONT><BR>

This glossary contains definitions of some of the new terms,
acronyms, and abbreviations you may encounter as you set up
your own corporate intranet. We start with a few symbols and
numbers, then dive right into the alphabetical
listing.<BR><BR>

<CENTER>
<FONT SIZE ="+1" face="arial, helvetica">
<A HREF="#A">A</A> <A HREF="#B">B</A> <A HREF="#C">C</A>
<A HREF="#D">D</A> <A HREF="#E">E</A>
<A HREF="#F">F</A> <A HREF="#G">G</A> <A HREF="#H">H</A>
<A HREF="#I">I</A> <A HREF="#J">J</A>
```

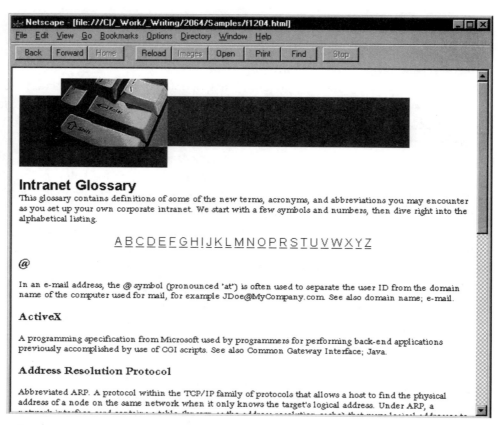

FIGURE 12.4: A sample glossary

```
<A HREF="#K">K</A> <A HREF="#L">L</A> <A HREF="#L">M</A>
<A HREF="#L">N</A> <A HREF="#L">O</A>
<A HREF="#L">P</A> <A HREF="#L">R</A> <A HREF="#L">S</A>
<A HREF="#L">T</A> <A HREF="#L">U</A>
<A HREF="#L">V</A> <A HREF="#L">W</A> <A HREF="#L">X</A>
<A HREF="#L">Y</A> <A HREF="#L">Z</A>
</FONT>
</CENTER>

<H3>@</H3>
In an e-mail address, the @ symbol (pronounced "at") is often
used to separate the user ID from the domain name of the
```

```
computer used for mail, for example JDoe@MyCompany.com. See
also domain name; e-mail.
```

`<H3><A NAME="A">ActiveX</A></H3>`

```
A programming specification from Microsoft used by programmers
for performing back-end applications previously accomplished
by use of CGI scripts. See also Common Gateway Interface;
Java.
```

To save screen space, when you click on a letter, you jump directly to the first entry for that letter, rather than to a stand-alone letter. You use the same HTML coding for either effect. See Chapter 9, "Creating Intranet Pages with HTML," for more information on using HTML.

If you use a lot of symbols and odd characters in your company, add an entry just for symbols. If your products all have numbers instead of names (do the numbers 386 and 486 ring any bells?), you can always add numbers too. Some authorities place numbers and symbols together at the beginning or at the end of the glossary, and others locate them at the appropriate point in the alphabet, as in *three eighty-six* and *four eighty-six,* for example.

You might also consider adding phonetic entries to help new users or users who have only read a term but have never heard it pronounced. After all, who would have thought that the acronym for *Small Computer System Interface,* or SCSI, would be pronounced *scuzzy?*

> **TIP**
>
> For users whose first language isn't English, consider adding a glossary in other languages. Because HTML supports the ISO-Latin-1 character set, you can create a glossary of terms in most of the common European languages. List the terms according to that language's rules for alphabetic order.

In addition to phonetic entries, you can add entries for graphical elements, such as a figure illustrating a concept, a program icon, or other useful image.

Once the glossary is ready for your intranet, don't forget to add links to it from other documents on your intranet so readers of these documents can access the glossary. For example, say you have an entry in the glossary for *SCSI.* To give readers the opportunity to jump to this definition in the glossary from the document they are currently reading, you'd include a link like this one:

```
The <A HREF="glossary.htm#scsi">SCSI</A> interface must be
properly terminated to prevent signals from echoing on the bus.
```

By specifying the named bookmark, this link allows the reader to go directly to the definition of SCSI in the glossary You can even use this technique to link terms inside the glossary. If a definition mentions a term that is itself an entry in the glossary, you can link them.

Developing Troubleshooting Procedures

Another popular addition to a technical support site is a page or set of pages that cover troubleshooting procedures. These might fall into the following categories:

- Procedures that customers use on their own to locate a problem
- Procedures that a service technician dials in to access from a customer site when experiencing particular difficulties servicing a unit in the field
- Procedures that technical support personnel in the office use as an aid when talking a customer through a specific problem over the phone

The page should begin with a statement that lets the reader know that he or she is in the right place. You might end the page with information on what to do if this troubleshooting procedure has not solved the problem; add your help desk phone number and extension and invite the person to call for more information. And if you don't normally add a `mailto` link to your e-mail address, consider adding one here. The last thing you want is frustrated users getting to the end of the troubleshooting information only to find nowhere else to go for help. They are stuck.

> **TIP**
>
> If you find that your troubleshooting procedure page looks like it will evolve into a long procedure, break it into several smaller pages. Sort the problems into categories (and even subcategories if you have to), and make the lower categories separate HTML documents. This lets readers find their way from the general to the specific as they work down the hierarchy of categories.

Just as you do with traditional printed troubleshooting guides, you'll have to take pains to make your intranet troubleshooting guide as straightforward and intuitive to use as possible, bearing in mind that in all probability the person who is using it is angry and frustrated. Only people who have a problem that they can't fix on their own access this kind of information; most people don't read this stuff for fun. If your troubleshooting procedures are hard to use and difficult to follow, you're actually compounding their difficulties by giving them another problem to deal with, rather than giving them an easy-to-use and elegant solution.

Developing a Download Page

A download page is a convenient way to give your users or customers easy access to new software, updates and bug fixes, product documentation, and any other material that can be transmitted electronically. Figure 12.5 shows you a sample download page.

You can also use a download page to save both you and the users of your intranet a great deal of time by distributing browser plug-in, or helper, applications. Add them as an option on your download page, and you'll save yourself the time you would have spent distributing the software manually. By placing the file or files on your intranet, users who want a copy of a new plug-in (or an update to an older one) can simply click on an item in a Web page and download it using their browser.

> **WARNING** Check the distribution license on any software or shareware before you make the plug-in available on the intranet.

Your download page tells users what they can find on your intranet and contains instructions on how to download files, as well as information on the file type and its approximate size. Users need to know information about the file type so they can decide if they can run it on their system after they have downloaded it. If the file is in a compressed or zipped form, add details about the compression program, or better still, as an additional option, make the compression program available for download from this page.

Collecting all the separate components of a large software package into a single zipped file is a convenient way to distribute a software package; you can also be confident all the pieces will make it to their destination and not get lost. Another way to distribute software is as a *self-extracting archive*—a zipped file that knows how to unzip itself and does not require a separate utility program to do the job.

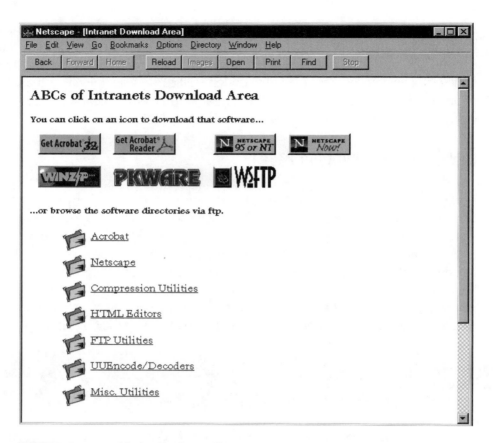

FIGURE 12.5:   This download page allows users to download directly by clicking on a button or by browsing a directory for the files they need.

TIP   One such program is WinZip, and you can copy an evaluation version of it to your hard drive or to your intranet server from the Internet using FTP or the Web. Start at the WinZip Web site, http://www.winzip.com.

So they can evaluate their hard disk space options, users also need some idea of the file size. Although the actual speed of the download isn't usually a big deal to networked users, it's extremely important to users who log on from a remote site using a modem and telephone connection.

The links used in your download page use the FTP (File Transfer Protocol) part of the TCP/IP family of networking protocols to actually do the work of moving the file from the server to the user's system. To retrieve a file, you simply click on its link, and the rest is automatic. (For details about TCP/IP, see Appendix B, "Intranet Protocols—TCP/IP.")

If you think back to the discussion of HTML links in Chapter 9, you'll remember that links can contain URLs. URLs not only specify a resource, they also specify an access method. Using FTP as the access method works much like using HTTP links. The HTML code used to do this looks like this:

```
<P> <A HREF="ftp://ftp.MyIntranet.com/Software/filename.ext">
<IMG SRC="filename.gif" ALT="software"> Program file</A> (file
type, nnK file size) for product-name. </P>
<BR>
```

In this case, the URL specifies the sample address:

```
ftp://ftp.MyIntranet.com/Software/filename.ext
```

Substitute the appropriate file and directory names of your own FTP server for the sample address listed here. Many of the server products we looked at in Chapter 7, "Choosing Intranet Hardware and Software," include FTP and Gopher servers in addition to Web servers. Microsoft's Peer Web servers for Windows 95 and Windows NT Workstation and the Internet Information Server for NT Server include all three services—HTTP, FTP, and Gopher.

> **TIP**
>
> If you or your users plan to use FTP to move files on a regular basis, consider providing dedicated FTP-client software rather than a browser. Dedicated FTP clients can't do everything that a browser can, but they're much more efficient at processing simple FTP transfers.

Creating a Help Desk

As an alternative to a traditional help desk, staffed by people answering the phone, you can create an intranet help desk. Think about what your current help desk actually does and how that can be transferred to an intranet-based system. Your help desk probably performs at least some, if not all, of the following functions:

- Receives information on real and perceived problems with your products from customers by telephone, e-mail, and conventional mail
- Records the information from these contacts into some form of database or retrieval system
- Tracks the status of these reports or trouble tickets
- Works with other departments to determine the cause of the reported problem and to arrive at a timetable to implement a solution
- Reports a solution to the customer
- Monitors the quality and efficiency of the help desk itself for accurate, timely, and courteous answers
- Writes service bulletins summarizing ways to avoid problems until a more permanent solution can be found

Chances are good that you already have a large number of help-desk documents available, some in electronic form on disk. You can use the tools we described in Chapter 11, "Using Intranet Authoring and Management Tools," to convert them to HTML.

> **TIP**
>
> Help desks are asked the same questions time and again; an intranet is a good way to answer those frequently asked questions. We'll show you how to manage your technical FAQ in the next section, so leave a slot for an FAQ on the intranet help desk.

After the usual opening text at the top of the page, you could add a help link for new or infrequent users. In the center, you could create a menu of items accessible from this page, arranged as an unordered list with square bullets (`<UL TYPE=SQUARE>`), and as we mentioned previously in the section "Developing Troubleshooting Procedures," remember to include an e-mail address and telephone number for those users who want to take things further.

FedEx and Package Tracking

One of the most widely used help-desk applications to be found anywhere is the package-tracking system implemented by FedEx on its World Wide Web site. Strictly speaking, this is an Internet application, not an intranet application, but it's so well designed and easy to use that it is well worth a mention here. Take a look at `http://www.fedex.com/`.

All a customer has to do is enter the airbill tracking number, the destination country, and the approximate ship date, and then click on the Request Tracking Info button. The system shows the path of the package through the delivery process, from initial pickup to final delivery, with time and date stamps.

Even though this site does only one thing, it does it very well and can serve as a model of efficient design to all of us.

If you're also using your intranet to monitor the help-desk function, you might add a separate page for help-desk administrators. The administrator may need the ability to search the problem database by trouble ticket number or problem type, along with the means to list and display all the pending or unresolved trouble tickets, and the rights and permissions to close a trouble ticket once the problem has been successfully resolved.

If you want to password protect the help-desk administrator page, use the `<INPUT>` tag in a form with the input field type specified as a password, like this:

```
<INPUT TYPE=PASSWORD>
```

The `PASSWORD` modifier is a variation on the `TEXT` modifier; the only difference is that `PASSWORD` echoes (or displays on the screen) a series of bullets rather than the letters typed by the user. This information isn't encrypted when it's submitted; it's only hidden from the curious as it's entered.

NOTE See the section "Designing a Form" in Chapter 9, "Creating Intranet Pages with HTML," for more on how to get the most from `<INPUT>` tags.

Managing Technical FAQs

Technical support and help desk staff are constantly answering the same questions, so it makes good sense to add a Frequently Asked Questions (FAQ) document to your technical support intranet. Using an FAQ is a good way to get answers to people quickly, and in a way that boosts their satisfaction and helps to increase your status. They also feel like they're participating in that they can easily find the answers themselves without having to crack a book or chase down a support staff member.

Many of the questions people ask concern locating something—a software update, configuration information, and so on. You can tell them where to find that information in your FAQ; but better still, if the information they're requesting is available on your intranet, you can include a link to it. For example you may have two links in your FAQ answer, one to the download page and one to the help desk's home page.

The FAQ should contain the answers to those perennial questions, which might include the following:

- Where can I find up-to-date versions of in-house software?
- How do I access the intranet from a remote location or from a satellite office?
- I have a problem with my PC. Who do I contact for help?
- How do I report a network problem?
- How can I access the Internet from my desktop computer?
- How do I send a fax from my desktop computer?
- How do I order upgrades to commercial software packages?
- How do I send e-mail from my desktop computer?
- How often should I change my password?
- How often should I back up my hard disk and can I back it up to the server?
- Why does the network go down so often?

Another frequently-asked-question is a request for a new account on the server, and that sort of question is best dealt with by e-mail. The answer to this question can contain an embedded `mailto` link.

No doubt your organization will have its own set of frequently asked questions that you can add to this list.

Preparing to Set Up the Site

Before bringing your technical support site online, you'll want to develop a pilot project to test the suitability of the concept in your own department and also to catch the eye and the imagination of people who will use it every day. Getting the technical support people involved early in the project will pay dividends down the line when the system is in use for real, all day, every day.

At the same time, you'll want to establish criteria you can use to define your success in converting from the traditional telephone and mail support to intranet and e-mail support. These criteria will be substantially different from those used in other departments, such as human resources, and may include better problem reporting and tracking, fewer and shorter telephone calls, lower printing and distribution costs for technical bulletins and service notes, and more complete feedback to the engineering and research and development departments.

On a practical note, you'll need staff trained and ready to maintain and update your intranet if it's to continue to provide essential and reliable backup to the staff on the front line. Decide who will be responsible for providing updated content material and develop procedures for loading that new content onto the server in a timely way; usually a single point of contact works best. Be sensitive to feedback from your users, the people on the phones and talking to the customers; if the intranet is not helping them to do their job better and faster, a redesign may be in order.

You'll also have to communicate with other important departments within your organization as you respond to genuine problems from customers. You'll be talking to the manufacturing department if the problem is in fabrication, to your manufacturing engineers if the problem is a procedure- or materials-related problem, and even to engineering and R & D itself if the problem represents a fundamental flaw in the product.

A complete technical support intranet implementation requires much more than simply adding HTML tags to existing documents and forms. You'll come to view the intranet as integral to your technical support needs.

Setting Up a Training Site on Your Intranet

An application that fits well in the intranet world is training. According to a recent International Data Corporation report, the online training market is expected to expand to well over $1 billion by the end of the century. One of the key elements driving this growth is the need for training programs to be changed and updated quickly and cheaply as a company's training needs change. Many corporations are finding that moving the training function to the intranet is the answer.

Using an intranet brings other benefits too, as we have seen in earlier chapters. Communications improve as trainees use e-mail to respond to course material and ask questions. Because training has always been an area that requires heavy use of paper products, converting to an intranet for training saves in paper and printing costs. With an intranet, you can easily make last-minute changes as course material changes, and you can avoid the tight production deadlines imposed by traditional printed training documentation. By using links carefully, you can add cross-references to other material quickly and easily, even if the material was prepared by someone else or is only available at a distant networked location.

If you've used video-based training in an international company, you've confronted the problems of different video standards throughout the world—NTSC (*National Television System Committee*) in North America and PAL (*Phase Alteration Line*) in most of Europe, for example. You have to create the video in one format and then pay to have it converted to the other format for distribution. That particular problem goes away completely when you convert to intranet-based training. Simply produce the video as you would normally, and then make it available on the intranet. With this method, the video format is irrelevant.

In this part of the chapter, we'll look at some ways to get your training site up and running fast.

Deciding on Content

Using an intranet for training opens up all sorts of creative possibilities, not only in the corporate world, but also in universities and colleges, private and public schools, and government agencies as well. Any institution that performs any kind of training can benefit from using an intranet.

Here's a high-level look at some of the things you can do with an intranet training site:

- Use your training site for technical presentations
- Publish course descriptions
- Register for courses
- Create a how-to procedure
- Present white papers to your training site participants
- Schedule seminars with and on your training site
- Make a training FAQ available

The Original Web-Based Training Course

While most people know that NCSA (*National Center for Supercomputing Applications*) originally led the way with Mosaic, the first graphical browser, they don't know that NCSA also pioneered Web-based training with outstanding tutorials.

Quite apart from their content, these tutorials are excellent examples of how to do Web-based training. A good place to start is at

```
http://hoohoo.ncsa.uiuc.edu/docs
```

Here you'll find a discussion of how to set up the NCSA Unix-based server. Each page is arranged in a logical sequence, with links to the next page and to other related material. Like any well-organized, paper-based manual, you start at the top and work your way logically through to the end.

The intranet is also the perfect place to keep all sorts of training-related materials. Here are some possible candidates:

- Lesson plans
- Seminar outlines
- Class schedules
- Training manuals
- Presentations
- Videos
- Recommended reading lists
- Subject bibliographies

- Lists of faculty members and lecturers
- Survey forms and questionnaires

If this material is already on disk in some form, you can use the procedures outlined in Part 2, "Planning Your Intranet," and in Chapter 11, "Using Intranet Authoring and Management Tools," to translate the material into HTML and into a form suitable for viewing with a browser.

Taking Advantage of Technology

Using an intranet for training can be superior to any other single technology, simply because you can take advantage of many other technologies in support of your overall training effort. You aren't limited to simple text. If you need to show a picture to make a point, simply add a link to a GIF file. If you want to play an audio snippet, add a link to an AV or a WAVfile. If you want to show a video or an animated sequence, you can do that too.

If you have a special training need not met by the traditional browser functions or add-on programs, you have two options. You can create your own browser plug-in application to do the job for you, or you can configure a proprietary application as a browser helper.

An intranet also makes the development of the course material easier than many conventional systems, and it's particularly useful if the course creators are widely dispersed geographically. Electronic discussions using intranet collaboration tools and e-mail eliminate the need for traveling to attend face-to-face meetings. Developing the content on an intranet also brings a certain level of consistency to the material, particularly if several people will be teaching the same class at the same time in many different physical locations.

IBTauthor: CBT Moves to the Intranet

CBT, or computer-based training, has arrived on the intranet in the form of IBTauthor from Stanford Testing Systems of Spokane, Washington. CBT has been around for a long time, so how is IBTauthor different? IBTauthor is specifically designed for creating intranet and Internet training applications. It uses all the components of Internet technology that make the intranet work. If you have a Web server in place and your users have access to browsers, all you have to add is the IBTauthor package.

You create your training modules in standard HTML, and these modules are then compiled by a program called IBTmaker into a form that IBTauthor understands. This software manages all the detailed work, such as creating the links between questions and explanations, creating the answer database, and building the table of contents.

The entire system is overseen by another element called IBTclass, which administers your courses to your trainees.

Two versions of IBTauthor are available. The Departmental version is for a maximum of 500 trainees, taking as many as 100 simultaneous courses that consist of a maximum of 1,000 lessons each. The Enterprise version is for more than 10,000 trainees, taking as many as 10,000 courses that consist of a maximum of 1,000 lessons per course. Here are some of the other important features of IBTauthor:

- Runs on Windows 95 and Windows NT
- Works with any modern browser
- Requires no proprietary programming
- Supports standard HTML, including tables and frames
- Includes sample courses
- Can link to material outside the course
- Supports multimedia, including audio and video
- Can access ODBC systems from Microsoft, Oracle, Sybase, and others
- Can include configurable tests with multiple choice, random, imagemap, fill-in-the-blanks, or automatic test selection
- Can be administered from a remote browser

Trainees can take a pre-quiz test to assess their strengths and then take a post-quiz test to see how well they learned the material or to allow you to evaluate the effectiveness of your teaching material. You can even assign different score variables so you can look at the kinds of questions on which the trainees did well (or poorly). If a trainee gets 90 percent of the hardware questions wrong and 90 percent of the software questions right, it's easy to see where more training is needed. Find out more at

    http://ibt.testprep.com/

Adding Course Descriptions

Once your training manuals are converted to HTML and are available on your intranet, it's time to get the word out by advertising the courses you have available. This might involve department-, company-, or campuswide communications.

WARNING Because HTML pages that describe training courses are often part of a larger set of pages detailing other educational opportunities, be sure to give all of the educational opportunity pages a similar look and feel. It is important that they all follow the same design rules and contain equivalent content.

Be sure to include the course length, fee, starting and ending times for each day of instruction, and any prerequisite courses potential attendees must have already completed. You should also explain any certification that attendees who successfully complete the course will receive. If the course description gets too cumbersome, simply use a shortened version here and add a link to a longer, more detailed description on another page.

Use second-level headings to cover who should attend the course and what they'll learn from it and to present a list of the materials provided as part of the course fee, including text books and any product samples.

Making Technical Reports Available on Your Intranet

Another great way to use your intranet is to distribute technical information in the form of reports or white papers. Readers of technical reports on your intranet are always looking at the most up-to-date material. As we've said before, the printing and distribution costs associated with intranet use are negligible when compared with traditional paper-based methods. An intranet *technical report* is the equivalent of a technical paper published by a scholarly journal, but you can also adapt it to encompass technical *white papers,* which are condensed presentations of technical material, position papers, strategic reports, discussions of survey results, focus-group studies, technical marketing information, and so on.

> **TIP**
>
> Placing technical papers on your intranet makes it easy for people who are widely scattered throughout the organization to collaborate on the same project.

Begin the report with the name and e-mail address of the author or authors, and add links to biographical information and photographs if they're available. Add department affiliations and technical qualifications if they're appropriate.

Your technical report might include some of the following parts:

Executive Summary	Summarizes the report in a short paragraph, sometimes called an *abstract*.
Table of Contents	May contain direct links to its sections if the report is long.
Introduction	States the nature of the topic covered in the report and may reference previous work in the field.
Scope	Defines the scope of the project and justifies the research.

Method	Describes the investigative methods used in the research project to the degree that other interested researchers could replicate the work if they wished.
Results	Describes the results of the project and presents any statistical data derived from the results.
Discussion	Further describes the results, giving information about possible avenues for future research.
Conclusion	Interprets the results and derives general principles from the detailed results described earlier.
Biography	Lists the references cited in the paper.
Appendix	Contains material, such as tabulations of raw data, that is too bulky to fit in the main body of the document. Reference material is also included in the appendices.

In any section of the technical report, you can also include appropriate graphics, tables, and other art. If the image is small enough, you can include it inline; if you want to use a large image, add a link to the image instead. Don't forget to add sound and video as well if they add value to the presentation.

Breaking the Short-Page Rule

Earlier, we told you to keep your pages relatively short. Well, there is always an exception to every rule, and here is the exception to that particular rule. In a technical report, you can permit the document to grow to whatever length best serves the material. If the content is very technical, most people probably won't read the whole thing on the screen; they'll read a portion of the report to decide whether they're interested in reading more. If they want to continue, they'll most likely print out the report and read it later.

If you want to be certain that this printout is complete, consider putting the whole report onto a single Web page. This neatly eliminates the need for the reader to track down all the other pages that form part of the technical paper and print them one by one.

To close this section, let's take a look at a real-world example of how a prominent company has presented highly technical information in the form of a white paper. The design of a report should target the audience. For example, if your audience is made up of members of the conservative academic community and you want to make sure they read your report, don't make it look like a page from *Wired* magazine.

The paper shown in Figure 12.6 is part of a white paper on Java shown on Sun Microsystems's World Wide Web site. You can read the whole paper at

```
http://www.sun.com/javacomputing
```

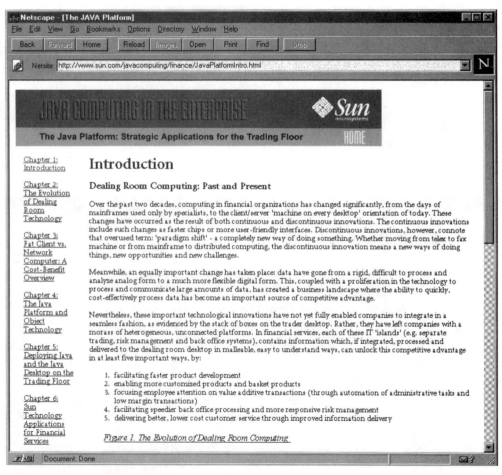

FIGURE 12.6: Example white paper on Sun Microsystem's site

> **NOTE**
>
> You can find more examples on Microsoft's Web site at `http://www.microsoft.com/intranet` and on Netscape's Web site at `http://www.netscape.com/comprod/at_work/white_paper`.

While this example is from the World Wide Web, that's not particularly important. What is important is that you look at it and translate what you learn into something you can use on your own intranet.

> **TIP**
>
> Don't forget that you can look at the HTML source code used in the report shown in Figure 12.6 (and the HTML used in any other page on the Web) by selecting View ≻ Source in both Netscape Navigator and Internet Explorer. This is a great way to observe and learn how some of the trickier things are accomplished in HTML. In no time at all, you'll be muttering "So that's how they did it."

Sun Microsystems and Intranet Training

As you might imagine, the intranet at Sun Microsystems plays an important role in several company operations, including training. It also contains a journal of articles on several technical subjects, a searchable archive of technical e-mail messages, and a projects registry.

Sun has made training modules available on the intranet as an alternative to classroom training, which is still available. Engineers can use the Web-based modules to access the information they need immediately, without having to wait for a class to roll around on the schedule and without having to wade through material that they already know and understand. Training is provided in several formats, including plain text, interactive modules, and even some video, although video is used sparingly because of the high bandwidth requirements it places on the system. All training tools contain "hack" sections full of tips and tricks, often contributed by the engineers themselves.

Using a Training FAQ

And just as we said earlier in this chapter, there is always a place for a FAQ page on your intranet. In this case, it will contain some of the questions (as well as the answers to these questions) in the following list:

- How do I register for a class?
- Must my manager approve my attending this class?
- What is the last date I can register for this class?
- What happens if I can't complete the class?
- What is the procedure for dropping a class, and is there an associated penalty?
- What is the last date for adding a class or changing to a different class?
- If I fail the test at the end of the class, how long must I wait before I can take it again, and do I have to retake the class?
- Why isn't this class available on our intranet?

So people can always get answers to their questions, create links between course outlines, seminar schedules, and the FAQ—as well as between registration forms and the FAQ. Figure 12.7 shows you a sample FAQ.

FIGURE 12.7: A sample frequently asked questions (FAQ) list

Creating a Sales and Marketing Site on Your Intranet

Hard on the heels of corporate training come sales and marketing intranet sites. In addition to considering all the intranet planning and design issues we looked at in Part 2, you need to ask yourself several additional questions when planning a sales and marketing intranet. Many of these questions are specific to this sort of department; for example, many sales reps are seldom in the office to answer questions, and pricing, availability, and other vital product or service information must be accurate and accessible to sales and marketing personnel at all times. Some of the usual organizational questions that must be answered before setting up a sales and marketing intranet include:

- What initial information will you provide on your Intranet? And what information will you provide later in the project once the pilot plan has proved to be a success?
- How will the sales and marketing home page be assembled and organized?
- Will the home page include links to other intranets within the corporation? If so, which ones?
- Who will manage the content and provide updated material?
- How often will updates be needed?
- What form will the updates take: e-mail containing the new pricing structure, printed material, database output, word processor files automatically converted to HTML form, or a complete new set of linked HTML files? And what level of effort will be required to translate that new information from the source documents into a final, proofed, and approved HTML page you can upload to the server?
- Who will be the primary contact between the sales and marketing department and the other groups in the corporate office who need to give their input?
- Will people outside the company ever see the content on this intranet? If so, is the material they'll see presented in a professional and attractive way?
- Will you be able to phase out traditional printed sales materials? If so, how long will the process take?
- Are there special problems introduced by international operations?
- Who will inform the outside-sales staff that the intranet is up and running and available for their use?

- Who will train the outside-sales staff in how to access the intranet from a remote site? Who will tell them what it can and can't do for them, and who will collect their suggestions for future additions and improvements?
- Who will take the responsibility for informing the field sales staff about content updates and the availability of new sections on the intranet?

Additionally, there are all the administrative duties that need to be performed, including making backups and installing new content files and software updates. Many sales and marketing departments have technically capable people who can take on these new jobs; others don't.

If you feel that your department is in the latter category, plan to add staff to help with the workload. Setting up a successful sales and marketing intranet is not something you can ask a few salespeople to do one quiet Friday afternoon. Do it once and do it right. In the next section, we'll look at some of the areas in sales and marketing that can benefit from a corporate intranet.

Deciding on Content

Exactly how you use your intranet depends on your company, the corporate culture, and the tasks you want the intranet to perform. Some of the typical sales and marketing uses for an intranet include the following:

- New product announcements
- Marketing bulletins
- Surveys
- Sales kits
- Pricing information
- Availability information
- Data sheets
- Competitor analysis
- Customer testimonials
- Distributor information
- Product specification and testing information
- Lead generation and contact lists
- Marketing presentations
- Frequently asked questions
- Newsletters for contractors and suppliers

In the sections that follow, we'll look at creating new product announcements, sales kits, expense reports, and FAQs.

Posting New Product Announcements

An important function in sales and marketing is to get the word out about new products or upgrades to existing products. This announcement might be for internal release, for release to strategic partners, contractors, and targeted customers, or it might also go on your Internet site for release to the outside world. You can also use this type of page to announce your new vice president or your new research project.

> **TIP**
>
> If your new product announcement will also be a press release at some point, be sure it answers the simple questions that every journalist is taught to ask: who, what, when, where, why, and how.

Rethinking Sales Kits

An intranet offers a way to distribute sales kits that is cheaper than the mail and that eliminates the possibility of lost packages. Intranets lend themselves particularly well to new product announcements made simultaneously to a worldwide sales force. Unlike traditional shrink-wrapped printed materials, last-minute changes can be accommodated quickly, easily, and, best of all, cheaply, when using an intranet.

In changing over from traditional packaging to an intranet, be careful to publicize your planned schedule to everyone in your organization so no one is left in doubt about the available sales tools. Also, decide whether your products and services can be sold directly from the intranet without backup from traditional sales materials, whether you need parallel print material, and whether you can phase out some or all of your printed material over time.

You'll also have to pay special attention to the detailed requirements of your sales kits. For example, should all sales materials be accompanied by fancy graphics, audio, and video, or should those features be kept in reserve for major new product announcements?

Data General Corporation and Sales Kits

Data General Corporation uses its intranet to distribute sales and marketing information worldwide. Data General used to publish monthly "Sales Survival Kits" to its sales staff. These kits included new product information, sales guides, demo disks, slide presentations, and other sales tools. All this information is now available as "Information Libraries" on Data General's intranet. Information about new material and updates to the intranet are sent out to the sales staff by e-mail. By using an intranet, Data General saves a bundle of money in printing and distribution costs, and the sales staff can access up-to-the-minute information on the products they're interested in selling in their region.

Now, let's look at some of the sales kit components you can distribute via your intranet.

Creating New Product Specifications and Data Sheets

It makes good sense to have product specifications, configuration information, testing results, data sheets, and price lists available on your intranet. This is particularly true for a high-tech environment in which changes are both frequent and expected and in which configuration can be complex. New and emerging companies are likely to adopt the intranet approach, particularly for materials that have a short shelf life or are modified frequently.

Pricing information on the intranet may need additional security protection, but it's quicker and less expensive to update on an intranet than it is to update and distribute hard-copy price lists.

Collecting Survey Results

You can use a survey form to collect information on customer wants and needs, and you can use it to collect opinions from a focus group looking at a prototype version of a new product or evaluating a possible new service. You can even use it to collect sales reports from outlying offices.

Filling in an Expense Report

Many companies use their intranet for some sort of reporting function. For example, Olivetti uses a page on its intranet to capture the hours each researcher spends working on each project. You can also use your intranet as a way to file expense reports. On-site employees can submit their time and expense reports without leaving their desks, and remote workers in outlying satellite offices can dial in and submit their reports using a modem and telephone line.

A typical expense report is divided into these sections:

Personal Information   This section collects the name, employee number, department, and e-mail address of the person completing the expense report.

Travel Expenses   This section allows for the entry of a date, a description of the type of travel, and a dollar amount.

Accommodation Expenses   This section allows for the entry of a date, the name of a hotel, and a dollar amount.

Entertainment Expenses   This section allows you to enter a date, the name, job title, and company affiliation of the person entertained, as well as a dollar amount.

Supplies   In this section, you can enter a date, a description of the supplies purchased, and the dollar amount.

Other categories you might consider adding to this report include a section for mileage expenses, a text area for comments, such as notes on foreign exchange rates used in calculating final expense totals or a justification for any unusual amounts. Unfortunately, your company's finance department will probably still want to see those receipts, so you'll have to submit the actual receipts another way.

The whole report relies on the `<FORM></FORM>` tags to create the appropriate data items you can collect using a CGI script. To ensure that data isn't lost if travel and accommodation occur on different dates, save each date in the form into a unique variable. For example, save your travel date using the variable `DateTravel` and your hotel reservations date in `DateHotel`.

MTC and International Sales

MTC, a company with 140 employees based in Petaluma, California, sells international telecommunications services, such as cellular phones that work in a number of countries. MTC also sells switching services that allow long-distance calls to be routed in the most cost-effective way. Sales are made by 15,000 sales representatives operating in more than 160 countries.

The sales force was linked to company headquarters by long-distance phone and by fax. But as sales grew, so did the cost of doing business. To bring down these costs, MTC decided to use an intranet linked to the Internet by a Windows NT server running a firewall to preserve system security.

To save time and money, MTC decided to keep its existing databases—housed in Microsoft Access—and to use a Web browser as the front end for the sales force. The firewall isolates the intranet from the Internet and accepts only a limited number of *remote procedure calls* (RPC). The sales force requests information, and the firewall queries the appropriate ODBC database, collects the information, and then formats it in a way suitable for display on the Web browser. By isolating the two parts of the system with ODBC, MTC can upgrade its SQL databases at any point, and the upgrade will have no effect on the front end used by the sales staff.

For security purposes, each member of the sales force has a password and a user ID, and all international transactions are encrypted in both directions. MTC notes that not only is this system saving the company a considerable amount of money previously spent on long-distance phone calls, but that it also allows for a substantial increase in the worldwide sales force without requiring any additional support staff in Petaluma.

Using a FAQ Page on Your Sales and Marketing Intranet

There is almost always a place on an intranet for a FAQ page, and the sales and marketing intranet is no exception. Here are some of the questions that sales staff new to your organization might have:

- How do I book an order?
- How do I change or cancel an order?

- How and when does my customer get shipping and delivery details for their order?
- What are the cutoff points for volume discounts?
- When and where are sales conferences held?
- Does the company offer special discounts to clients? If so, how does a new client qualify for such a discount?
- Does the department provide boilerplate proposal text? If so, can I get it from a download page on the intranet?
- Where is the latest corporate slide show located and how can I review a copy?
- How often is marketing information updated?
- Where do I find out about new product releases?
- How can I order additional sales literature?
- Are there any special problems associated with international orders?

This chapter should get you thinking about the ways you can add practical applications to your intranet. We've given you ideas for some specific sites and some pointers to more information on the Web. Next, we'll discuss how to train your staff to use your intranet to its fullest.

Chapter 13

GETTING PEOPLE TO USE YOUR INTRANET

FEATURING

- **Updating your intranet plan**
- **Getting the word out—publicizing your intranet**
- **Creating a training plan**
- **Keeping the content fresh**

Now that you've created your intranet, you'll need to let your users know that it's there, how to access it, what they can use it for, and why they want to use it. To do those things, you'll need to become a trainer, marketing specialist, and evangelist for your intranet.

To get you started, we'll use the intranet plan you created in Part 2 to help you answer the how, what, why, and who questions.

Revisiting Your Intranet Plan

To effectively communicate what your intranet is and in what ways it will help your users, you'll need to use the information in your intranet plan. You originally decided many things—organization, content, security, hardware, and software. You also decided on a mission or goal for your intranet. You may have modified your original plan as your needs developed and you became more intranet-savvy.

> **TIP** Your intranet plan should be a living, adaptable tool. Continue to revise your plan as your intranet changes. Keeping it up-to-date also keeps you thinking about your intranet in new ways as it grows.

As you revisit your intranet plan, look for key items that you'll need to pass on to your users. Think of areas or concepts that gave you problems. Chances are those same areas will give your users problems as well. For example, if the technical issues involved in setting up your intranet were difficult to resolve during the planning process, these same issues will probably come up for your users as well. Once you've set up your intranet, tested it for bugs, and refined your plan if necessary, it's time to publicize your intranet to your users.

Publicizing Your Intranet

Next to getting content for your intranet, getting people to use it is your greatest challenge. People by nature like the security of the familiar and need to be shown the benefit of change. To paraphrase a great Dilbert cartoon, "Change is good. You go first."

Most companies already have some sort of publicity mechanisms in place. You may have a large marketing department or just one publicist, but there's probably someone you can use as an avenue into the marketing process. You also have tools your company uses to convey information. For example, press releases, corporate graphics and photos, or a MarComm (Marketing Communications) writer. You can adapt and use these same tools to publicize your intranet internally.

Here are some effective ways to publicize your intranet:

Use your marketing department's know-how   Your marketing department already knows how to get the word out. Use them to help publicize your intranet. By working with them, you'll learn the techniques and become more self-reliant and develop a solid partnership along the way.

Write an article for the company newsletter   The company newsletter reaches everyone, and an article, or better yet a monthly column, can generate interest and keep your intranet in your user's minds. Your newsletter column can also be used to help train users on new features.

Hold training sessions   The type of training sessions are determined by the complexity of your intranet and your corporate culture. A high-tech company with a casual environment will respond to a more relaxed training program than a large insurance firm. One approach might be as simple as an e-mail announcement, a self-help section on the intranet, and a lunchtime training overview. The opposite end of the training spectrum is a formalized handbook and classes on using an intranet.

Of course, this is only a beginning. As your intranet grows, you'll learn which types of promotions work best. You may find that the techies in your organization never read the newsletter but will use your intranet if they get an e-mail telling them a useful piece of technical documentation is on the intranet. Other less technical users may feel more comfortable using an intranet if they've had some formal training. Let's look at a simple training plan next.

Creating a Training Program

As you think about publicizing your intranet, you first need to realize that not all users are interested in learning a new way of organizing information or learning the technologies needed to access the information. Some people just don't adapt well to change; others are fearful of technology. Other users will instantly grasp the new medium—maybe they're familiar with the Web and Internet and feel comfortable enough to shift effortlessly to an intranet. In either case, some training may be a good way to publicize your intranet, let users know what they can expect to find there, and minimize nontechnical users' anxieties about this new technology.

Let's look at a some things you might including in you intranet training program:

- A live demo
- Overview handouts, including a glossary, basic intranet technology info, and so on
- An online tutorial
- A printed "map" of your intranet
- Procedures for logging on to your intranet
- Contact information for both general help and specific technical problems

Remember to include the trainer's name, phone number, and e-mail address on all handouts. You may also want to include the same information for your Webmaster or the person responsible for maintaining your intranet.

> **NOTE** Training programs are as diverse as intranets—this book only covers basic training. If you need extensive training, your HR or training department should be able to give you tips on developing more in-depth programs.

Of course, you can add to this list and include regular classes on the intranet, online multimedia tutorials, and other extensive intranet training materials. On the low end, your training program may consist of your Webmaster giving a lunchtime presentation once a quarter on the basics we've listed above.

After you've decide what to include, you'll need to publicize the training. Use all the methods we discussed in the previous section. You may also want to put up a flyer in the lunch room and in the HR department and personally invite as many people as possible. The day before the training, send out a brief reminder via e-mail about the training including the date, time, and place. And remember to include a notice on your intranet itself!

> **NOTE** If an intranet is a new concept at your company, don't be surprised if your intranet traffic doesn't go up until after the second or third training session. That's because people may not feel comfortable enough with the technology until it's been around the company for a while.

Now that you've publicized your intranet and your users are trained, you need to keep them coming back. Next, we'll look at ways to keep your intranet content up-to-date and beneficial for users.

Keeping Your Content Fresh

One of the most difficult tasks in any project is maintenance. Creating your intranet will pose problems and challenges, but maintaining your intranet is more difficult because the sense of accomplishment and challenge isn't as high. Updating the phone list or the conference areas on your intranet are much less exciting than creating them for the first time. It's natural to say "done that" and move on. Rethink your natural tendencies, however, and remember that you must change and adapt your intranet to keep it alive. Let's look at some ways to get the information you need to keep your intranet from slowly dying.

Looking for Existing Information

Look for new ways to use existing information by repackaging, rewriting, or restructuring the content for use on your intranet. Possibilities include the following:

- *E-mail* about new company information, procedures, policies, and general information is often sent to various groups, subgroups, or even the whole company. Adding e-mail capability to your intranet is useful, but repackaging that information into a reusable, searchable format can add more value than an easily lost or deleted e-mail. For example, you may choose to convert procedures you've received via e-mail into HTML pages so the information is more readily available, or you may also choose to save information from e-mail in a database for storage.
- *Newsletters* offer a lot of corporate or departmental information. Putting that information on your intranet allows your users an easy way to get the newsletter without printing out a copy for everyone. Of course, some users will still print a copy, but remote users will now be able to get the newsletter as soon as it's published without waiting for a printed copy to be mailed. The company saves some paper and mailing costs while the users benefit by having instant access to the information and if they choose, the option to print the newsletter. Another advantage of putting a newsletter on your intranet is that it generates traffic.
- Posting *press releases* that have been released to the public allows your intranet users to feel connected to the company's vision. Sometimes the outward perception of your company isn't what the employees see. By including press releases and other marketing information on your intranet you help build a consistent vision both inside and outside the company.

Getting Hooked into the Information Pipeline

One potential problem in any group or corporation is that even if the correct information is available, the people who need it may not know about it. That includes your intranet team. If they don't know the information exists, they can't evaluate its usefulness for your intranet. Here are some of the "info pipelines" you can use to gather information for your intranet:

- E-mail distribution lists
- Voicemail distribution
- Marketing department
- Human resources department
- IS department

Contact your IS manager about including your intranet team on key e-mail and voicemail distribution lists. Also encourage departments and teams within your company to include the intranet team, or at least the team leader or manager, in any informational messages. We've already discussed ways to use your marketing department's skills to promote your intranet. Now use the connections you've made to keep you up-to-date on information the marketing department is publicizing outside the company. Many companies forget to send public information to the staff, leaving them feeling a little lost. By adding your names to the distribution of press releases, marketing brochures, and white papers you'll be able to evaluate and include the appropriate information on your intranet, improving communication within the company.

Browsing the Web

The Web is a great place for information—especially intranet information. Because the Web and intranets are technologically connected, you can use any ideas, tips, or tactics you find on a Web site on your intranet. When you browse the Web, keep your mind open to new applications that might be adapted for your intranet. For example, a particular layout might present your intranet's information in a more useful way, or a new Java-based applet might allow your users a powerful communication tool if it were implemented on your intranet. You'll find some excellent starting points for exploration in Table 13.1

Reading Books and Magazines

There are many excellent books and magazines available covering intranet, Web, and networking technologies. We'll only list a few here; explore any large bookstore or an extensive online bookstore, for example, Amazon Books at `http://www.amazon.com`, for many more titles.

TIP	You'll notice many intranet and Web magazines are free to "qualified readers." That means you may fill out an application and if your job has enough to do with intranets or the Internet and you have some buying authority, the magazine "pays" for your free subscription by selling your advertising profile. This doesn't necessarily mean you'll be added to every junk mail list in the world—I get very little junk mail, and I subscribe to several industry magazines.

As with anything intranet-related, new resources are springing up every day and old, reliable sources move on, so I've given you contact info as a phone number, or more likely, a URL, so you can find out the latest edition and pricing. Some of the magazines have offline editions, others are completely online. Table 13.1 lists some of the available resources.

Table 13.1: Intranet Print and Web Resources

Book, Magazine, or Web Resource	Description	URL
Books		
The ABCs of the Internet	A cousin to this book, *The ABCs of the Internet* discusses the Internet and its components—the Web, e-mail, Telnet, Gopher, and Usenet in plain, concise English. If you need to know about the Internet quickly without all the hype and jargon, this is the book to pick up.	`http://www.sybex.com`
Mastering Internet Information Server and *Mastering Netscape FastTrack Server*	Two Sybex titles providing detailed coverage of two of the most popular intranet servers.	`http://www.sybex.com`

Table 13.1: Intranet Print and Web Resources (continued)

Book, Magazine, or Web Resource	Description	URL
Books		
Mastering Intranets	"The big book," *Mastering Intranets* is an in-depth look at intranets, with expanded coverage of intranet technology, detailed hardware and software installation information, and expanded intranet case-studies. Includes a CD-ROM with intranet templates.	http://www.sybex.com
WebMaster in a Nutshell	An excellent overview book from O'Reilly.	http://www.ora.com
The Whole Internet for Windows 95	Another O'Reilly title, an updated version of a classic Internet book.	http://www.ora.com
Magazines		
C|NET	Online magazine covering computer news, tips, and software reviews.	http://www.cnet.com/
Inter@ctive Week	A weekly Web and intranet magazine. Good coverage of industry-specific usage of intranets. Subscription is free to qualified readers. Paid subscriptions are $99.	http://web1.zdnet.com/intweek/

Table 13.1: Intranet Print and Web Resources (continued)

Book, Magazine, or Web Resource	Description	URL
Magazines		
Intranet Design Magazine	An online intranet magazine with lots of useful, well-organized information.	`http://www.innergy.com/`
Intranet Executive	Netscape's online intranet magazine for intranet information.	`http://www.netscape.com/comprod /columns/intranet/index.html`
Webmaster	A slick monthly with good industry profiles. Webmaster also has a good online intranets section. Free to qualified readers or $29.97/year.	`http://www.web-master.com/`
WebWeek	Weekly Web and intranet magazine. Complimentary subscriptions are available to qualified readers. Regular subscriptions are $129.	`http://www.webweek.com/`
Wired and *HotWired*	Print and online magazines from Wired.	`http://www.wired.com` `http://www.hotwired.com`
Web Resources		
32bit.com	A software archive and discussion area site focusing on 32-bit software.	`http://www.32bit.com/ newhomepage/`

Table 13.1: Intranet Print and Web Resources (continued)

Book, Magazine, or Web Resource	Description	URL
Web Resources		
Acropolis	A Web site dedicated to electronic publishing using Adobe Acrobat. One of the site editors is the co-author of *Web Publishing with Adobe Acrobat and PDF*	`http://plaza.interport.net/acropolis/`
Adobe Plug-in Source Catalog	Adobe's commercial source for plug-ins to Acrobat, Photoshop, PageMaker, and other Adobe products.	`http://www.pluginsource.com/`
Adobe Systems Incorporated	As you create your intranet, you'll need tools and Adobe has them. From Acrobat to Photoshop, you'll find information and downloadable software on Adobe's Web site.	`http://www.adobe.com/`
Cafe del Sol	Sun Microsystem's Java connection. Always something interesting to read here.	`http://www.hotjava.com/`
Claremont Intranet Study	Available on the Web or as a downloadable Acrobat file, this site offers a whitepaper approach to intranets with lots of excellent information for you to use as you develop your site.	`http://www.sgi.com/Products/WebFORCE/Solutions/Claremont/`

Table 13.1: Intranet Print and Web Resources (continued)

Book, Magazine, or Web Resource	Description	URL
Web Resources		
Dictionary of PC Hardware and Data Communications Terms	This page is for the dictionary from O' Reilly. You can use the page to search for PC terms and definitions.	`http://www.ora.com/reference/dictionary/`
DoctorHTML v5	A Web page analysis tool that retrieves an HTML page and generates a report on any problems with your tagging.	`http://www2.imagiware.com/RxHTML/htdocs/intro.html`
Emerge	An Acrobat reseller that provides lots of online information about Acrobat and PDF and a large collection of other online Acrobat resources.	`http://www.emrg.com/`
Excite Search	Another excellent search engine. Excite also has a free, downloadable search engine you can install on your intranet.	`http://www.excite.com`
fine.com INTERACTIVE Response Marketing	An intranet gallery that should give you some ideas on setting up your intranet.	`http://www.fine.com/shots_intranet.htm`
The Free, Online Computing Dictionary	Not fancy, but a functional search of computing terminology	`http://wfn-shop.princeton.edu/cgi-bin/foldoc`

Table 13.1: Intranet Print and Web Resources (continued)

Book, Magazine, or Web Resource	Description	URL
Web Resources		
Gamelan	Many Java and JavaScript applets plus lots of information. A must-see if you're interested in Java.	`http://www.gamelan.com/`
HTML Quick Reference (including Explorer and Netscape extensions)	Very basic, but useful HTML reference guide.	`http://sdcc8.ucsd.edu/ ~mlwilson/htmlref.html`
HTMLedPro(1.1)	A popular, shareware HTML editor for Windows machines.	`http://www.ist.ca/htmledpro`
Intranet Data Sheet	From Microsoft, this piece is titled "What Is an Intranet, and Why Should I Use One in My Business?" and should be useful as you publicize your intranet.	`http://www.microsoft.com/ intranet/datasheet.htm`
Intranet Links	A Netscape list of intranet links not duplicated here.	`http://home.netscape.com/ comprod/at_work/linklist.html`
Intranet Solutions Center	Microsoft's online Intranet site. Lots of technical information.	`http://www.microsoft.com/ intranet/default.asp`
Lycos Search	Web-based search engine.	`http://www.lycos.com/ customsearch.html`
Microsoft Site Builder Multimedia Workshop	Internet themes you can freely use on your intranet.	`http://www.microsoft.com/ workshop/design/mmgallry/`

Table 13.1: Intranet Print and Web Resources (continued)

Book, Magazine, or Web Resource	Description	URL
Web Resources		
Microsoft Site Builder Workshop	An Internet technologies site from Microsoft. The information is just as useful for your intranet as it is for your Web site.	`http://www.microsoft.com/ workshop/default.asp`
Microsoft Technical Support Software Library	Search the Microsoft site for software, service packs, upgrades, and patches.	`http://www.microsoft.com/kb/ softlib/`
Netscape's "Creating Net Sites"	Information on Web sites that you'll find useful as you create your intranet.	`http://www.netscape.com/ assist/net_sites/index.html`
Netscape Intranet Product Line	An intranet white paper from Netscape. This is a good source document for you to use as you plan your intranet.	`http://www.netscape.com/ comprod/at_work/white_paper/ intranet/vision.html`
Netscape Navigator Software	The latest version available online.	`http://www.netscape.com/comprod /mirror/client_download.html`
O'Reilly Home Page	Lots of good Internet and intranet information online	`http://www.ora.com/`
OpenText Index-Power Search	Wait, another search engine.	`http://index.opentext.net/main/ powersearch.html`
Project Cool—the Acrobat Developer's Zone	A very cool, PDF-only look at the potential of Acrobat-based information delivery.	`http://www.projectcool.com/ developer/acrobat/`

Table 13.1: Intranet Print and Web Resources (continued)

Book, Magazine, or Web Resource	Description	URL
Web Resources		
SandyBay Software's *PCWebopaedia*	An excellent Web-based PC dictionary. You can also download a version of the Webopaedia in Windows Help format.	`http://www.sandybay.com/pc-web/`
Shareware.com	A sister site to CNET, Shareware.com is a great starting point when you're looking for low-cost utility programs, HTML editors, or other software.	`http://www.shareware.com/`
Sherlock@-The Internet Consulting Detective	An Internet learning site with a Sherlock Holmes theme. A site like this may be useful for your intranet users if they're intimidated by the Web and intranets.	`http://www.intermediacy.com/sherlock/`
Web Master's Intranet Resource Center	Webmaster magazine's online intranet information center. Lots of good intranet information—Free!	`http://www.cio.com/WebMaster/wm_irc.html`
Webber	An excellent shareware HTML editor for Windows. Webber has Wizards to help you create the more complex HTML tags like frames, tables, and forms.	`http://www.csdcorp.com/webber.htm`

Table 13.1: Intranet Print and Web Resources (continued)

Book, Magazine, or Web Resource	Description	URL
Web Resources		
WebCrawler	Yet another search engine.	`http://www.webcrawler.com/`
Welcome to Real Audio set	Get information on streaming audio on your intranet. You can learn about server options as well as download a free Real Audio player plug-in.	`http://www.realaudio.com/`
The Willcam Group-Compact Index of HTML Tags	An online HTML reference in compact form. Very useful as a quick tag lookup.	`http://www.willcam.com/cmat/ html/crossref.html`
WUGNET Shareware Hall of Fame	An excellent source for intranet and Internet shareware.	`http://www.wugnet.com/ shareware/`
Yahoo! and Yahoo! Advanced Search	A great way to find information on the Internet. We've already mentioned Yahoo! several times throughout this book. Here's the base URL to start your search.	`http://www.yahoo.com/` `http://www.yahoo.com/search.html`
Yahoo!-Computers and Internet: Communications and Networking: Intranet	A large listing of intranet information available on the Web.	`http://www.yahoo.com/Computers_ and_Internet/Communications_and _Networking/Intranet/`

This list is far from complete. Use it as a starting point and you'll discover links and pointers to other resources that can help you get new information that you can use on your intranet. Remember, too, that this list is only a tool to get you started. If you've effectively publicized your intranet and your users feel comfortable using it, they'll become the best source of new content and ideas to keep your intranet going.

This chapter gave you some starting points for publicizing your intranet and expanding your user base, using traditional marketing methods and online technologies. You can take advantage of both to make your intranet an invaluable resource for users.

We've come a long way since Chapter 1—you've learned about intranets and related technologies, browsers, intranet planning, security, and training. We've introduced you to a lot of new terms and acronyms and the TCP/IP protocol. To give you a little more information, we've added two appendices for your reference. Appendix A is a glossary of intranet-related terminology, and Appendix B gives you an overview of the TCP/IP protocol underlying your intranet.

Appendix A

INTRANET GLOSSARY

This appendix contains definitions of some of the new terms, acronyms, and abbreviations you may encounter as you set up your own corporate intranet. We start with a symbol and then dive right into the alphabetical listing.

@ In an e-mail address, the @ symbol (pronounced "at") is often used to separate the user ID from the domain name of the computer used for mail, for example `JDoe@MyCompany.com`. *See also* domain name; e-mail.

access server A computer that provides access to remote users who dial into the system and access network resources as though their computer was connected to the network directly. Also called a *remote access server.*

ActiveX A programming specification from Microsoft used by programmers for performing back-end applications previously accomplished using of CGI scripts. *See also* Common Gateway Interface; Java.

Address Resolution Protocol Abbreviated ARP. A protocol within the TCP/IP family of protocols that allows a host to find the physical address of a node on the same network when it only knows the target's logical address. *See also* protocol; Transmission Control Protocol/Internet Protocol.

anchor   A hypertext link, in the form of text or a graphic, that when you click on it takes you to the linked file. An anchor may be at the source or the destination of the hypertext link. *See also* hypertext; link.

anonymous FTP   A method used to access an Internet host with FTP that doesn't require you to have an account on the target computer system. Just log on to the Internet computer with the user name *anonymous* and use your e-mail address as your password. This access method was originally provided as a courtesy so system administrators could see who had logged on to their systems, but now it's often required to gain access to an Internet computer that has FTP service.

You can't use anonymous FTP with every computer on the Internet—only with those that have been set up to offer the service. The system administrator decides which files and directories will be open to public access, and the rest of the system is considered off limits and cannot be accessed by anonymous FTP users. Some sites only allow you to download files from them; as a security precaution, you aren't allowed to upload files to them. All this aside, the world open to anonymous FTP users is enormous; you can access tens of thousands of computers, and you can download hundreds of thousands of files. *See also* File Transfer Protocol.

API   Application Programming Interface; the complete set of operating system functions that an application can use to perform such tasks as managing files and displaying information. An API provides a standard way to write an application, and it also describes how the application should use the functions that it provides. Using an API is quicker and easier than developing functions from scratch and helps to ensure some level of consistency among all applications developed on a specific operating system. *See also* Internet Server API; Netscape Server API.

applet   A self-contained program designed to be run in a specific environment, such as a Java applet running within a browser.

Application Programming Interface   *See* API.

Archie   A system used on the Internet to locate files available by anonymous FTP. Archie was written by students and volunteers at McGill University's School of Computer Science in Montreal, Canada, and is available on servers worldwide. You can use an Archie client on your system, log on to an Archie server using Telnet, or send e-mail to an Archie server. When you ask Archie to look for a file, it looks in a database rather than searching the whole Internet; once Archie finds the file, use anonymous FTP to retrieve it.

archive file   A single file that contains one or more files or directories that may have been compressed to save space. Archives are often used to transport large numbers of files across the Internet. An archive file created by the Unix operating system may have the filename extension `TAR` (for tape archive); archives created with DOS, OS/2, and Windows archive utilities usually have the filename extension `ZIP` and are sometimes called Zip files. The name *Zip* comes from the PKZIP program, although other programs, including WinZip, can create zip files. Archive files created on the Macintosh will probably have the extension `SAE` or `SIT` from the StuffIt program.

> **TIP**   You can get the most recent copies of popular archive utilities off the Internet. PKZip is available from `http://www.pkware.com/`, StuffIt from `http://www.aladdinsys.com/`, TAR from `ftp://prep.ai.mit.edu/pub/gnu/`, and WinZip from `http://www.winzip.com/`.

ASCII   ASCII is the acronym for *American Standard Code for Information Interchange.* ASCII is a standard coding scheme that assigns values to letters, numbers, punctuation marks, and control characters to achieve compatibility between computer systems. In ASCII, each character is represented by a unique integer value composed of seven bits. The values from 0 to 31 are used for nonprinting control characters, and the values from 32 to 127 are used to represent the letters of the alphabet, numbers, and common punctuation marks. All computers that use ASCII can understand the Standard ASCII Character Set. It's used to represent everything from source code to written text and is used when exchanging information between computers.

asynchronous transmission   A method of data transmission that uses start bits and stop bits to coordinate the flow of information so the time intervals between individual characters do not have to be equal. Parity is often used to check the accuracy of the data received.

attribute   A quantity that defines a special property or characteristic of an HTML element. An attribute is defined within the start tag. *See also* element; Hypertext Markup Language; tag.

auditing   The process of scrutinizing network security-related events and transactions to ensure that they are accurate, particularly reviewing attempts to create, access, and delete files and directories. Records of these events are stored in the Event Log, which can only be examined by the system administrator. *See also* system administrator.

audit trail   An automatic feature of certain programs (or of some operating systems) that creates a running record of all transactions. An audit trail allows you to track a piece of data from the moment it enters the system to the moment it leaves and to determine the origin of any changes to that data. You can then use that information to confirm who's accessing your intranet.

authentication   In a network or multiuser operating system, the process that validates a user's logon information. Authentication usually involves comparing the user name and password to a list of authorized users and their password. If a match is found, the user can log on and access the system in accordance with the rights or permissions assigned to his or her account.

authorization   The provision of rights or permissions based on identity. Authorization and authentication go hand in hand in networking; your access to services is based on your identity, and the authentication process confirms that you are who you say you are.

> **TIP**
>
> **If you see or hear about an intranet term that we haven't covered, you can still find out what it means by looking on the Internet. Two good sources are the PCWebopaedia at** http://www .sandybay.com/pc-web/ **and the Dictionary of PC Hardware and Data Communications Terms at** http://www.ora.com/ reference/dictionary/.

backbone   The portion of the network that manages the bulk of the traffic. The backbone may connect several locations or buildings, and other smaller networks may be attached to it. A backbone often uses a higher-speed communications system than the individual LAN segments. *See also* local area network.

bandwidth   The transmission capacity of a communications channel, usually stated in megabits per second (Mbps). For example, Ethernet has a bandwidth of 10Mbps, and FDDI has a bandwidth of 100Mbps.

bang path From the Unix world, a *bang* is an exclamation point, and a *bang path* is a series of host names used to direct e-mail from one user to another. *See also* e-mail.

bastion host A computer system that is the main connection to the Internet for users of a local area network. A bastion host is usually configured in such a way as to minimize the risk of intruders gaining access to the main LAN. It gets its name from the fortified projections on the outer walls of medieval European castles. *See also* firewall; proxy server.

bits per second Abbreviated bps. The number of bits transmitted every second during a data-transfer procedure.

bridge A hardware device used to connect local area networks so they can exchange data. A bridge can connect networks that use different wiring or network protocols. Bridges work at the Data Link layer of the ISO/OSI model and manage the flow of traffic between two LANs by reading the address of every data packet. *See also* gateway; router.

browser Short for Web browser. A browser is a program used to explore Internet or intranet resources. Browsers let you see text, graphics, and other file types. A browser presents the information—text, graphics, sound, or video—as a document, or *page*, on the screen. Most people use Netscape Navigator or Microsoft Internet Explorer. See Chapter 2, "Using a Browser to Access Your Intranet," for basic information on using both these browsers.

callback modem Also known as a *dialback modem.* A special modem that does not answer an incoming call, but instead requires the caller to enter a code and then hang up so the modem can return the call. As long as the entered code matches a previously authorized number, the modem dials the number. Callback modems are used in installations for which communications lines must be available for remote users but data must be protected from intruders. *See also* modem.

CERN CERN, the Centre Europeen pour la Recherche Nucleaire, is the European laboratory for particle physics where the concept of the World Wide Web first originated in 1989.

CERT Another acronym, this time for Computer Emergency Response Team. Founded in 1988 at Carnegie-Mellon University, CERT works with the Internet community to increase awareness of security issues; it conducts research into improving existing systems and provides a 24-hour technical assistance service for responding to security incidents. You can reach CERT by e-mail at `cert@cert.org` or by telephone at (412) 268-7090.

CGI *See* Common Gateway Interface.

client An application that uses information or services provided by a server. Many of the common intranet tools, including Gopher, FTP, and the Web browsers, are all client applications interacting with the appropriate server. *See also* client-server.

client-server A network model that distributes processing between the client (or front end) and the server (or back end) on the network. Clients, including many popular intranet tools—such as Gopher, FTP, and the Web browsers—request information from the servers. The servers store data and programs and provide network-wide services to clients. *See also* client; server.

collaboration software A set of network-based applications that let users share information quickly and easily. *See also* whiteboard.

Common Gateway Interface Abbreviated CGI. A standard way that programs can interface with Web servers and allow them to run applications, such as search engines, and to access databases and other back-end applications. *See also* search engine.

congestion A condition that occurs when the load exceeds the capacity of a communications circuit. The server may respond, or a message may appear, telling you that no ports are available for the service or host you're requesting.

connectionless A term that describes a communications model in which the source and destination addresses are included in each packet, so a direct connection between nodes is not required for communications. *See also* node.

connection-oriented A term that describes a communications model that goes through three well-defined stages: establishment of the connection, transfer of the data, and release of the connection. TCP is a connection-oriented protocol. *See also* protocol; Transmission Control Protocol.

cracker   An unauthorized person who breaks into a computer system planning to do harm or damage or with criminal intent. The popular press often portrays crackers as programmers with exceptional talent, and some of them are, but most of them use a set of well-worn tricks to exploit common security weaknesses in the systems they target. *See also* hacker.

daemon   A background program that runs unattended, collecting information or performing administrative tasks. The term comes from the Unix world. Daemons manage all sorts of tasks, including mail, networking, Internet and intranet services, and FTP, Gopher, and Web services. Some daemons are triggered automatically by events to perform their work; others operate at set time intervals. Because they spend most of their time waiting for something to do, daemons do not consume large quantities of system resources.

Data Encryption Standard   Abbreviated DES. Developed by the U.S. National Bureau of Standards, a standard method of encrypting and decrypting data. DES works by combining transposition and substitution. It is used by the U.S. government and most banks and money-transfer systems to protect all sensitive computer information.

data packet   One unit of information transmitted as a discrete entity from one node on the network to another. More specifically, in packet-switched networks, a packet is a transmission unit of a fixed maximum length that contains a header, a set of data, and error-control information. *See also* node.

DCOM   *See* Distributed Common Object Model.

dedicated line   A communications circuit used for one specific purpose and not used by or shared between other users. You need only dial a dedicated line to restore service after an unscheduled interruption. Also known as a *dedicated circuit* or a *direct connection.* An ISDN connection to the Internet qualifies as a dedicated line. *See also* direct connection; ISDN.

DES   *See* Data Encryption Standard.

dial-up line   A nondedicated communications channel in which a connection is established by dialing the destination code and is then broken once the call is complete.

direct connection   A communications circuit used for one specific purpose and not used by or shared between other users. You need only dial a dedicated line to restore service after an unscheduled interruption. Also known as a *dedicated circuit* or a *direct line.* An ISDN connection to the Internet qualifies as a direct connection. *See also* dedicated line; ISDN.

Distributed Common Object Model   Abbreviated DCOM. A specification from Microsoft that enables communications between distributed objects.

DNS   An acronym for Domain Name Service and sometimes referred to as *Domain Name System.* The distributed database system used to map host names to numeric IP addresses. DNS lets you use the Internet without having to remember long lists of cryptic numbers. *See also* IP address.

DNS alias   A host name that the DNS server knows points to another host. Computers always have one real name, but they can also have several aliases. DNS aliases are sometimes called *CNAMEs* or *canonical names. See also* DNS.

DNS name server   A server containing information that is part of the DNS distributed database, which makes computer names available to client programs querying for name resolution on the Internet. *See also* DNS.

document database   A carefully organized collection of related documents; for example, a set of technical support bulletins.

document root   On an Internet server, a directory that contains the files, images, and data you want to present to all users who access the server with a browser. *See also* browser.

domain   A description of a single computer, a whole department, or a complete site, used for naming and administrative purposes. Top-level domains must be registered to receive e-mail from outside the organization; local domains have meaning only inside their own enterprise. Depending on the context, domains can have several slightly different meanings:
   • On the Internet, a domain is part of the DNS.
   • In Windows NT, a user can log in to the local computer and be authenticated to access just that one system or can log in to a domain and be authenticated to access other servers within that domain.

- In IBM's SNA (Systems Network Architecture), a domain includes all the terminals and other network resources controlled by a single processor or processor group.
- In Novell's NetWare 4.*x*, a domain is a special area of memory where a NetWare Loadable Module (NLM) can run without corrupting the operating system memory.

domain name   In DNS, an easy-to-remember name that identifies a specific host, as opposed to the hard-to-remember numeric IP address. *See also* DNS; IP address.

download   In communications, to transfer a file or other information from the server to another computer over a network link or via modem. *See also* upload.

element   A unit of structure in HTML. Some elements have start and stop tags; others have only a single tag. Certain elements can contain other elements. *See also* Hypertext Markup Language; tag.

e-mail   Also called *electronic mail.* The use of a network to transmit text messages, memos, and reports. Users can send a message to one or more individual users, to a predefined group, or to all users on the system. When you receive an e-mail message, you can read, print, forward, answer, or delete it. E-mail has several advantages over conventional mail systems, including: It's fast; it's extensive; and it allows you to send files as attachments to messages. The problems with e-mail are similar to those associated with online communications in general, such as security (always assume that your e-mail is not private) and the legal status of documents exchanged via e-mail.

encapsulation   The process of inserting the header and data from a higher-level protocol into the data frame of a lower-level protocol. *See also* protocol.

encryption   The process of encoding information in an attempt to make it secure from unauthorized access. The reverse of this process is known as decryption. The two main encryption schemes in common use are *private (symmetrical) key scheme,* which is an encryption algorithm based on a private encryption key known to both the sender and the recipient of the information, and *public (asymmetrical) key scheme,* which is an encryption scheme based on using the two halves of a long bit sequence as encryption keys.

encryption key   A unique and secret number used to encrypt data to protect it from unauthorized access.

enterprise   A term used to encompass an entire business group, organization, or corporation, including all local, remote, and satellite offices.

enterprise network   A network that connects every computer in every location of a business group, organization, or corporation and runs the company's mission-critical applications. In many cases, an enterprise network includes several types of computers running several operating systems.

Ethernet   A popular network protocol and cabling scheme with a transfer rate of 10Mbps, originally developed by Xerox in 1976. Ethernet uses a bus topology, and network nodes are connected by thick or thin coaxial cable, fiber-optic cable, or twisted-pair cabling.

Ethernet address   The address assigned to a network interface card by the original manufacturer. This address identifies the local device address to the rest of the network and allows messages to find the correct destination. Also known as the MAC (*media access control*) address or the hardware address.

Exchange   A groupware product from Microsoft that allows users to discuss corporate-wide issues, set up meetings, and send e-mail containing links to pages on the World Wide Web. Exchange competes with Lotus Notes from IBM and with GroupWise from Novell.

FAQ   Abbreviation for *Frequently Asked Questions.* Originally a Usenet document that contained the answers to the questions that new users asked when they first subscribed to a newsgroup. Recent use has spread beyond Usenet, although the concept remains the same: to distribute answers to questions that the seasoned users have grown tired of answering. A FAQ is often an excellent introduction to a technically difficult subject. *See also* newsgroup; Usenet.

Fast Ethernet   A version of the Ethernet standard that permits data-transfer rates of 10Mbps or 100Mbps or both, and uses CSMA/CD access methods. *See also* Ethernet.

fiber-optic cable　A transmission technology that sends pulses of light along specially manufactured optical fibers. Each fiber consists of a core, thinner than a human hair. Light signals introduced at one end of the cable are conducted along the cable as the signal reflects from the sheath. Fiber-optic cable is lighter and smaller than traditional copper cable, is immune to electrical interference, offers better security, and has better signal-transmitting qualities.

File Transfer Protocol　Abbreviated FTP. The TCP/IP protocol used to log on to a computer, list files and directories, and transfer files. FTP supports a range of file-transfer types and formats, including ASCII, EBCDIC, and binary. *See also* anonymous FTP; Transmission Control Protocol/Internet Protocol.

firewall　A barrier established in hardware or in software, or sometimes in both, that allows traffic to flow only one way—outward from the protected network. A firewall is a device commonly used to protect an internal network from unwanted intruders.

form　An HTML element that allows users to complete information in fill-in-the-blanks boxes, checklists, or other formats, and then submit that data as an application to be processed. The `FORM` element is specified in level 2 HTML. *See also* Hypertext Markup Language.

FTP　*See* File Transfer Protocol.

fully qualified domain name　Abbreviated FQDN. A host name with the appropriate domain name appended. For example, on a host with the host name `wallaby` and the DNS domain name `my-company.com`, the FQDN is `wallaby.my-company.com`. *See also* domain name; DNS.

gateway　A shared connection between a LAN and a larger system, such as a mainframe computer or a large packet-switching network, whose protocols are different. Often slower than a bridge or a router, a gateway is a combination of hardware and software with its own processor and memory used to perform protocol conversions. *See also* bridge; router.

GIF　*See* Graphics Interchange Format.

Gopher   A popular client-server application that presents Internet resources as a series of menus, shielding the user from the underlying mechanical details of IP addresses and different access methods. Developed at the University of Minnesota, home of the Golden Gophers. *See also* client-server; IP address.

Gopherspace   A collective term used to describe all the Internet resources accessible using Gopher.

Graphics Interchange Format   Abbreviated GIF. A graphics file format, originating on CompuServe, that results in relatively small graphics files. A graphic in this format can be used as an inline image in an HTML document. *See also* Hypertext Markup Language; inline image.

groupware   Network software designed for use by a group of people all working on the same project or needing access to the same data.

hacker   In the programming community, a hacker is a person who pursues knowledge of computer systems for its own sake—someone willing to "hack through a problem." More recently, particularly in popular culture, the term has come to mean a person who breaks into other people's computers with malicious intent (what some programmers call a *cracker*). *See also* cracker.

helper application   A program launched or used by a Web browser to process a file that the browser cannot handle. A helper may view a JPEG file, play a sound file, or expand compressed files. Sometimes called a *plug-in.* A helper that deals with video, graphics, or animation is called a *viewer;* a helper that deals with sound files is called a *player. See also* JPEG; player; viewer.

hit   A hit on a Web or intranet page occurs whenever you access any file, whether it is an HTML document, a graphic, a CGI script, or an audio or video clip on that page. If you access three files on an HTML page, you generate three hits. This means that a hit is not usually a good estimate of the number of individual people visiting a site because the number of hits simply reflects the number of files accessed. *See also* Common Gateway Interface; Hypertext Markup Language.

home page   An initial starting page on an intranet or a Web site. A home page may be associated with a single person, a specific subject, a corporation, a nonprofit organization, or a school and is a convenient jumping-off place for links to other pages or Internet resources. Think of it as a front door to a site.

host   The central or controlling computer in a networked environment, providing services that other computers or terminals can access via the network. A large system accessible on the Internet is also known as a host. Sometimes known as a *host system* or a *host computer*.

HotJava   An interactive Web browser from Sun Microsystems. HotJava is the browser related to Java, the programming language designed to create small executable programs that can be downloaded quickly and run using a small amount of memory. *See also* Java.

HTML   *See* Hypertext Markup Language.

HTTP   *See* Hypertext Transfer Protocol.

hypertext   A method of presenting information so the user can view it in a nonsequential way, regardless of how the topics were originally arranged. In a hypertext application, you can browse through the information flexibly, choosing to follow a new path each time you access the information. When you click on a hot spot or link, you activate a jump to another hypertext document, which may be located on the same server or can be on a completely different system thousands of miles away.

Hypertext Markup Language   Abbreviated HTML. A markup or structuring language used to describe Web and intranet documents. Originally only used to define structure, HTML now defines the structure, appearance, and placement of HTML elements, including fonts, graphics, text, hypertext links to other sites, and many more details. HTML is a subset of Standard Generalized Markup Language, or SGML. *See also* hypertext.

Hypertext Transfer Protocol   Abbreviated HTTP. An underlying protocol used by intranets and the Web. HTTP defines how messages are formatted and transmitted and what the software, in this case intranet Web servers and browsers, should do with the various commands.

HTTP is called a *stateless protocol,* which means each HTTP command is executed independently, not relying on any other command. This protocol is more stable, but adding interactive content can be difficult. *See also* hypertext; link.

imagemap   A graphical inline image on an HTML page that potentially connects each region of the image with a Web resource; you can click on the image to retrieve the resource. *See also* inline image; Hypertext Markup Language.

inline image   An image merged with text displayed on an HTML page. *See also* Hypertext Markup Language.

International Standards Organization/Open System Interconnection model
Abbreviated ISO/OSI model. A network reference model defined by the ISO that divides computer-to-computer communications into seven connected layers. Such layers are known as a *protocol stack.*
    Each successively higher layer builds on the functions provided by the layers below, as follows:

Application layer 7	The highest level of the model. It defines the manner in which applications interact with the network, including database management, e-mail, and terminal-emulation programs.
Presentation layer 6	Defines the way in which data is formatted, presented, converted, and encoded.
Session layer 5	Coordinates communications and maintains the session for as long as it is needed, performing security, logging, and administrative functions.
Transport layer 4	Defines protocols for structuring messages and supervises the validity of the transmission by performing some error checking.
Network layer 3	Defines protocols for data routing to ensure that the information arrives at the correct destination node.
Data Link layer 2	Validates the integrity of the flow of data from one node to another by synchronizing blocks of data and controlling the flow of data.
Physical layer 1	Defines the mechanism for communicating with the transmission medium and the network-interface hardware.

internet   Short for *internetwork.* Two or more networks using different networking protocols, connected by means of a router. Users on an internetwork can access the resources of all connected networks.

The Internet   The world's largest computer network, consisting of millions of computers supporting tens of millions of users in more than 100 countries. The Internet is growing at such a phenomenal rate that any size estimates are quickly out of date. The Internet was originally established to meet the needs of the U.S. defense industry, but it has quickly grown into a huge global network serving universities, academic researchers, commercial interests, and government agencies, both in the United States and overseas.

   The Internet uses TCP/IP protocols, and Internet computers run many operating systems, including several variations of Unix, Windows NT, and VMS.

Internet Architecture Board   Abbreviated IAB. The coordinating committee for management of the Internet. IAB has two main subcommittees:

- The *Internet Engineering Task Force* (IETF) specifies protocols and recommends Internet standards.
- The *Internet Research Task Force* (IRTF) researches new technologies and refers them to the IETF.

Previously, the abbreviation stood for *Internet Activities Board.*

Internet Content Provider   Abbreviated ICP. A company that will design and deliver content for your Web site. For a fee, of course!

Internet Control Message Protocol   Abbreviated ICMP. That portion of TCP/IP that provides the functions used for Network layer management and control. *See also* International Standards Organization/Open System Interconnection model; Transmission Control Protocol/Internet Protocol.

Internet NFS   A TCP/IP-based protocol from Sun Microsystems used for sharing and accessing files remotely over the Internet. *See also* Network File System.

Internet Protocol   Abbreviated IP. The TCP/IP Session-layer protocol that regulates packet forwarding by tracking Internet addresses, routing outgoing messages, and recognizing incoming messages. IP does not guarantee the delivery of a packet, nor does it specify the order of delivery. *See also* Transmission Control Protocol/Internet Protocol.

Internet Server API   Abbreviated ISAPI. An Internet Information Server programming interface for back-end applications developed by Microsoft and Process Software Corporation. *See also* Netscape Server API.

Internet service provider   Abbreviated ISP. The company that provides you or your organization with access to the Internet via a dial-up or a dedicated connection. An ISP will normally have several servers and a high-speed connection to an Internet backbone. *See also* backbone; dedicated line; dial-up line.

InterNIC   The organization that maintains unique addresses for all the computers on the Internet using DNS. *See also* DNS.

intranet   In the most general sense, a private, corporate network that uses Internet software and TCP/IP protocol standards. Many companies use intranets for tasks as simple as distributing a company newsletter and for tasks as complex as posting and updating technical support bulletins to service personnel worldwide. An intranet does not always include a permanent connection to the Internet. *See also* The Internet; Transmission Control Protocol/Internet Protocol.

intruder   An unauthorized user of a computer system, usually a person having malicious intent. *See also* cracker.

IP   *See* Internet Protocol.

IP address   A set of four numbers (4 bytes, or 32 bits), separated by dots, that specifies the actual location of a computer on the Internet or other TCP/IP-based network. These numbers are difficult for most people to remember, so humans tend to refer to Internet computers by their domain names instead. *See also* domain name; Transmission Control Protocol/Internet Protocol.

ISDN   An acronym for Integrated Services Digital Network. A standard for a worldwide digital-communications network intended to replace all current systems with a completely digital, synchronous, full-duplex transmission system. Computers and other devices connect to ISDN via simple, standardized interfaces. When complete, ISDN systems will be capable of transmitting voice, video, and data all on the same line—a task that currently requires three separate connections.

ISO/OSI model   *See* International Standards Organization/Open System Interconnection model.

ISP   *See* Internet service provider.

Java   An object-oriented programming language developed by programmers at Sun Microsystems and designed to create distributed, executable applications for use with special Web browsers. Java technology has been licensed by many companies, including Microsoft, IBM, Adobe Systems, Oracle, Borland, Symantec, and other companies developing Web applications. *See also* ActiveX; HotJava; Java Database Connectivity.

Java Database Connectivity   Abbreviated JDBC. An API that allows developers to write Java applets that can access a database. *See also* API.

JavaScript   A scripted, noncompiled subset of Java.

JPEG   Acronym for *Joint Photographic Experts Group.* An image-compression standard and file format that defines a set of compression methods for high-quality images, such as photographs, single video frames, or scanned pictures; JPEG doesn't work very well when compressing text, line art, or vector graphics.

JPEG uses lossy compression methods that result in some loss of original data; when you decompress the image, you don't get exactly the same image you originally compressed (although JPEG was specifically designed to discard information not easily detected by the human eye). JPEG can store 24-bit color images in as many as 16 million colors; files in GIF format can only store a maximum of 256 colors. *See also* Graphics Interchange Format; lossy compression.

kilobits per second   Abbreviated Kbps. The number of bits transmitted every second, measured in multiples of 1024 bits per second; used as an indicator of transmission rates.

LAN   *See* local area network.

legacy system   A computer system that has been in use for a long time, either in a corporation (in the case of a mainframe computer) or in a home or small office (in the case of an older PC system).

link   In a hypertext document, a connection between one element and another in the same or in a different document. *See also* hypertext.

local area network   Abbreviated LAN. A group of computers and associated peripheral devices connected by a communications channel, capable of sharing files and other resources between several users. *See also* wide area network.

lossless compression   Any data-compression method that compresses a file by rerecording the data it contains in a more compact fashion. With lossless compression, no original data is lost when the file is decompressed. Lossless compression methods are used on program files and on images such as medical X rays, where losing data can't be tolerated. *See also* lossy compression.

lossy compression   Any data-compression method that compresses a file by discarding any data that the compression method decides isn't needed. Use lossy compression to shrink audio or images files if absolute accuracy isn't required and if the loss of some data won't be noticed. *See also* lossless compression.

megabits per second   Abbreviated Mbps. A measurement of the amount of information moving across a network or communications link in one second, measured in multiples of 1,048,576 bits.

MIME   *See* Multipurpose Internet Mail Extensions.

modem   Contraction of *mod*ulator/*dem*odulator; a device that allows a computer to transmit information over a telephone line by translating between the digital signals used by the computer and the analog signals suitable for use by the telephone system. When transmitting, the modem modulates the digital information onto a carrier signal on the telephone line. When receiving, the modem performs the reverse process to demodulate the data from the carrier signal.

Mosaic   A World Wide Web client program or Web browser, originally written by the National Center for Supercomputing Applications (NCSA) at the University of Illinois. There are several excellent commercial browsers descended from Mosaic, the most common being Netscape Navigator from Netscape Communications. *See also* browser; Web browser.

MPEG   An acronym for Motion Picture Experts Group. An image compression standard and file format that defines a compression method for desktop audio, animation, and video. MPEG is a lossy compression method that results in some data loss when a video clip is decompressed. *See also* lossy compression.

multicast backbone   Abbreviated MBONE. An experimental method of transmitting digital video over the Internet in real time. MBONE requires the creation of another backbone service with special hardware and software to accommodate video and audio transmissions. The TCP/IP protocols used for Internet transmissions are unsuitable for real-time audio or video; they were designed to deliver text and other files reliably, but often with some delay. *See also* Transmission Control Protocol/ Internet Protocol.

Multipurpose Internet Mail Extensions   Abbreviated MIME. An Internet specification that allows users to send multiple-part and multimedia messages rather than simple ASCII-text messages. A MIME-enabled e-mail application can send Acrobat files, binary files, audio messages, and digital video over the Internet.

National Center for Supercomputing Applications   Abbreviated NCSA. At the University of Illinois at Urbana-Champaign, NCSA is credited with the creation of Mosaic, the first graphical Web browser. *See also* Mosaic; Web browser.

National Computer Security Center   Abbreviated NCSC. A branch of the U.S. National Security Agency that defines security for computer products. The Department of Defense Standard 5200.28, also known as the Orange Book, specifies several levels of increasingly complex security measures.

NC   A simplified computer used to access the Internet or an intranet, developed by Microsoft and Intel and backed by most of the PC manufacturers, including Compaq, Hewlett-Packard, Digital Equipment Corporation, Gateway 2000, NEC, and Toshiba. The NetPC is aimed at alleviating the costs of maintaining and upgrading PCs in large corporations. Based on an Intel chip and a version of the Microsoft Windows operating system, NetPCs will allow users to continue to use their current software stored on a local hard-disk drive and to load software from the network. Also called a network computer or NetPC.

NCSA   *See* National Center for Supercomputing Applications.

NCSC   *See* National Computer Security Center.

Netscape Server API   Abbreviated NSAPI. A programming specification used by Netscape servers when performing back-end applications. *See also* ActiveX; Internet Server API.

network-centric   An imprecise term often used to describe an approach to software development that includes a strong client-server component.

Network File System   Abbreviated NFS. A distributed file-sharing system developed by Sun Microsystems more than 10 years ago that has been licensed and implemented by more than 300 vendors.

Network News Transfer Protocol   Abbreviated NNTP. A protocol used for posting and retrieving news articles on Usenet newsgroups. *See also* newsgroup; protocol; Usenet.

newsgroup   A Usenet discussion group devoted to a single topic. Subscribers to the newsgroup post articles that can be read by all the other subscribers.

Newsgroup names fit into a formal structure in which each component of the name is separated from the next by a period. The leftmost portion of the name represents the category of the newsgroup, and the name gets more specific from left to right. *See also* Usenet.

newsreader   An application used to read the articles posted to Usenet newsgroups. Newsreaders are of two kinds: *threaded* newsreaders group the posts into threads of related articles; *unthreaded* newsreaders present the articles in their original order of posting. Of the two, threaded newsreaders are much easier to use. *See also* newsgroup; Usenet.

NFS   *See* Network File System.

NNTP   *See* Network News Transfer Protocol.

node   Any device attached to the network that is capable of communicating with other network devices.

NSAPI   *See* Netscape Server API.

NT file system   Abbreviated NTFS. The file system native to Windows NT and Windows NT Server. There are several advantages to using NTFS, including long file names, reduced file fragmentation, improved fault tolerance, increased system security, and much better recovery after a system crash.

octet   The Internet's own term for eight contiguous bits, or a *byte*. Some computer systems attached to the Internet used a byte with more than eight bits, hence the need for this term.

ODBC   An acronym for Open Database Connectivity. A programming interface developed by Microsoft that allows clients to access many types of database and file formats. *See also* client; client-server.

ODSI   Abbreviation for Open Directory Services Interface. A standard from Microsoft that enables client software to query Internet directories by providing a common API for naming.

page   A single file of text in HTML. *See also* Hypertext Markup Language.

password   A security method that identifies a specific, authorized user of a computer system or network by a specific string of characters. In general, passwords should be a mixture of upper- and lowercase letters and numbers and should be longer than six characters. Passwords should be kept secret and changed often. The worst passwords are the obvious ones: people's names or initials, place names, birth dates, and anything to do with computers or Star Trek.

PDF   *See* Portable Document Format.

Perl   An acronym formed from Practical Extraction and Report Language (or Pathologically Eclectic Rubbish Lister, depending on who you believe); a scripting language written by Larry Wall that you can use to write powerful data and text manipulation routines quickly and easily. For this reason, Perl has become a popular language for writing CGI applications. Perl doesn't suffer from the arbitrary limitations that plague other languages; lines can be of any length, arrays can be of any size, variable names can be as long as you care to make them, and binary data doesn't cause any problems. *See also* Common Gateway Interface.

permanent virtual circuit   Abbreviated PVC. A fixed communications circuit, created and maintained even when no data is being transmitted. A PVC has no setup overhead and gives improved performance for periodic transmissions that require an immediate connection.

permissions In many operating systems, the ability of a user to access certain system resources, including files and directories. Permissions are based on the rights granted to user accounts by the system administrator. *See also* rights; system administrator.

PGP Abbreviation for Pretty Good Privacy. A popular shareware public-key-encryption program, written by Phil Zimmermann and available at no cost from certain Internet sites. *See also* encryption.

player A program launched or used by a Web browser to process a file that the browser can't handle. A player is a program that deals with sound files. *See also* helper application; plug-in; viewer.

plug-in A small program that you link in to your browser to add a special capability. Plug-ins are available from a variety of companies and are usually free.

point of presence Abbreviated POP. A connection to the telephone company or to long-distance carrier services.

Point-to-Point Protocol Abbreviated PPP. A TCP/IP protocol used to transmit over serial lines and telephone connections. PPP allows a user to establish a temporary direct connection to the Internet via a modem that appears to the host system as if it were an Ethernet port on the host's network. PPP also provides an automatic method of assigning an IP address so mobile users can connect to the network at any point. *See also* Ethernet; IP address; protocol; Transmission Control Protocol/Internet Protocol.

Point-to-Point Tunneling Protocol Abbreviated PPTP. A proprietary networking protocol from Microsoft that supports virtual private networks, allowing remote users to access NT Server systems across the Internet without compromising security.

POP *See* point of presence.

Portable Document Format Abbreviated PDF. A file-format standard that was developed by Adobe Systems and others. A file in this format usually has a PDF file-name extension.

port number   The default input/output location identifier for an Internet application. For example, FTP, Gopher, HTTP, and Telnet are all assigned unique port numbers so the computer knows how to respond when it's contacted on a specific port; Gopher servers usually talk at port 70, HTTP servers use port 80, and SMTP e-mail is always delivered to port 25. You can override these defaults by specifying different values in a URL. *See also* File Transfer Protocol; Hypertext Transfer Protocol; SMTP; Telnet; Uniform Resource Locator.

PPP   *See* Point-to-Point Protocol.

Presentation layer   The sixth of the seven layers that make up the ISO/OSI model of computer communications. The Presentation layer defines the way in which data is formatted, presented, converted, and encoded. *See also* International Standards Organization/Open System Interconnection model.

privacy enhanced mail   Abbreviated PEM. An e-mail system that uses RSA encryption to provide a confidential method of authentication.

Private Key Scheme   *See* encryption.

protocol   In networking and communications, the formal specification that defines the procedures to follow when transmitting and receiving data. Protocols define the format, timing, sequence, and error checking used on the network.

protocol stack   A layered set of protocols that work together to provide a set of network functions. Internet and intranet computers use a TCP/IP stack. *See also* protocol; Transmission Control Protocol/Internet Protocol.

proxy server   A program running on a server positioned between your LAN or intranet and the Internet. In an attempt to conceal the underlying network structure from any intruders, this program filters all outgoing connections so they all appear to come from the same machine. A proxy server will also forward your request to the Internet, intercept the response, and then forward the response to you at your network node. A system administrator can also regulate the outside points to which the LAN users may connect. *See also* The Internet; intranet; local area network; node; system administrator.

Public Key Scheme   *See* encryption.

PVC   *See* permanent virtual circuit.

RealAudio   Technology developed by Progressive Networks that lets you play audio files as they're in the process of being downloaded rather than waiting until the complete file has arrived, which gives a much faster response time.

Registry   In Windows NT, the system database that contains information on hardware, software, and users on the system.

remote access   Using a modem and telephone circuit, a workstation-to-network connection that allows data to be sent or received over large distances. Remote access is handled in different ways in different operating systems. Also known as *remote connection.*

remote connection   *See* remote access.

replication   The process of synchronizing data stored on two or more computers.

resource   In HTML, any URL, directory, or application that the server can access and send to a requesting client. *See also* Hypertext Markup Language; Uniform Resource Locator.

rights   The privileges granted to a user or a group of users by the system administrator that determine the operations they can perform on the system. *See also* system administrator; permissions.

robot   A World Wide Web application that automatically locates and collects information about new Web sites. Robots are most often used to create large databases of Web sites.

router   A device that forwards packets between networks, using information from the Network layer or from routing tables. The networks connected by a router may use the same or different networking protocols. There are several different types of routers; some only perform traffic-routing functions, and others can also perform file-storage tasks. *See also* bridge; gateway.

Routing Information Protocol Abbreviated RIP. A widely used protocol that distributes routing information on TCP/IP networks. *See also* protocol; Transmission Control Protocol/Internet Protocol.

search engine A special Web server that lets you perform keyword searches to locate interesting Web pages. The Excite, Yahoo, and WebCrawler Web sites each contain examples of different search engines.

secure sockets layer Abbreviated SSL. An interface developed by Netscape that provides an encrypted data transfer between client and server applications over the Internet. *See also* client-server.

Serial Line Internet Protocol Abbreviated SLIP. A protocol used to run IP over serial lines or telephone connections using modems. SLIP allows you to establish a temporary direct connection to the Internet via a modem and appear to the host as though you were using a port on the host's network. SLIP is slowly being replaced by PPP. *See also* Internet Protocol; modem; protocol; Point-to-Point Protocol.

server Any computer that makes access to files, printing, communications, and other services available to users on the network. On a small network, one single server may perform all these tasks; on larger networks, individual servers tend to specialize and perform a particular function. Server is also used to describe the software that powers a shared computer resource. *See also* client.

server root A directory on an Internet server that contains the server program as well as configuration and information files.

Session layer The fifth of the seven layers of the ISO/OSI model for computer communications. The Session layer coordinates communications and maintains the session for as long as it's needed, performing security, logging, and administrative functions. *See also* International Standards Organization/Open System Interconnection model.

Simple Network Management Protocol Abbreviated SNMP. A standard protocol, part of the TCP/IP suite, used to manage and monitor nodes on a network. *See also* node; protocol; Transmission Control Protocol/Internet Protocol.

SLIP *See* Serial Line Internet Protocol.

SMTP   An acronym for Simple Mail Transfer Protocol. The TCP/IP protocol for exchanging e-mail on the Internet. *See also* e-mail; protocol; Transmission Control Protocol/Internet Protocol.

sniffer   A small program loaded onto your system by an intruder, designed to monitor specific traffic on the network. The sniffer program watches for the first part of any remote logon session that includes logon ID, password, and host name of a person logging on to another machine. Once this information is in the hands of the intruder, he or she can log on to that system at will. One weakly secured network can therefore expose not only other local systems, but also any remote systems to which the local users connect.

SNMP   *See* Simple Network Management Protocol.

spider   A World Wide Web application that automatically locates and collects information about new Web sites. Spiders are most often used to create large databases of Web sites that in turn are accessed by search engines responding to user requests for information. *See also* search engine.

SSL   *See* secure sockets layer.

subnet   A logical network created from a single IP address. A mask is used to identify bits from the host portion of the address to be used for subnet addresses. *See also* IP address.

subnet address   The subnet portion of an IP address. In a subnetted network, the host part of the IP address is divided into a subnet portion and a host portion by a subnet mask.

subnet mask   A number, or more correctly, a bit pattern, that identifies which parts of an IP address correspond to the network, subnet, and host portions of the address. Also referred to as an *address mask*.

system administrator   Often abbreviated SA. The person charged with the responsibility of managing a computer system. In a large installation, the system administrator may actually be several people or even a small department. The tasks performed by the system administrator include installing, updating, and removing software packages; installing operating system upgrades; installing and configuring hardware, such as printers, terminals, modems, routers, gateways, and firewalls; and monitoring system performance and making tuning adjustments as needed.

T1   A long-distance point-to-point circuit, providing 24 channels of 64Kbps, giving a total bandwidth of 1.544Mbps. The standard T1 frame is 193 bits long and consists of twenty-four 8-bit voice samples and one synchronization bit. It transmits 8,000 frames per second. When a T1 service is made available in single 64Kbps increments, it is known as fractional T1. T2, T3, and T4 services are also available. *See also* kilobits per second; megabits per second.

tag   An element in HTML used to annotate a document. A tag is text enclosed by less than and greater than symbols that tells the browser what each part of the document means. For example, the tag <H1> indicates the start of a level one heading, and the tag </H1> marks the end of a level one heading. *See also* element; Hypertext Markup Language.

TCP   *See* Transmission Control Protocol.

TCP/IP   *See* Transmission Control Protocol/Internet Protocol.

Telnet   A terminal emulation protocol, part of the TCP/IP suite of protocols, that provides remote connection services. *See also* protocol; Transmission Control Protocol/Internet Protocol.

TFTP   *See* Trivial File Transfer Protocol.

token ring network   In networking, a ring topology that uses token-passing to regulate traffic and to avoid collisions. On a token ring network, the controlling network interface card generates a token that controls the right to transmit. This token is continuously passed from one node to the next around the network. When a node has information to transmit, it captures the token, sets its status to busy, and adds the message and the destination address.

   All other nodes continuously read the token to determine if they're the recipient of the message. If they are, they collect the token, extract the message, and return it to the sender. The sender then removes the message and sets the token status to free, indicating that it can be used by the next node waiting to send a message.

top-level domain   The highest category of host name, which either signifies the type of institution or the country of its origin. For more information, see Chapter 1.

Transmission Control Protocol   Abbreviated TCP. The connection-oriented– transport-level protocol used in the TCP/IP suite of protocols. *See also* protocol; Transmission Control Protocol/Internet Protocol.

Transmission Control Protocol/Internet Protocol   Abbreviated TCP/IP. A set of communications protocols first developed by the Defense Advanced Research Projects Agency (DARPA) in the late 1970s. The TCP/IP protocols encompass media access, packet transport, session communications, file transfer, e-mail, and terminal emulation.
   TCP/IP is supported by a large number of hardware and software vendors and is available on many computer systems, from PCs to mainframes. Many corporations, universities, and government agencies use TCP/IP, and it's also the basis for the Internet. *See also* e-mail; The Internet; protocol.

Transport layer   The fourth of seven layers of the ISO/OSI model for computer communications. The Transport layer defines protocols for message structure and supervises the validity of the transmission by performing some error checking. *See also* International Standards Organization/Open System Interconnection model; protocol.

Trivial File Transfer Protocol   Abbreviated TFTP. A simplified version of the TCP/IP File Transfer Protocol that does not include password protection or user-directory capability. *See also* File Transfer Protocol; Transmission Control Protocol/Internet Protocol.

tunneling   The encapsulation of one protocol inside another. Tunneling is used to create pseudo-connections across connectionless networks, such as the Internet, and may be referred to as *protocol encapsulation* or *synchronous pass-through*. *See also* encapsulation; Point-to-Point Tunneling Protocol.

UDP   *See* User Datagram Protocol.

unauthorized access   To gain entry to a computer system using stolen or guessed passwords. *See also* password.

Unicode   A 16-bit character code, defined by the Unicode Consortium and by the ISO 10646 standard, that supports a maximum of 65,536 unique characters rather than the 256 characters available in the current ASCII character set.

Uniform Resource Locator   Abbreviated URL. A method of accessing Internet resources. URLs contain information about both the access method to use and the resource itself and are used by Web browsers to connect you directly to a specific document or home page on the World Wide Web, without your having to know where that resource is physically located. *See also* browser; home page; World Wide Web.

uninterruptible power supply   Abbreviated UPS. An alternative power source, usually consisting of a set of batteries, used to power a computer system if the normal power service is interrupted or falls below acceptable levels.

upload   In communications, to transfer a file or other information from your computer to the server over a network link or via a modem. *See also* download.

URL   *See* Uniform Resource Locator.

Usenet   A contraction formed from *User Network*. An international, noncommercial network linking many thousands of sites. Although Usenet and the Internet are closely related, they are not the same thing. Not every Internet computer is part of Usenet, and not every Usenet system can be reached from the Internet. Like the Internet, Usenet has no central governing body; it's run by the people who use it. With well over 10,000 newsgroups, Usenet is accessed by millions of people in more than 100 countries every day. *See also* newsgroup; newsreader.

user account   A security mechanism that is used to control access to a network and that is established and maintained by the system administrator. Elements of a user account include password information, rights, and information about the groups to which the user belongs. *See also* password; system administrator.

User Datagram Protocol   Abbreviated UDP. The connectionless transport-level protocol used in the TCP/IP suite of protocols and usually bundled with IP-layer software. Because UDP doesn't add overhead, as connection-oriented TCP does, UDP is often used with SNMP applications. *See also* Internet Protocol; protocol; Simple Network Management Protocol; Transmission Control Protocol/Internet Protocol.

viewer   An application launched by a Web browser to view a file that the browser cannot handle by itself. Sometimes called a *helper application.* A viewer displays video clips and animation files. *See also* helper application; plug-in.

Virtual Reality Modeling Language   Abbreviated VRML. A draft specification for three-dimensional rendering used in conjunction with Web browsers. *See also* browser; Web browser.

VMS   A multiuser, multitasking virtual memory operating system from Digital Equipment Corporation (DEC) for the popular VAX line of computers and workstations.

VRML   *See* Virtual Reality Modeling Language.

WAN   *See* wide area network.

The Web   *See* World Wide Web.

Web browser   A World Wide Web client application that you use to look at hyper-text documents and follow links to other HTML documents on the Web. *See also* browser; hypertext; Hypertext Markup Language; World Wide Web.

Web page   Information placed on a Web server for viewing with a Web browser. A Web page may contain text, graphics, audio or video clips, and links to other Web pages. *See also* browser; Web browser.

Web server   A hardware and software package that provides services to Web clients. *See also* client; client-server; server.

whiteboard   An application that lets several network users look at and share images, data, and text simultaneously, as they all participate in a common conference call. Each person's comments and suggestions are labeled and separated from the comments made by others participating in the call.

wide area network   Abbreviated WAN. A network that connects users across large distances, often crossing the geographical boundaries of cities or states. *See also* local area network.

WinCGI   A Common Gateway Interface for Windows applications.

workflow software   Software that allows users to move and manage information among themselves, combining the functions of e-mail, imaging, and document management. A document moves through various stages of processing as it's edited, signed, or validated by the various members of the workgroup. *See also* e-mail.

workgroup   A group of individuals who work together and share the same files and databases over a LAN. Workgroups use workflow software to edit and exchange files and update databases as a group. *See also* local area network.

World Wide Web   Abbreviated WWW, W3, or simply called *the Web*. A huge collection of hypertext pages on the Internet. Web traffic is growing faster than most other Internet services, and the reason for this becomes obvious when you try out a capable Web browser. *See also* browser; hypertext; The Internet.

Appendix B

INTRANET PROTOCOLS—TCP/IP

FEATURING

- **Understanding TCP/IP's history and design goals**
- **Understanding TCP**
- **Understanding IP**
- **Assigning IP Addresses**
- **Using the name resolution methods**

One of the most important elements of intranet technology—the element that makes intranets so easy to set up and use—is the networking protocol that provides the foundation to the Internet. This protocol is known as *TCP/IP;* it's actually a whole family of protocols, with its name coming from only two of them—the *Transmission Control Protocol* and the *Internet Protocol.* Before you can do anything with your intranet, you must first set up TCP/IP on the server and on all the workstations.

> **NOTE** Because the TCP/IP protocol is much more technical than the rest of this book, we put it in a separate appendix. While you might not need to know everything about TCP/IP, this appendix should give you a good foundation to start from.

This appendix describes the TCP/IP family of protocols, IP addressing, and address classifications, and goes on to describe several of the name resolution services available. *Name resolution* allows you to use names in place of numbers to identify your intranet server and clients, but more on this later.

This is a completely self-contained appendix; most of the TCP/IP information is concentrated here, rather than being spread throughout the other chapters in this book. Obviously, this appendix is just a starting point to learn about TCP/IP. If you are not interested in learning about how TCP/IP works, you can safely skip this appendix.

Introducing TCP/IP

We have referred to TCP/IP many times throughout this book, so by now you have some idea of how central it is to intranet (and Internet) technology. Now let's look at it in detail by first giving some background on TCP/IP and how it came about.

A Brief History of TCP/IP

The TCP/IP protocol was first proposed in 1973, but it was not until 1983 that a standardized version was developed and adopted for wide area use. In that same year, TCP/IP became the official transport mechanism for all connections to ARPAnet, a forerunner of the Internet.

Much of the original work on TCP/IP was done at the University of California at Berkeley, where computer scientists were also working on the Berkeley version of Unix (which eventually grew into the Berkeley Software Distribution [BSD] series of Unix releases). TCP/IP was added to the BSD releases, which in turn was made available to universities and other institutions for the cost of a distribution tape. Thus, TCP/IP began to spread in the academic world, laying the foundation for today's explosive growth of the Internet—and of intranets as well.

During this time, the TCP/IP family continued to evolve and add new members. One of the most important aspects of this growth was the continuing development of the certification and testing program carried out by the U.S. government to ensure that the published standards, which were free, were met. Publication ensured that the developers did not change anything or add any features specific to their own needs. This open approach has continued to the present day; use of the TCP/IP family of protocols virtually guarantees a trouble-free connection between many hardware and software platforms.

TCP/IP Design Goals

When the U.S. Department of Defense began to define the TCP/IP network protocols, their design goals included the following:

- It had to be independent of all hardware and software manufacturers. Even today, this is fundamentally why TCP/IP makes such good sense in the corporate world; it's not tied to IBM, Novell, Microsoft, DEC, or any other specific company.
- It had to have good built-in failure recovery. Because TCP/IP was originally a military proposal, the protocol had to be able to continue operating even if large parts of the network suddenly disappeared from view, say after an enemy attack. But they might only disappear to one segment of users, not to all of them, hence the term *view*.
- It had to handle high error rates and still provide completely reliable end-to-end service.
- It had to be efficient with a low data overhead. The majority of data packets using the IP protocol have a simple, 20-byte header, which means better performance in comparison with other networks. A simple protocol translates directly into faster transmissions, giving more efficient service.
- It had to allow the addition of new networks without any service disruptions.

As a result, TCP/IP was developed with each component performing unique and vital functions that solved all the problems involved in moving data between machines over networks in an elegant and efficient way.

Benefits of Using TCP/IP

Now that we have described how TCP and IP are used, let's take a look at the major benefits of using TCP/IP rather than other networking protocols:

- TCP/IP is a routable protocol, which means it can send datagrams over a specific route, thus reducing traffic on other parts of the network.
- TCP/IP has reliable and efficient data-delivery mechanisms.
- TCP/IP is a widely published open standard and is completely independent of any hardware or software manufacturer.
- TCP/IP can send data between different computer systems running completely different operating systems, from small PCs all the way to mainframes and everything in between.
- TCP/IP is separated from the underlying hardware and will run over Ethernet, Token Ring, or X.25 networks and even over dial-up telephone lines.
- TCP/IP uses a common addressing scheme. Therefore, any system can address any other system, even in a network as large as the Internet. (We will look at this addressing scheme in the "Understanding IP Addressing" section later in this appendix.)

The popularity that the TCP/IP family of protocols enjoys isn't because the protocols were there or even because the U.S. government mandated their use. They're popular because they're robust, solid protocols that solve many of the most difficult networking problems.

Using the Transmission Control Protocol

As we've mentioned previously, the transmission layer of the protocol is called *Transmission Control Protocol* (TCP). TCP serves to ensure reliable, verifiable data exchange between hosts on a network. TCP breaks data into pieces, wrapping it with the information needed to route it to its destination and reassembling the pieces at the receiving end of the communications link. The wrapped and bundled pieces are called *datagrams*. TCP puts a header on the datagram that provides the information needed to get the data to its destination. The most important information in the header includes the source and destination port numbers, a sequence number for the datagram, and a checksum.

The *source port number* and the *destination port number* allow the data to be sent back and forth to the correct process running on each computer. The *sequence number* allows the datagrams to be rebuilt in the correct order in the receiving computer, and the *checksum* allows the protocol to check whether the data sent is the same as the data received. It does this by first totaling the contents of a datagram and inserting that number in the header. This is when IP enters the picture. Once the header is in the datagram, TCP passes the datagram to IP to be routed to its destination. The receiving computer then performs the same calculation, and if the two calculations don't match, an error occurred somewhere along the line, and the datagram is resent.

Figure B.1 shows the layout of the datagram with the TCP header in place.

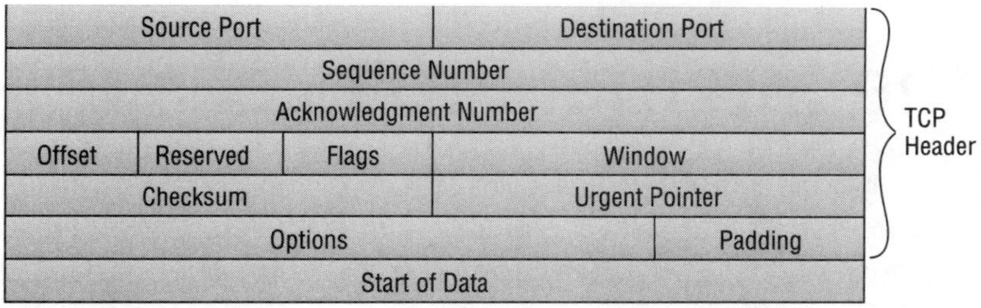

FIGURE B.1: A datagram with its TCP header

In addition to the source and destination port numbers, the sequence number, and the checksum, a TCP header contains the following information:

Acknowledgment Number	Indicates that the data was received successfully. If the datagram is damaged in transit, the receiver throws the data away and does not send an acknowledgment back to the sender. After a predefined time-out expires, the sender retransmits data for which no acknowledgment was received.
Offset	Specifies the length of the header.
Reserved	Indicates variables set aside for future use.
Flags	Indicates that this packet is the end of the data or that the data is urgent.
Window	Provides a way to increase packet size, which improves efficiency in data transfers.

Urgent Pointer	Gives the location of urgent data.
Options	Indicates a set of variables reserved for future use or for special options as defined by the user of the protocol.
Padding	Ensures that the header ends on a 32-bit boundary.

The data in the packet immediately follows this header information.

TCP communications can be summarized as follows:

- Flow control allows two systems to cooperate in datagram transmission to prevent overflows and lost packets.
- Acknowledgment lets the sender know that the recipient has received the information.
- Sequencing ensures that packets arrive in the proper order.
- Checksums allow easy detection of lost or corrupted packets.
- Retransmission of lost or corrupted packets is managed in a timely way.

Using the Internet Protocol

The Network layer portion of TCP/IP is called *Internet Protocol.* This is what actually moves the data from Point A to Point B, a process that is referred to as *routing*.

IP is *connectionless*; that is, it doesn't swap control information (or handshaking information) before establishing an end-to-end connection and starting a transmission. The Internet Protocol must rely on TCP to determine that the data has arrived successfully at its destination and to retransmit the data if it didn't. IP's only job is to route the data to its destination. In this effort, IP inserts its own header in the datagram once it's received from TCP. The main contents of the IP header are the source and destination addresses, the protocol number, and a checksum.

> **NOTE**   You may sometimes hear IP described as unreliable because it contains no error detection or recovery code.

Without the header provided by IP, intermediate routers between the source and destination, commonly called *gateways*, would not be able to determine where to route the datagram. Figure B.2 shows the layout of the datagram with the TCP and IP headers in place.

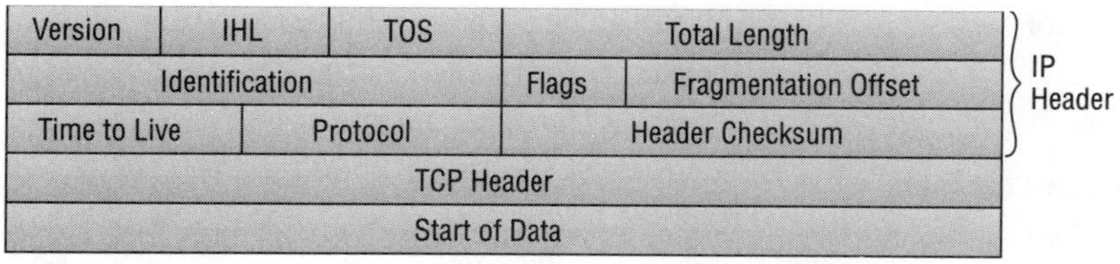

Version	IHL	TOS	Total Length	
Identification		Flags	Fragmentation Offset	IP Header
Time to Live	Protocol	Header Checksum		
TCP Header				
Start of Data				

FIGURE B.2: A datagram with TCP and IP headers

Let's take a look at the fields in the IP header:

Version	Defines the IP version number. Version 4 is the current standard, and values of five or six indicate that special protocols are being used.
IHL (Internet Header Length)	Defines the length of the header information. The header length can vary; the default header is five 32-bit words, and the sixth word is optional.
TOS (Type of Service)	Indicates the kind or priority of the required service.
Total Length	Specifies the total length of the datagram, which can be a minimum of 576 bytes and a maximum of 65,536 bytes.
Identification	Provides information that the receiving system can use to reassemble fragmented datagrams.
Flags	Specifies, using the first flag bit, that the datagram should not be fragmented and must therefore travel over subnetworks that can handle the size without fragmenting it; the second flag bit indicates that the datagram is the last of a fragmented packet.
Fragmentation Offset	Indicates the original position of the data and is used during reassembly.
Time to Live	Originally indicated the time in seconds that the datagram could be in transit; if this time was exceeded, the datagram was considered lost. Now interpreted as a hop count and usually set to the default value 32 (for 32 hops); this number is decremented by each router through which the packet passes.

Protocol	Identifies the protocol type, allowing the use of non-TCP/IP protocols. A value of 6 indicates TCP, and a value of 17 indicates User Datagram Protocol (UDP).
Header Checksum	Specifies an error-checking value that is recalculated at each stopover point, necessary because certain fields change.
TCP Header	Indicates the header added by the TCP part of the protocol suite.

The data in the packet immediately follows this header information.

Gateways and Routing

As we mentioned previously, routing is the process of getting your data from Point A to Point B. Routing datagrams is similar to driving a car. Before you drive off to your destination, you determine which roads you'll take to get there. And sometimes along the way, you have to change your mind and alter your route.

The IP portion of the TCP/IP protocol inserts its header in the datagram, but before the datagram can begin its journey, IP determines whether it knows the destination. If it does know it, IP sends the datagram on its way. If it doesn't know and can't find out, IP sends the datagram to the host's gateway.

Each host on a TCP/IP network has a *gateway,* or an off-ramp for datagrams not destined for the local network. They're going somewhere else, and the gateway's job is to forward them to that destination if it knows where it is. Each gateway has a defined set of specific destinations, called routing tables, that tell the gateway the route to use.

Because gateways don't know the location of every IP address, they have their own gateways that act just like any TCP/IP host. In the event the first gateway doesn't know the way to the destination, it forwards the datagram to its own gateway. This forwarding, or routing, continues until the datagram reaches its destination. The entire path to the destination is known as the *route.*

> **NOTE** Routes can be predefined and made static, and alternate routes can also be predefined, providing a maximum probability that your datagrams travel via the shortest and fastest route.

Datagrams intended for the same destination may actually take different routes to get there. Many variables determine the route. For example, overloaded gateways may not respond in a timely manner or may simply refuse to route traffic and so time out. That time-out causes the sending gateway to seek an alternate route for the datagram.

Understanding IP Addressing

As you read in "The Internet Protocol" section earlier in this appendix, IP moves data between computer systems in the form of a datagram, and each datagram is delivered to the destination port number that is contained in the datagram header. This destination port number, or address, is a standard 16-bit number that contains enough information to identify the receiving network as well as the specific host on that network for which the datagram is intended.

In this section, we'll go over what IP addresses are, why they're so necessary, and how they're used in TCP/IP networking.

IP Addresses Explained

TCP/IP requires that each computer on a TCP/IP network have its own unique IP address. A consortium between AT&T and Network Solutions, called InterNIC (*Internet Network Information Center*), manages the task of assigning IP addresses. See the sidebar "InterNIC and Domain Names" for information on how to apply for an IP address from InterNIC. An *IP address* is a 32-bit number, usually represented as a four-part number, with each of the four parts separated by a period or decimal point. You may also hear this method of representation called *dotted decimal, dotted ip,* or *quad decimal.* In the IP address, each individual byte, or *octet* as it is sometimes called, can have a usable value in the range 1 to 254.

NOTE   The term *octet* is the Internet community's own term for an 8-bit byte and came into common use because some of the early computers attached to the Internet had bytes of more than 8 bits; some of DEC's early systems had bytes of 18-bits.

The way these addresses are used varies according to the network's class. We'll cover network classes in the next section. All you can say with certainty is that the 32-bit IP address is divided in some way to create an address for the network and an address for each host. In general, though, the higher-order bits of the address make up the network part of the address, and the rest constitutes the host part of the address. In addition, the host part of the address can be divided further to allow for a *subnetwork* address. We'll be looking at all this in more detail in the "IP Address Classification" and "Understanding IP Subnets" sections later in this discussion.

Some host addresses are reserved for special use. For example, in all network addresses, host numbers 0 and 255 are reserved. An IP host address with all bits set to zero identifies the network itself, so 52.0.0.0 refers to network 52. An IP address with all the bits set is known as a *broadcast address*. The broadcast address for network 204.176 is 204.176.255.255. A datagram sent to this address is automatically sent to every individual host on the 204.176 network.

A *domain name* is an alias for the TCP/IP address. For example, your company, Basset Hound, Inc. may have a TCP/IP address of 204.176.99.22 and a domain of `Bassethound.com`. The domain name is an easier way to find your address on the Internet.

InterNIC and Domain Names

As mentioned previously, InterNIC manages the task of assigning IP addresses and domain names to Internet users. A domain name is a unique but easy-to-remember name used in the place of the hard-to-remember 32-bit IP address.

Until recently, this service was provided for no charge by the National Science Foundation, but now a charge is levied for most services simply because the demand for domain registrations is so high. Since 1993, the NSF has funded the administration of domain name registration through a cooperative agreement with Network Solutions, and this agreement extends through to 1998.

Contact InterNIC at

`http://rs.internic.net`

or by e-mail at

`hostmaster@internic.net`

If you aren't connected to the Internet yet, you can send mail to this address:

Network Solutions
InterNIC Registration Services
505 Huntmar Park Drive
Herndon, VA 22070
Or you can phone or fax:
Telephone (703)742-4777
Fax (703)742-4811

InterNIC assigns and regulates IP addresses on the Internet; you can get one directly from the InterNIC, or you can ask your Internet service provider (ISP) to secure an IP address on your behalf.

InterNIC also lets you apply for any domain name you like, regardless of your company name; the only restriction is that the name must be available and not already reserved by someone else. To see if a domain name is available, use the InterNIC Whois service at

```
http://rs.internic.net/cgi-bin/whois
```

To use the Whois service, type your proposed name in the Query box, for example, **Bassethound.com**, and press Enter when you are ready to search the database. When the search is complete, you'll find out if anyone has already reserved the name you entered. If no one has registered your chosen name, you will see this message:

```
No match for "BASSETHOUND.COM".
```

To register your new name, go to

```
http://rs.internic.net/help/domain/new-domain-reg.html
```

Here you will be guided through the many steps in the registration process, and you can fill in your application form using your favorite Web browser. You can also apply to modify, transfer, or delete a domain name, and a help desk is always available if you need to ask a question or two.

When you're done, you can track the progress of your application. An invoice will be mailed to you automatically. The whole process can take several weeks, depending on the size of the current backlog. A commercial domain name costs $100 (`.edu` or `.org` domain names are still free), so plan ahead. The $100 fee covers the cost of your domain name for two years; InterNIC charges $50 a year to maintain an already existing domain name.

> **NOTE**
>
> If you're setting up an intranet and you don't want to connect to the outside world through the Internet, you don't need to register the IP addresses you use on your intranet with InterNIC. Registering your addresses with InterNIC simply ensures that the addresses you propose to use are unique over the entire Internet. If you never connect to the Internet, there's no reason to worry about whether those addresses are redundant with a computer that *isn't* on your network. Another strategy is to obtain your address from InterNIC and only use it internally until you are ready to connect to the Internet.

IP Address Classifications

In the 32-bit IP address, the number of bits used to identify the network and the host vary according to the network class of the address. As mentioned previously, if you never connect your intranet to the outside world and the Internet, you don't need to worry about this information. If you do plan to connect to the Internet, you'll need to know that the several classes are as follows:

- Class A is used for very large networks only. The high-order bit in a Class A network is always zero, which leaves 7 bits available to define 127 networks. The remaining 24 bits of the address allow each Class A network to hold as many as 16,777,216 hosts.
- Class B is used for medium-sized networks. The two high-order bits are always 10, and the remaining bits are used to define 16,384 networks, each with as many as 65,535 hosts attached.
- Class C is for smaller networks. The three high-order bits are always 110, and the remaining bits are used to define 2,097,152 networks, but each network can have a maximum of only 254 hosts.
- Class D is a special multicast address and cannot be used for networks. The four high-order bits are always 1110, and the remaining 28 bits allow access to more than 268 million possible addresses.
- Class E is reserved for experimental purposes. The first four bits in the address are always 1111.

Because the bits used to identify the class are combined with the bits that define the network address, we can draw the following conclusions from the size of the first octet, or byte, of the address:

- A value of 126 or less indicates a Class A address. The first octet is the network number; the next three, the host address.
- A value of exactly 127 is reserved as a loopback test address. If you send a message to 127.0.0.1, it should get back to you unless something is wrong with your network. Using this number as a special test address has the unfortunate effect of wasting more than 24 million possible IP addresses.
- A value of 128 through 191 is a Class B address. The first two octets are the network number, and the last two are the host address.
- A value of 192 through 223 is a Class C address. The first three octets are the network address, and the last octet is the host address.
- A value greater than 223 indicates a reserved address.

Using Name Resolution Methods

Internet host names are used because they're easier to remember than long dotted-decimal IP addresses. Host names are typically the name of a device that has a specific IP address. On the Internet, host names are part of what is known as a *fully qualified domain name*. A fully qualified domain name consists of a host name and a domain name. For example, in the fully qualified domain name `www.dyson.com`, the host name is `www`, and the domain name is `dyson.com`.

Although we all have Social Security numbers that we can generally remember when called for, life would be difficult if we had to remember the Social Security numbers of all our friends and associates. Likewise, it's easier to remember `www.microsoft.com` than it is to remember 198.105.232.6, Microsoft's IP address. The process of finding the host name for any given IP address is known as *name resolution,* and it can be performed in several ways. We'll look at all of them in the next few sections.

Using HOSTS

Several automatic conversion systems are available to translate an IP address into a host name, and HOSTS is one of the simplest. You create a file called `Hosts` and enter a line into it for every system, like this:

```
198.34.56.25 myserver.com
198.34.57.03 yourserver.com
```

Now comes the nasty part. You must store this ASCII file on *every single workstation*; when you make a change, you must change the contents of the `Hosts` file on *every single workstation*. Simple but painful on a network, but what happens if you want to go out to other networks or to the Internet? Fortunately, there are better solutions to this problem, as you'll see in the next two sections.

Using DNS

The abbreviation DNS stands for *Domain Name Service*. You use DNS to translate host names and domain names to IP addresses, and vice versa, by means of a standardized lookup table that the network administrator defines and configures.

Suppose you're using your browser to surf the Web, and you enter the URL **http://www.microsoft.com** to bring up the Microsoft home page. Your Web browser then asks the DNS server using the TCP/IP protocol for the IP address of `www.microsoft.com`. When your Web browser receives this address, it connects to the Microsoft Web server and downloads the home page. Simplifying the task of remembering addresses, DNS is an essential part of any TCP/IP network—all you have to remember is the host name and domain name.

DNS tables are composed of records. Each record is composed of a host name, a record type, and an address. There are several record types, including the address record, the mail exchange record, and the CNAME record.

The *address record*, commonly known as the A record, maps a host name to an IP address. The example below shows the address record for a host called `mail` in the `company.com` domain:

```
mail.company.com.    IN    A    204.176.47.9
```

The *mail exchange record* points to the mail exchanger for a particular host. DNS is structured so you can actually specify several mail exchangers for one host. This feature provides a higher probability that e-mail will actually arrive at its intended destination. The mail exchangers are listed in the record, with a priority code that indicates the order in which the mail exchangers should be accessed by other mail delivery systems.

If the first priority doesn't respond in a given amount of time, the mail delivery system tries the second one, and so on. Here are some sample mail exchange records:

```
hostname.company.com.    IN    MX    10 mail.company.com.
hostname.company.com.    IN    MX    20 mail2.company.com.
hostname.company.com.    IN    MX    30 mail3.company.com.
```

In this example, if the first mail exchanger, `mail.company.com`, does not respond, the second one, `mail2.company.com` is tried, and so on.

The *CNAME record,* or *canonical name record,* is also commonly known as the *alias record* and allows hosts to have more than one name. For example, your Web server has the host name `www`, but you want that machine to also have the name `ftp` so users can easily FTP in to manage Web pages. You can accomplish this with a CNAME record. Assuming you already have an address record established for the host name `www`, a CNAME record adding `ftp` as a host name would look something like this:

```
www.company.com.        IN    A       204.176.47.2
ftp.company.com.        IN    CNAME   www.company.com.
```

When you put all these record types together in a file, called a *DNS table,* it might look like this:

```
mail.company.com.       IN    A       204.176.47.9
mail2.company.com.      IN    A       204.176.47.21
mail3.company.com.      IN    A       204.176.47.89
yourhost.company.com.   IN    MX      10 mail.company.com.
yourhost.company.com.   IN    MX      20 mail2.company.com.
yourhost.company.com.   IN    MX      30 mail3.company.com.
www.company.com.        IN    A       204.176.47.2
ftp.company.com.        IN    CNAME   www.company.com.
```

You can establish other types of records for specific purposes, but we won't go into those in this book. DNS can become complex quickly for the novice; entire books are dedicated to the DNS system.

> **NOTE** For more information on DNS, see *DNS and BIND* from O'Reilly or Yahoo's DNS info on the Web at `http://www.yahoo.com/ Computers_and_Internet/Software/Protocols/DNS/`.

Using WINS

WINS, or *Windows Internet Naming Service,* is an essential part of the Microsoft networking topology. Before we get into a discussion of WINS, however, we must define a few new terms, including two new protocols: NetBIOS and NetBEUI.

- *NetBIOS* (pronounced net-bye-os or net-bye-ose) is an acronym formed from a *Network Basic Input/Output System*, a Session-layer network protocol originally developed by IBM and Sytek to manage data exchange and network access. NetBIOS provides an API with a consistent set of commands for requesting lower-level network services to transmit information from node to node, thus separating the applications from the underlying network operating system. Many vendors provide either their own version of NetBIOS or an emulation of its communications services in their products.
- *NetBEUI* (pronounced net-boo-ee) is an acronym formed from *NetBIOS Extended User Interface,* an implementation and extension of IBM's NetBIOS transport protocol from Microsoft. NetBEUI communicates with the network through Microsoft's NDIS (*Network Driver Interface Specification*). NetBEUI is shipped with all versions of Microsoft's operating systems today and is generally considered to have a lot of overhead, making it a poor choice for large networks.

WINS is used in conjunction with TCP/IP and maps NetBIOS names to IP addresses. For example, you have a print server on your LAN that you have come to know as PrintServer1. In the past, to print to that server you needed to remember only its name and to select that name from a list. TCP/IP, however, is a completely different protocol and doesn't understand NetBIOS names; it therefore has no way of knowing the location of those servers or their addresses. That's where WINS comes in. When you install TCP/IP on your Windows NT Server, you'll probably find that things work a lot better, and more seamlessly, if you also install WINS.

Each time you access a network resource on a Windows NT network using TCP/IP, your system needs to know the host name or IP address. If WINS is installed, you can continue using the NetBIOS names that you have previously used to access the resources because WINS provides the cross-reference from name to address for you.

When you install and configure TCP/IP, you'll see a place to specify the WINS server addresses. These addresses are stored with the configuration, and TCP/IP uses them to query for host names and addresses when necessary. WINS is similar to DNS in that it cross-references host names to addresses; however, as we mentioned earlier, WINS references NetBIOS names to IP addresses, and DNS references TCP/IP host names to IP address.

NOTE For more information on installing and configuring TCP/IP under Windows 95 or NT, see *Mastering Intranets*.

Another major difference between WINS and DNS is that WINS builds its own reference tables, and you have to configure DNS manually. When a workstation running TCP/IP is booted and attached to the network, it uses the WINS address settings in the TCP/IP configuration to communicate with the WINS server. The workstation gives the WINS server various pieces of information about itself, such as the NetBIOS host name, the actual user name logged on to the workstation, and the workstation's IP address. WINS stores this information for use on the network and periodically refreshes it to maintain accuracy.

Microsoft, however, has developed a new DNS record that allows the DNS server to work in perfect harmony with a WINS server. The Microsoft DNS Server software currently ships with Windows NT Server. Here's how it works: When a DNS query returns a WINS record, the DNS server then asks the WINS server for the host name address. Thus, you don't need to build complex DNS tables to establish and configure name resolution on your server; Microsoft DNS relies entirely on WINS to tell it the addresses it needs to resolve. And because WINS builds its tables automatically, you don't have to edit the DNS tables when addresses change; WINS takes care of this for you.

You can use both WINS and DNS on your network, or you can use one without the other. Your choice is determined by whether your network is connected to the Internet and whether your host addresses are dynamically assigned. When you're connected to the Internet, you must use DNS to resolve host names and addresses because TCP/IP depends on DNS service for address resolution.

If your network includes any mixture of Macintoshes, minicomputers, mainframe computers, Unix systems, PCs running Novell NetWare, and PCs running some version of Windows, you know that these computers normally can't communicate. But with TCP/IP installed on each of them, they can all communicate and transfer data back and forth with relative ease. That's simply not possible with any other networking protocol in existence today. And that's why you'll find the TCP/IP family of protocols in use almost everywhere computers are connected. This appendix gives you only the basics, but that should be enough to get you and your intranet started.

Index

Note to the Reader: First level entries are in **bold**. Page numbers in **bold** indicate the principal discussion of a topic or the definition of a term. Page numbers in *italic* indicate illustrations.

S

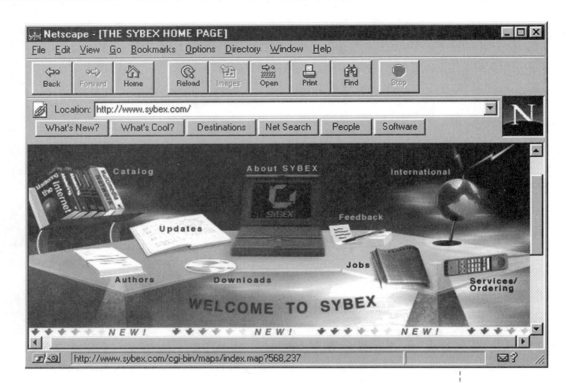